JAPAN'S RELIGIONS

Shinto and Buddhism

BY

LAFCADIO HEARN

CONTENTS

SOURCES

Selected from: Koizumi Edition
The writings of Lafcadio Hearn 16 vols.
Boston. Houghton Mifflin Company. 1922.

A QUESTION IN THE ZEN TEXTS

I

My friend opened a thin yellow volume of that marvelous text which proclaims at sight the patience of the Buddhist engraver. Movable Chinese types may be very useful; but the best of which they are capable is ugliness itself when compared with the beauty of the old block-printing.

"I have a queer story for you," he said.

"A Japanese story?"

"No — Chinese."

"What is the book?"

"According to Japanese pronunciation of the Chinese characters of the title, we call it 'Mu-Mon-Kwan,' which means, 'The Gateless Barrier.' It is one of the books especially studied by the Zen sect, or sect of Dhyâna. A peculiarity of some of the Dhyâna texts — this being a good example — is that they are not explanatory. They only suggest. Questions are put; but the student must think out the answers for himself. He must *think* them out, but not write them. You know that Dhyâna represents human effort to reach, through meditation, zones of thought beyond the range of verbal expression; and any thought once narrowed into utterance loses all Dhyâna quality. . . . Well, this story is supposed to be true; but it is used only for a Dhyâna

I

question. There are three different Chinese versions of it; and I can give you the substance of the three."

Which he did as follows:

II

THE story of the girl Ts'ing, which is told in the "Lui-shwo-li-hwan-ki," cited by the "Ching-tang-luh," and commented upon in the "Wu-mu-kwan" (called by the Japanese "Mu-Mon-Kwan"), which is a book of the Zen sect:

There lived in Han-yang a man called Chang-Kien, whose child-daughter, Ts'ing, was of peerless beauty. He had also a nephew called Wang-Chau — a very handsome boy. The children played together, and were fond of each other. Once Kien jestingly said to his nephew: "Some day I will marry you to my little daughter." Both children remembered these words; and they believed themselves thus betrothed.

When Ts'ing grew up, a man of rank asked for her in marriage; and her father decided to comply with the demand. Ts'ing was greatly troubled by this decision. As for Chau, he was so much angered and grieved that he resolved to leave home, and go to another province. The next day he got a boat ready for his journey, and after sunset, without bidding farewell to any one, he proceeded up the river. But in the middle of the night he was startled by a voice calling to him, "Wait! — it is I!" — and he saw a girl running along the bank toward the boat. It was Ts'ing. Chau was unspeakably delighted. She sprang into the boat; and the lovers found their way safely to the province of Chuh.

In the province of Chuh they lived happily for six years; and they had two children. But Ts'ing could not forget her parents, and often longed to see them again.

At last she said to her husband: "Because in former

2

time I could not bear to break the promise made to you, I ran away with you and forsook my parents — although knowing that I owed them all possible duty and affection. Would it not now be well to try to obtain their forgiveness?"

"Do not grieve yourself about that," said Chau; — "we shall go to see them."

He ordered a boat to be prepared; and a few days later he returned with his wife to Han-yang.

According to custom in such cases, the husband first went to the house of Kien, leaving Ts'ing alone in the boat. Kien welcomed his nephew with every sign of joy and said:

"How much I have been longing to see you! I was often afraid that something had happened to you."

Chau answered respectfully:

"I am distressed by the undeserved kindness of your words. It is to beg your forgiveness that I have come."

But Kien did not seem to understand. He asked:

"To what matter do you refer?"

"I feared," said Chau, "that you were angry with me for having run away with Ts'ing. I took her with me to the province of Chuh."

"What Ts'ing was that?" asked Kien.

"Your daughter Ts'ing," answered Chau, beginning to suspect his father-in-law of some malevolent design.

"What are you talking about?" cried Kien, with every appearance of astonishment. "My daughter Ts'ing has been sick in bed all these years — ever since the time when you went away."

"Your daughter Ts'ing," returned Chau, becoming angry, "has not been sick. She has been my wife for six years; and we have two children; and we have both returned to this place only to seek your pardon. Therefore please do not mock us!"

For a moment the two looked at each other in silence.

Then Kien arose, and motioning to his nephew to follow, led the way to an inner room where a sick girl was lying. And Chau, to his utter amazement, saw the face of Ts'ing — beautiful, but strangely thin and pale.

"She cannot speak," explained the old man; "but she can understand." And Kien said to her, laughingly: "Chau tells me that you ran away with him, and that you gave him two children."

The sick girl looked at Chau, and smiled; but remained silent.

"Now come with me to the river," said the bewildered visitor to his father-in-law. "For I can assure you — in spite of what I have seen in this house — that your daughter Ts'ing is at this moment in my boat."

They went to the river; and there, indeed, was the young wife, waiting. And seeing her father, she bowed down before him, and besought his pardon.

Kien said to her:

"If you really be my daughter, I have nothing but love for you. Yet though you seem to be my daughter, there is something which I cannot understand. . . . Come with us to the house."

So the three proceeded toward the house. As they neared it, they saw that the sick girl — who had not before left her bed for years — was coming to meet them, smiling as if much delighted. And the two Ts'ings approached each other. But then — nobody could ever tell how — they suddenly melted into each other, and became one body, one person, one Ts'ing — even more beautiful than before, and showing no sign of sickness or of sorrow.

Kien said to Chau:

"Ever since the day of your going, my daughter was dumb, and most of the time like a person who had taken too much wine. Now I know that her spirit was absent."

Ts'ing herself said:

"Really I never knew that I was at home. I saw Chau

4

going away in silent anger; and the same night I dreamed that I ran after his boat. . . . But now I cannot tell which was really I — the I that went away in the boat, or the I that stayed at home."

III

"THAT is the whole of the story," my friend observed. "Now there is a note about it in the 'Mu-Mon-Kwan' that may interest you. This note says: 'The fifth patriarch of the Zen sect once asked a priest — "In the case of the separation of the spirit of the girl Ts'ing, which was the true Ts'ing?"' It was only because of this question that the story was cited in the book. But the question is not answered. The author only remarks: 'If you can decide which was the real Ts'ing, then you will have learned that to go out of one envelope and into another is merely like putting up at an inn. But if you have not yet reached this degree of enlightenment, take heed that you do not wander aimlessly about the world. Otherwise, when Earth, Water, Fire, and Wind shall suddenly be dissipated, you will be like a crab with seven hands and eight legs, thrown into boiling water. And in that time do not say that you were never told about the *Thing*.'. . . Now the *Thing* —"

"I do not want to hear about the Thing," I interrupted — "nor about the crab with seven hands and eight legs. I want to hear about the clothes."

"What clothes?"

"At the time of their meeting, the two Ts'ings would have been differently dressed — very differently, perhaps; for one was a maid, and the other a wife. Did the clothes of the two also blend together? Suppose that one had a silk robe and the other a robe of cotton, would these have mixed into a texture of silk and cotton? Suppose that one was wearing a blue girdle, and the other a yellow girdle, would the result have been a green girdle? ... Or did one Ts'ing simply slip out of her costume, and leave it on the ground, like the cast-off shell of a cicada?"

"None of the texts say anything about the clothes," my friend replied: "so I cannot tell you. But the subject is quite irrelevant, from the Buddhist point of view. The doctrinal question is the question of what I suppose you would call the personality of Ts'ing."

"And yet it is not answered," I said.

"It is best answered," my friend replied, "by not being answered."

"How so?"

"Because there is no such thing as personality."

THE INTRODUCTION OF BUDDHISM

THE nature of the opposition which the ancient religion of Japan could offer to the introduction of any hostile alien creed, should now be obvious. The family being founded upon ancestor-worship, the commune being regulated by ancestor-worship, the clan-group or tribe being governed by ancestor-worship, and the Supreme Ruler being at once the high-priest and deity of an ancestral cult which united all the other cults in one common tradition, it must be evident that the promulgation of any religion essentially opposed to Shintō would have signified nothing less than an attack upon the whole system of society. Considering these circumstances, it may well seem strange that Buddhism should have succeeded, after some preliminary struggles (which included one bloody battle), in getting itself accepted as a second national faith. But although the original Buddhist doctrine was essentially in disaccord with Shintō beliefs, Buddhism had learned in India, in China, in Korea, and in divers adjacent countries, how to meet the spiritual needs of peoples maintaining a persistent ancestor-worship. Intolerance of ancestor-worship would have long ago resulted in the extinction of Buddhism; for its vast conquests have all been made among ancestor-worshiping races. Neither in India nor in China nor in Korea — neither in Siam nor Burmah nor Annam — did it attempt to extinguish ancestor-worship. Everywhere it made itself accepted as an ally, nowhere as an enemy, of social custom. In Japan it adopted the same policy which had secured its progress on the continent; and in order to form any clear conception of Japanese religious conditions, this fact must be kept in mind.

As the oldest extant Japanese texts — with the probable exception of some Shintō rituals — date from the eighth century, it is only possible to surmise the social conditions of that earlier epoch in which there was no form of religion but ancestor-worship. Only by imagining the absence of all Chinese and Korean influences can we form some vague idea of the state of things which existed during the so-called Age of the Gods — and it is difficult to decide at what period these influences began to operate. Confucianism appears to have preceded Buddhism by a considerable interval; and its progress, as an organizing power, was much more rapid. Buddhism was first introduced from Korea, about 552 A.D.; but the mission accomplished little. By the end of the eighth century the whole fabric of Japanese administration had been reorganized upon the Chinese plan, under Confucian influence; but it was not until well into the ninth century that Buddhism really began to spread throughout the country. Eventually it overshadowed the national life, and colored all the national thought. Yet the extraordinary conservatism of the ancient ancestor cult — its inherent power of resisting fusion — was exemplified by the readiness with which the two religions fell apart on the disestablishment of Buddhism in 1871. After having been literally overlaid by Buddhism for nearly a thousand years, Shintō immediately reassumed its archaic simplicity, and reëstablished the unaltered forms of its earliest rites.

But the attempt of Buddhism to absorb Shintō seemed at one period to have almost succeeded. The method of the absorption is said to have been devised, about the year 800, by the famous founder of the Shingon sect, Kūkai, or "Kōbōdaishi" (as he is popularly called), who first declared the higher Shintō gods to be incarnations of various Buddhas. But in this matter, of course, Kōbōdaishi was merely following precedents of Buddhist policy. Under the name of Ryōbu-Shintō,[1] the new compound of Shintō and Buddhism obtained Imperial approval and support. Thereafter, in hundreds of places, the two religions were domiciled within the same precinct — sometimes even within the same building: they seemed to have been veritably amalgamated. And nevertheless there was no real fusion; — after ten centuries of such contact they separated again, as lightly as if they had never touched. It was only in the domestic form of the ancestor cult that

[1] The term "Ryobu" signifies "two departments" or "two religions."

9

THE INTRODUCTION OF BUDDHISM

Buddhism really affected permanent modifications; yet even these were neither fundamental nor universal. In certain provinces they were not made; and almost everywhere a considerable part of the population preferred to follow the Shintō form of the ancestor cult. Yet another large class of persons, converts to Buddhism, continued to profess the older creed as well; and, while practicing their ancestor-worship according to the Buddhist rite, maintained separately also the domestic worship of the elder gods. In most Japanese houses to-day, the "god-shelf" and the Buddhist shrine can both be found; both cults being maintained under the same roof.[1] . . . But I am mentioning these facts only as illustrating the conservative vitality of Shintō, not as indicating any weakness in the Buddhist propaganda. Unquestionably the influence which Buddhism exerted upon Japanese civilization was immense, profound, multiform, incalculable; and the only wonder is that it should not have been able to stifle Shintō forever. To state, as various writers have carelessly stated, that Buddhism became the popular religion, while Shintō remained the official religion, is altogether misleading. As a matter of fact Buddhism became as much an official religion as Shintō itself, and influenced the lives of the high-

[1] The ancestor-worship and the funeral rites are Buddhist, as a general rule, if the family be Buddhist; but the Shintō gods are also worshiped in most Buddhist households, except those attached to the Shin sect. Many followers of even the Shin sect, however, appear to follow the ancient religion likewise; and they have their Ujigami.

est classes not less than the lives of the poor. It made monks of Emperors, and nuns of their daughters; it decided the conduct of rulers, the nature of decrees, and the administration of laws. In every community the Buddhist parish-priest was a public official as well as a spiritual teacher: he kept the parish register, and made report to the authorities upon local matters of importance.

By introducing the love of learning, Confucianism had partly prepared the way for Buddhism. As early even as the first century there were some Chinese scholars in Japan; but it was toward the close of the third century that the study of Chinese literature first really became fashionable among the ruling classes. Confucianism, however, did not represent a new religion: it was a system of ethical teachings founded upon an ancestor-worship much like that of Japan. What it had to offer was a kind of social philosophy — an explanation of the eternal reason of things. It reënforced and expanded the doctrine of filial piety; it regulated and elaborated preëxisting ceremonial; and it systematized all the ethics of government. In the education of the ruling classes it became a great power, and has so remained down to the present day. Its doctrines were humane, in the best meaning of the word; and striking evidence of its humanizing effect on government policy may be found in the laws and the maxims of that wisest of Japanese rulers — Iyéyasu.

THE INTRODUCTION OF BUDDHISM

But the religion of the Buddha brought to Japan another and a wider humanizing influence — a new gospel of tenderness — together with a multitude of new beliefs that were able to accommodate themselves to the old, in spite of fundamental dissimilarity. In the highest meaning of the term, it was a civilizing power. Besides teaching new respect for life, the duty of kindness to animals as well as to all human beings, the consequence of present acts upon the conditions of a future existence, the duty of resignation to pain as the inevitable result of forgotten error, it actually gave to Japan the arts and the industries of China. Architecture, painting, sculpture, engraving, printing, gardening — in short, every art and industry that helped to make life beautiful — developed first in Japan under Buddhist teaching.

There are many forms of Buddhism; and in modern Japan there are twelve principal Buddhist sects; but, for present purposes, it will be enough to speak, in the most general way, of popular Buddhism only, as distinguished from philosophical Buddhism, which I shall touch upon in a subsequent chapter. The higher Buddhism could not, at any time or in any country, have had a large popular following; and it is a mistake to suppose that its particular doctrines — such as the doctrine of Nirvana — were taught to the common people. Only such forms of doctrine were preached as could be made intelligible and attractive to very simple minds. There is a Buddhist proverb: "First observe the person; then preach the Law" — that is to say, Adapt your instruction to the capacity of the listener. In Japan, as in China, Buddhism had to adapt its instruction to the mental capacity of large classes of people yet unaccustomed to abstract ideas. Even to this day the masses do not know so much as the meaning of the word "Nirvana" (Néhan): they have been taught only the simpler forms of the religion; and in dwelling upon these, it will be needless to consider differences of sect and dogma.

To appreciate the direct influence of Buddhist teaching upon the minds of the common people, we must remember that in Shintō there was no doctrine of metempsychosis. As I have said before, the spirits of the dead, according to ancient Japanese thinking, continued to exist in the world: they mingled somehow with the viewless forces of nature, and acted through them. Everything happened by the agency of these spirits — evil or good. Those who had been wicked in life remained wicked after death; those who had been good in life became good gods after death; but all were to be propitiated. No idea of future reward or punishment existed before the coming of Buddhism: there was no notion of any heaven or hell. The happiness of ghosts and gods alike was supposed to depend upon the worship and the offerings of the living.

With these ancient beliefs Buddhism attempted

to interfere only by expanding and expounding them
— by interpreting them in a totally new light.
Modifications were effected, but no suppressions:
we might even say that Buddhism accepted the
whole body of the old beliefs. It was true, the new
teaching declared, that the dead continued to exist
invisibly; and it was not wrong to suppose that
they became divinities, since all of them were
destined, sooner or later, to enter upon the way to
Buddhahood — the divine condition. Buddhism
acknowledged likewise the greater gods of Shintō,
with all their attributes and dignities — declaring
them incarnations of Buddhas or Bodhisattvas:
thus the Goddess of the Sun was identified with
Dai-Nichi-Nyōrai (the Tathâgata Mahâvairokana);
the deity Hachiman was identified with Amida
(Amitâbha). Nor did Buddhism deny the existence
of goblins and evil gods: these were identified with
the pretas and the Marakâyikas; and the Japanese
popular term for goblin, "ma," to-day reminds us
of this identification. As for wicked ghosts, they
were to be thought of as pretas only — gaki — self-
doomed by the errors of former lives to the Circle
of Perpetual Hunger. The ancient sacrifices to the
various gods of disease and pestilence — gods of
fever, small-pox, dysentery, consumption, coughs,
and colds — were continued with Buddhist approval; but converts were bidden to consider such
maleficent beings as pretas, and to present them
with only such food-offerings as are bestowed upon

14

pretas — not for propitiation, but for the purpose of relieving ghostly pain. In this case, as in the case of the ancestral spirits, Buddhism prescribed that the prayers to be repeated were to be said *for* the sake of the haunters, rather than *to* them. . . . The reader may be reminded of the fact that Roman Catholicism, by making a similar provision, still practically tolerates a continuance of the ancient European ancestor-worship. And we cannot consider that worship extinct in any of those Western countries where the peasants still feast their dead upon the Night of All Souls.

Buddhism, however, did more than tolerate the old rites. It cultivated and elaborated them. Under its teaching a new and beautiful form of the domestic cult came into existence; and all the touching poetry of ancestor-worship in modern Japan can be traced to the teaching of the Buddhist missionaries. Though ceasing to regard their dead as gods in the ancient sense, the Japanese converts were encouraged to believe in their presence, and to address them in terms of reverence and affection. It is worthy of remark that the doctrine of pretas gave new force to the ancient fear of neglecting the domestic rites. Ghosts unloved might not become "evil gods" in the Shintō meaning of the term; but the malevolent gaki was even more to be dreaded than the malevolent kami — for Buddhism defined in appalling ways the nature of the gaki's power to harm. In various Buddhist funeral rites, the dead are actually addressed as gaki — beings to be pitied, but also to be feared — much needing human sympathy and succor, but able to recompense the food-giver by ghostly help.

One particular attraction of Buddhist teaching was its simple and ingenious interpretation of nature. Countless matters which Shintō had never attempted to explain, and could not have explained, Buddhism expounded in detail, with much apparent consistency. Its explanations of the mysteries of birth, life, and death were at once consoling to pure minds, and wholesomely discomforting to bad consciences. It taught that the dead were happy or unhappy not directly because of the attention or the neglect shown them by the living, but because of their past conduct while in the body.[1] It did not attempt to teach the higher doctrine of successive rebirths — which the people could not possibly have understood — but the merely symbolic doctrine of transmigration, which everybody could understand. To die was not to melt back into nature, but to be reincarnated; and the character of

[1] The reader will doubtless wonder how Buddhism could reconcile its doctrine of successive rebirths with the ideas of ancestor-worship. If one died only to be born again, what could be the use of offering food or addressing any kind of prayer to the reincarnated spirit? This difficulty was met by the teaching that the dead were not immediately reborn in most cases, but entered into a particular condition called "Chū-U." They might remain in this disembodied condition for the time of one hundred years, after which they were reincarnated. The Buddhist services for the dead are consequently limited to the time of one hundred years.

the new body, as well as the conditions of the new existence, would depend upon the quality of one's deeds and thoughts in the present body. All states and conditions of being were the consequence of past actions. Such a man was now rich and powerful, because in previous lives he had been generous and kindly; such another man was now sickly and poor, because in some previous existence he had been sensual and selfish. This woman was happy in her husband and her children, because in the time of a former birth she had proved herself a loving daughter and a faithful spouse; this other was wretched and childless, because in some anterior existence she had been a jealous wife and a cruel mother. "To hate your enemy," the Buddhist preacher would proclaim, "is foolish as well as wrong: he is now your enemy only because of some treachery that you practiced upon him in a previous life, when he desired to be your friend. Resign yourself to the injury which he now does you: accept it as the expiation of your forgotten fault. . . . The girl whom you hoped to marry has been refused you by her parents — given away to another. But once, in another existence, she was yours by promise; and you broke the pledge then given. . . . Painful, indeed, the loss of your child; but this loss is the consequence of having, in some former life, refused affection where affection was due. . . . Maimed by mishap, you can no longer earn your living as before. Yet this mishap is really due to the fact that in some previous existence you wantonly inflicted bodily injury. Now the evil of your own act has returned upon you: repent of your crime, and pray that its Karma may be exhausted by this present suffering." . . . All the sorrows of men were thus explained and consoled. Life was expounded as representing but one stage of a measureless journey, whose way stretched back through all the night of the past, and forward through all the mystery of the future — out of eternities forgotten into the eternities to be; and the world itself was to be thought of only as a traveler's resting-place, an inn by the roadside.

Instead of preaching to the people about Nirvana, Buddhism discoursed to them of blisses to be won and pains to be avoided: the Paradise of Amida, Lord of Immeasurable Light; the eight hot hells called To-kwatsu, and the eight icy hells called Abuda. On the subject of future punishment the teaching was very horrible: I should advise no one of delicate nerves to read the Japanese, or rather the Chinese accounts of hell. But hell was the penalty for supreme wickedness only: it was not eternal; and the demons themselves would at last be saved. . . . Heaven was to be the reward of good deeds: the reward might indeed be delayed, through many successive rebirths, by reason of lingering Karma; but, on the other hand, it might be attained by virtue of a single holy act in this present life. Besides, prior to the period of supreme reward, each succeeding rebirth could be made happier than the preceding one by persistent effort in the holy Way. Even as regarded conditions in this transitory world, the results of virtuous conduct were not to be despised. The beggar of to-day might to-morrow be reborn in the palace of a daimyō; the blind shampooer might become, in his very next life, an Imperial minister. Always the recompense would be proportionate to the sum of merit. In this lower world to practice the highest virtue was difficult; and the great rewards were hard to win. But for all good deeds a recompense was sure; and there was no one who could not acquire merit.

Even the Shintō doctrine of conscience — the god-given sense of right and wrong — was not denied by Buddhism. But this conscience was interpreted as the essential wisdom of the Buddha dormant in every human creature — wisdom darkened by ignorance, clogged by desire, fettered by Karma, but destined sooner or later to fully awaken and to flood the mind with light.

It would seem that the Buddhist teaching of the duty of kindness to all living creatures, and of pity for all suffering, had a powerful effect upon national habit and custom, long before the new religion found general acceptance. As early as the year 675, a decree was issued by the Emperor Temmu forbidding the people to eat "the flesh of kine, horses, dogs, monkeys, or barn-door fowls," and prohibiting the use of traps or the making of pitfalls in catching game.[1] The fact that all kinds of flesh-meat were not forbidden is probably explained by this Emperor's zeal for the maintenance of both creeds; — an absolute prohibition might have interfered with Shintō usages, and would certainly have been incompatible with Shintō traditions. But, although fish never ceased to be an article of food for the laity, we may say that from about this time the mass of the nation abandoned its habits of diet, and forswore the eating of meat, in accordance with Buddhist teaching. . . . This teaching was based upon the doctrine of the unity of all sentient existence. Buddhism explained the whole visible world by its doctrine of Karma — simplifying that doctrine so as to adapt it to popular comprehension. The forms of all creatures — bird, reptile, or mammal; insect or fish — represented only different results of Karma: the ghostly life in each was one and the same; and, in even the lowest, some spark of the divine existed. The frog or the serpent, the bird or the bat, the ox or the horse — all had had, at some past time, the privilege of human (perhaps even superhuman) shape: their present conditions represented only the consequence of ancient faults. Any human being also, by reason of like faults, might hereafter be reduced to the same dumb state — might be reborn as a reptile, a fish, a bird, or a beast of burden. The consequence of wanton

[1] See Aston's translation of the *Nihongi*, vol. II, p. 328.

cruelty to any animal might cause the perpetrator of that cruelty to be reborn as an animal of the same kind, destined to suffer the same cruel treatment. Who could even be sure that the goaded ox, the overdriven horse, or the slaughtered bird, had not formerly been a human being of closest kin — ancestor, parent, brother, sister, or child? . . .

Not by words only were all these things taught. It should be remembered that Shintō had no art: its ghost-houses, silent and void, were not even decorated. But Buddhism brought in its train all the arts of carving, painting, and decoration. The images of its Bodhisattvas, smiling in gold — the figures of its heavenly guardians and infernal judges, its feminine angels and monstrous demons — must have startled and amazed imaginations yet unaccustomed to any kind of art. Great paintings hung in the temples, and frescoes limned upon their walls or ceilings, explained better than words the doctrine of the Six States of Existence, and the dogma of future rewards and punishments. In rows of kakemono, suspended side by side, were displayed the incidents of a Soul's journey to the realm of judgment, and all the horrors of the various hells. One pictured the ghosts of faithless wives, for ages doomed to pluck, with bleeding fingers, the rasping bamboo-grass that grows by the Springs of Death; another showed the torment of the slanderer, whose tongue was torn by demon-pincers; in a third appeared the spectres of lustful men, vainly seeking to flee the embraces of women of fire, or climbing, in frenzied terror, the slopes of the Mountain of Swords. Pictured also were the circles of the preta-world, and the pangs of the Hungry Ghosts, and likewise the pains of rebirth in the form of reptiles and of beasts. And the art of these early representations — many of which have been preserved — was an art of no mean order. We can hardly conceive the effect upon inexperienced imagination of the crimson frown of Emma (Yama), Judge of the dead — or the vision of that weird Mirror which reflected to every spirit the misdeeds of its life in the body — or the monstrous fancy of that double-faced Head before the judgment seat, representing the visage of the woman Mirumé, whose eyes behold all secret sin; and the vision of the man Kaguhana, who smells all odors of evil-doing. . . . Parental affection must have been deeply touched by the painted legend of the world of children's ghosts — the little ghosts that must toil, under demon-surveillance, in the Dry Bed of the River of Souls. . . . But pictured terrors were offset by pictured consolations — by the beautiful figure of Kwannon, white Goddess of Mercy — by the compassionate smile of Jizō, the playmate of infant ghosts — by the charm also of celestial nymphs, floating on iridescent wings in light of azure. The Buddhist painter opened to simple fancy the palaces of heaven, and guided hope, through gardens of jewel-trees, even to the shores of that lake where the souls of the blessed are reborn in lotus-blossoms, and tended by angel nurses.

Moreover, for people accustomed only to such simple architecture as that of the Shintō miya, the new temples erected by the Buddhist priests must have been astonishments. The colossal Chinese gates, guarded by giant statues; the lions and lanterns of bronze and stone; the enormous suspended bells, sounded by swinging beams; the swarming of dragon-shapes under the eaves of the vast roofs; the glimmering splendor of the altars; the ceremonial likewise, with its chanting and its incense-burning and its weird Chinese music — cannot have failed to inspire the wonder-loving with delight and awe. It is a noteworthy fact that the earliest Buddhist temples in Japan still remain, even to Western eyes, the most impressive. The Temple of the Four Deva Kings at Ōsaka — which, though more than once rebuilt, preserves the original plan — dates from 600 A.D.; the yet more remarkable temple called Hōryūji, near Nara, dates from about the year 607.

Of course the famous paintings and the great statues could be seen at the temples only; but the Buddhist image-makers soon began to people even the most desolate places with stone images of Buddhas and of Bodhisattvas. Then first were made those icons of Jizō, which still smile upon the traveler from every roadside — and the images of Kōshin, protector of highways, with his three symbolic Apes — and the figure of that Batō-Kwannon, who protects the horses of the peasant — with other figures in whose rude but impressive art suggestions of Indian origin are yet recognizable. Gradually the graveyards became thronged with dreaming Buddhas or Bodhisattvas — holy guardians of the dead, throned upon lotus-flowers of stone, and smiling with closed eyes the smile of the Calm Supreme. In the cities everywhere Buddhist sculptors opened shops, to furnish pious households with images of the chief divinities worshiped by the various Buddhist sects; and the makers of ihai, or Buddhist mortuary tablets, as well as the makers of household shrines, multiplied and prospered.

Meanwhile the people were left free to worship their ancestors according to either creed; and if a majority eventually gave preference to the Buddhist rite, this preference was due in large measure to the peculiar emotional charm which Buddhism had infused into the cult. Except in minor details, the two rites differed scarcely at all; and there was no conflict whatever between the old ideas of filial piety and the Buddhist ideas attaching to the new ancestor-worship. Buddhism taught that the dead might be helped and made happier by prayer, and that much ghostly comfort could be given them by food-offerings. They were not to be offered flesh or wine; but it was proper to gratify them with fruits and rice and cakes and flowers and the smoke of incense. Besides, even the simplest food-offerings might be transmuted, by force of prayer, into celestial nectar and ambrosia. But what especially helped the new ancestor cult to popular favor, was the fact that it included many beautiful and touching customs not known to the old. Everywhere the people soon learned to kindle the hundred and eight fires of welcome for the annual visit of their dead — to supply the spirits with little figures made of straw, or made out of vegetables, to serve for oxen or horses [1] — also to prepare the ghost-ships (shōryōbuné), in which the souls of the ancestors were to return, over the sea, to their under-world. Then too were instituted the Bon-odori, or Dances of the Festival of the Dead,[2] and the custom of suspending white lanterns at graves, and colored lanterns at house-gates, to light the coming and the going of the visiting dead.

[1] An eggplant, with four pegs of wood stuck into it, to represent legs, usually stands for an ox; and a cucumber, with four pegs, serves for a horse. . . . One is reminded of the fact that, at some of the ancient Greek sacrifices, similar substitutes for real animals were used. In the worship of Apollo, at Thebes, apples with wooden pegs stuck into them, to represent feet and horns, were offered as substitutes for sheep.

[2] The dances themselves — very curious and very attractive to witness — are much older than Buddhism; but Buddhism made them a feature of the festival referred to, which lasts for three days. No person who has not witnessed a Bon-odori can form the least idea of what Japanese dancing means: it is something utterly different from what usually goes by the name — something indescribably archaic, weird, and nevertheless fascinating. I have repeatedly sat up all night to watch the peasants dancing. Japanese dancing-girls, be it observed, do not dance; they pose. The peasants dance.

THE INTRODUCTION OF BUDDHISM

But perhaps the greatest value of Buddhism to the nation was educational. The Shintō priests were not teachers. In early times they were mostly aristocrats, religious representatives of the clans; and the idea of educating the common people could not even have occurred to them. Buddhism, on the other hand, offered the boon of education to all — not merely a religious education, but an education in the arts and the learning of China. The Buddhist temples eventually became common schools, or had schools attached to them; and at each parish-temple the children of the community were taught, at a merely nominal cost, the doctrines of the faith, the wisdom of the Chinese classics, calligraphy, drawing, and much besides. By degrees the education of almost the whole nation came under Buddhist control; and the moral effect was of the best. For the military class indeed there was another and special system of education; but samurai scholars sought to perfect their knowledge under Buddhist teachers of renown; and the Imperial household itself employed Buddhist instructors. For the common people everywhere the Buddhist priest was the schoolmaster; and by virtue of his occupation as teacher, not less than by reason of his religious office, he ranked with the samurai. Much of what remains most attractive in Japanese character — the winning and graceful aspects of it — seems to have been developed under Buddhist training.

It was natural enough that to his functions of public instructor, the Buddhist priest should have added those of a public registrar. Until the period of disendowment, the Buddhist clergy remained, throughout the country, public as well as religious officials. They kept the parish records, and furnished at need certificates of birth, death, or family descent.

To give any just conception of the immense civilizing influence which Buddhism exerted in Japan would require many volumes. Even to summarize the results of that influence by stating only the most general facts, is scarcely possible — for no general statement can embody the whole truth of the work accomplished. As a moral force, Buddhism strengthened authority and cultivated submission, by its capacity to inspire larger hopes and fears than the more ancient religion could create. As teacher, it educated the race, from the highest to the humblest, both in ethics and in æsthetics. All that can be classed under the name of art in Japan was either introduced or developed by Buddhism; and the same may be said regarding nearly all Japanese literature possessing real literary quality — excepting some Shintō rituals, and some fragments of archaic poetry. Buddhism introduced drama, the higher forms of poetical composition, and fiction, and history, and philosophy. All the refinements of Japanese life were of Buddhist introduction, and at least a majority of its diversions and pleasures. There is even to-day scarcely one interesting or beautiful thing, produced in the country, for which the nation is not in some sort indebted to Buddhism. Perhaps the best and briefest way of stating the range of such indebtedness is simply to say that Buddhism brought the whole of Chinese civilization into Japan, and thereafter patiently modified and reshaped it to Japanese requirements. The elder civilization was not merely superimposed upon the social structure, but fitted carefully into it, combined with it so perfectly that the marks of the welding, the lines of the juncture, almost totally disappeared.

THE HIGHER BUDDHISM

PHILOSOPHICAL Buddhism requires some brief consideration in this place — for two reasons. The first is that misapprehension or ignorance of the subject has rendered possible the charge of atheism against the intellectual classes of Japan. The second reason is that some persons imagine the Japanese common people — that is to say, the greater part of the nation — believers in the doctrine of Nirvana as extinction (though, as a matter of fact, even the meaning of the word is unknown to the masses), and quite resigned to vanish from the face of the earth, because of that incapacity for struggle which the doctrine is supposed to create. A little serious thinking ought to convince any intelligent man that no such creed could ever have been the religion of either a savage or a civilized people. But myriads of Western minds are ready at all times to accept statements of impossibility without taking the trouble to think about them; and if I can show some of my readers how far beyond popular comprehension the doctrines of the higher Buddhism really are, something will have been accomplished for the cause of truth and common sense. And besides the reasons already given for dwelling upon the subject, there is this third and special reason — that it is one of extraordinary interest to the student of modern philosophy.

Before going further, I must remind you that the metaphysics of Buddhism can be studied anywhere else quite as well as in Japan, since the more important sutras have been translated into various European languages, and most of the untranslated texts edited and published. The texts of Japanese Buddhism are Chinese; and only Chinese scholars are competent to throw light upon the minor special phases of the subject. Even to read the Chinese Buddhist canon of seven thousand volumes is commonly regarded as an impossible feat — though it has certainly been accomplished in Japan. Then there are the commentaries, the varied interpretations of different sects, the multiplications of later doctrine, to heap confusion upon confusion. The complexities of Japanese Buddhism are incalculable; and those who try to unravel them soon become, as a general rule, hopelessly lost in the maze of detail. All this has nothing to do with my present purpose. I shall have very little to say about Japanese Buddhism as distinguished from other Buddhism, and nothing at all to say about sect differences. I shall keep to general facts as regards the higher doctrine — selecting from among such facts only those most suitable for the illustration of that doctrine. And I shall not take up the subject of Nirvana, in spite of its great importance — having treated it as fully as

JAPAN

I was able in my "Gleanings in Buddha-Fields" —
but confine myself to the topic of certain analogies
between the conclusions of Buddhist metaphysics
and the conclusions of contemporary Western
thought.

In the best single volume yet produced in English on the subject of Buddhism,[1] the late Mr.
Henry Clarke Warren observed: "A large part of
the pleasure that I have experienced in the study
of Buddhism has arisen from what I may call the
strangeness of the intellectual landscape. All the
ideas, the modes of argument, even the postulates
assumed and not argued about, have always seemed
so strange, so different from anything to which I
have been accustomed, that I felt all the time as
though walking in Fairyland. Much of the charm
that the Oriental thoughts and ideas have for me
appears to be because they so seldom fit into Western categories." . . . The serious attraction of Buddhist philosophy could not be better suggested: it is
indeed "the strangeness of the intellectual landscape," as of a world inside-out and upside-down,
that has chiefly interested Western thinkers heretofore. Yet after all, there *is* a class of Buddhist concepts which can be fitted, or very nearly fitted, into
Western categories. The higher Buddhism is a kind
of Monism; and it includes doctrines that accord, in

[1] *Buddhism in Translations*, by Henry Clarke Warren (Cambridge,
Massachusetts, 1896). Published by Harvard University.

31

the most surprising manner, with the scientific theories of the German and the English monists. To my thinking, the most curious part of the subject, and its main interest, is represented just by these accordances — particularly in view of the fact that the Buddhist conclusions have been reached through mental processes unknown to Western thinking, and unaided by any knowledge of science. . . . I venture to call myself a student of Herbert Spencer; and it was because of my acquaintance with the Synthetic Philosophy that I came to find in Buddhist philosophy a more than romantic interest. For Buddhism is also a theory of evolution, though the great central idea of our scientific evolution (the law of progress from homogeneity to heterogeneity) is not correspondingly implied by Buddhist doctrine as regards the life of this world. The course of evolution as we conceive it, according to Professor Huxley, "must describe a trajectory like that of a ball fired from a mortar; and the sinking half of that course is as much a part of the general process of evolution as the rising." The highest point of the trajectory would represent what Mr. Spencer calls Equilibration — the supreme point of development preceding the period of decline; but, in Buddhist evolution, this supreme point vanishes into Nirvana. I can best illustrate the Buddhist position by asking you to imagine the trajectory line upside-down — a course descending out of the infinite, touching ground, and ascending again to mystery. . . . Nevertheless, some Buddhist ideas do offer the most startling analogy with the evolutional ideas of our own time; and even those Buddhist concepts most remote from Western thought can be best interpreted by the help of illustrations and of language borrowed from modern science.

I think that we may consider the most remarkable teachings of the higher Buddhism — excluding the doctrine of Nirvana, for the reason already given — to be the following:

> That there is but one Reality;
> That the consciousness is not the real Self;
> That Matter is an aggregate of phenomena created by the force of acts and thoughts;
> That all objective and subjective existence is made by Karma — the present being the creation of the past, and the actions of the present and the past, in combination, determining the conditions of the future. . . .

(Or, in other words, that the universe of Matter, and the universe of [conditioned] Mind, represent in their evolution a strictly moral order.)

It will be worth while now to briefly consider these doctrines in their relation to modern thought — beginning with the first, which is Monism.

All things having form or name — Buddhas, gods, men, and all living creatures — suns, worlds, moons, the whole visible cosmos — are transitory phenomena. . . . Assuming, with Herbert Spencer, that the test of reality is permanence, one can scarcely question this position; it differs little from the statement with which the closing chapter of the "First Principles" concludes:

Though the relation of subject and object renders necessary to us these antithetical conceptions of Spirit and Matter, the one is no less than the other to be regarded as but a sign of the Unknown Reality which underlies both.[1]

For Buddhism the sole reality is the Absolute — Buddha as unconditioned and Infinite Being. There is no other veritable existence, whether of Matter or of Mind; there is no real individuality or personality; the "I" and the "Not-I" are essentially nowise different. We are reminded of Mr. Spencer's position, that "it is one and the same Reality which is manifested to us both subjectively and objectively." Mr. Spencer goes on to say:

Subject and Object, as actually existing, can never be contained in *the consciousness produced by the coöperation of the two*, though they are necessarily implied by it; and the antithesis of Subject and Object, never to be transcended while consciousness lasts, renders impossible all knowledge of that Ultimate Reality in which Subject and Object are united. . . .

I do not think that a master of the higher Buddhism would dispute Mr. Spencer's doctrine of Transfigured Realism. Buddhism does not deny the actuality of phenomena as phenomena, but

[1] Edition of 1894.

denies their permanence, and the truth of the appearances which they present to our imperfect senses. Being transitory, and not what they seem, they are to be considered in the nature of illusions — impermanent manifestations of the only permanent Reality. But the Buddhist position is not agnosticism: it is astonishingly different, as we shall presently see. Mr. Spencer states that we cannot know the Reality so long as consciousness lasts — because while consciousness lasts we cannot transcend the antithesis of Object and Subject, and it is this very antithesis which makes consciousness possible. "Very true," the Buddhist metaphysician would reply; "we cannot know the sole Reality while consciousness lasts. *But destroy consciousness, and the Reality becomes cognizable.* Annihilate the illusion of Mind, and the light will come." This destruction of consciousness signifies Nirvana — the extinction of all that we call Self. Self is blindness: destroy it, and the Reality will be revealed as infinite vision and infinite peace.

We have now to ask what, according to Buddhist philosophy, is the meaning of the visible universe as phenomenon, and the nature of the consciousness that perceives. However transitory, the phenomenon makes an impression upon consciousness; and consciousness itself, though transitory, has existence; and its perceptions, however delusive, are perceptions of actual relation. Buddhism answers that both the universe and the consciousness are merely aggregates of Karma — complexities incalculable of conditions shaped by acts and thoughts through some enormous past. All substance and all conditioned mind (as distinguished from unconditioned mind) are products of acts and thoughts: by acts and thoughts the atoms of bodies have been integrated; and the affinities of those atoms — the polarities of them, as a scientist might say — represent tendencies shaped in countless vanished lives. I may quote here from a modern Japanese treatise on the subject:

The aggregate actions of all sentient beings give birth to the varieties of mountains, rivers, countries, etc. They are caused by aggregate actions, and so are called aggregate fruits. Our present life is the reflection of past actions. Men consider these reflections as their real selves. Their eyes, noses, ears, tongues, and bodies — as well as their gardens, woods, farms, residences, servants, and maids — men imagine to be their own possessions; but, in fact, they are only results endlessly produced by innumerable actions. In tracing everything back to the ultimate limits of the past, we cannot find a beginning: hence it is said that death and birth have no beginning. Again, when seeking the ultimate limit of the future, we cannot find the end.[1]

This teaching that all things are formed by Karma — whatever is good in the universe representing the results of meritorious acts or thoughts; and whatever is evil, the results of evil acts or thoughts — has the approval of five of the great

[1] *Outlines of the Mahâyâna Philosophy*, by S. Kuroda.

sects; and we may accept it as a leading doctrine of Japanese Buddhism. . . . The cosmos is, then, an aggregate of Karma; and the mind of man is an aggregate of Karma; and the beginnings thereof are unknown, and the end cannot be imagined. There is a spiritual evolution, of which the goal is Nirvana; but we have no declaration as to a final state of universal rest, when the shaping of substance and of mind will have ceased forever. . . . Now the Synthetic Philosophy assumes a very similar position as regards the evolution of phenomena: there is no beginning to evolution, nor any conceivable end. I quote from Mr. Spencer's reply to a critic in the "North American Review":

That "absolute commencement of organic life upon the globe," which the reviewer says I "cannot evade the admission of," I distinctly deny. The affirmation of universal evolution is in itself the negation of an absolute commencement of anything. Construed in terms of evolution, every kind of being is conceived as a product of modification wrought by insensible gradations upon a preëxisting kind of being; and this holds as fully of the supposed "commencement of organic life" as of all subsequent developments of organic life. . . . That organic matter was not produced all at once, but was reached through steps, we are well warranted in believing by the experiences of chemists.[1] . . .

Of course it should be understood that the Buddhist silence, as to a beginning and an end, concerns only the production of phenomena, not any particu-

[1] *Principles of Biology*, vol. 1, p. 482.

lar existence of groups of phenomena. That of which no beginning or end can be predicated is simply the Eternal Becoming. And, like the older Indian philosophy from which it sprang, Buddhism teaches the alternate apparition and disparition of universes. At certain prodigious periods of time, the whole cosmos of "one hundred thousand times ten millions of worlds" vanishes away — consumed by fire or otherwise destroyed — but only to be reformed again. These periods are called "World-Cycles," and each World-Cycle is divided into four "Immensities" — but we need not here consider the details of the doctrine. It is only the fundamental idea of an evolutional rhythm that is really interesting. I need scarcely remind the reader that the alternate disintegration and reintegration of the cosmos is also a scientific conception, and a commonly accepted article of evolutional belief. I may quote, however, for other reasons, the paragraph expressing Herbert Spencer's views upon the subject:

Apparently the universally coexistent forces of attraction and repulsion, which, as we have seen, necessitate rhythm in all minor changes throughout the Universe, also necessitate rhythm in the totality of changes — produce now an immeasurable period during which the attractive forces, predominating, cause universal concentration; and then an immeasurable period during which the repulsive forces, predominating, cause diffusion — alternate eras of Evolution and Dissolution. And thus there is suggested to us the conception of a past during which there have been successive Evolutions analogous to that which is now going on; and a future during which successive other such Evolutions may go on — ever the same in principle, but never the same in concrete result.[1]

Farther on, Mr. Spencer has pointed out the vast logical consequence involved by this hypothesis:

If, as we saw reason to think, there is an alternation of Evolution and Dissolution in the totality of things — if, as we are obliged to infer from the Persistence of Force, the arrival at either limit of this vast rhythm brings about the conditions under which a counter-movement commences — if we are hence compelled to entertain the conception of Evolutions that have filled an immeasurable past, and Evolutions that will fill an immeasurable future — we can no longer contemplate the visible creation as having a definite beginning or end, or as being isolated. It becomes unified with all existence before and after; and the Force which the Universe presents falls into the same category with its Space and Time as admitting of no limitation in thought.[2]

The foregoing Buddhist positions sufficiently imply that the human consciousness is but a temporary aggregate — not an eternal entity. There is no permanent self: there is but one eternal principle in all life — the supreme Buddha. Modern Japanese call this Absolute the "Essence of Mind."

[1] *First Principles*, § 183. This paragraph, from the fourth edition, has been considerably qualified in the definitive edition of 1900.

[2] *First Principles*, § 190. Condensed and somewhat modified in the definitive edition of 1900; but, for present purposes of illustration, the text of the fourth edition has been preferred.

THE HIGHER BUDDHISM

"The fire fed by fagots," writes one of these, "dies when the fagots have been consumed; but the essence of fire is never destroyed. . . . All things in the Universe are Mind." So stated, the position is unscientific; but as for the conclusion reached, we may remember that Mr. Wallace has stated almost exactly the same thing, and that there are not a few modern preachers of the doctrine of a "universe of mind-stuff." The hypothesis is "unthinkable." But the most serious thinker will agree with the Buddhist assertion that the relation of all phenomena to the unknowable is merely that of waves to sea. "Every feeling and thought being but transitory," says Mr. Spencer, "an entire life made up of such feelings and thoughts being but transitory — nay, the objects amid which life is passed, though less transitory, being severally in course of losing their individualities quickly or slowly — we learn that the one thing permanent is the Unknown Reality hidden under all these changing shapes." Here the English and the Buddhist philosophers are in accord; but thereafter they suddenly part company. For Buddhism is not agnosticism, but gnosticism, and professes to know the unknowable. The thinker of Mr. Spencer's school cannot make assumptions as to the nature of the sole Reality, nor as to the reason of its manifestations. He must confess himself intellectually incapable of comprehending the nature of force, matter, or motion. He feels justified in accepting the hypothesis that all known

40

elements have been evolved from one primordial undifferentiated substance — the chemical evidence for this hypothesis being very strong. But he certainly would not call that primordial substance a substance of mind, nor attempt to explain the character of the forces that effected its integration. Again, though Mr. Spencer would probably acknowledge that we know of matter only as an aggregate of forces, and of atoms only as force-centres, or knots of force, he would not declare that an atom *is* a force-centre, and nothing else. . . . But we find evolutionists of the German school taking a position very similar to the Buddhist position — which implies a universal sentiency, or, more strictly speaking, a universal potential-sentiency. Haeckel and other German monists assume such a condition for all substance. They are not agnostics, therefore, but gnostics; and their gnosticism very much resembles that of the higher Buddhism.

According to Buddhism there is no reality save Buddha: all things else are but Karma. There is but one Life, one Self: human individuality and personality are but phenomenal conditions of that Self. Matter is Karma; Mind is Karma — that is to say, mind as we know it: Karma, as visibility, represents to us mass and quality; Karma, as mentality, signifies character and tendency. The primordial substance — corresponding to the "protyle" of our monists — is composed of Five Elements, which are mystically identified with Five Buddhas, all of whom are really but different modes of the One. With this idea of a primordial substance there is necessarily associated the idea of a universal sentiency. Matter is alive.

Now to the German monists also matter is alive. On the phenomena of cell-physiology, Haeckel claims to base his conviction that "even the atom is not without rudimentary form of sensation and will — or, as it is better expressed, of feeling (æsthesis), and of inclination (tropesis) — that is to say, a universal soul of the simplest kind." I may quote also from Haeckel's "Riddle of the Universe" the following paragraph expressing the monistic notion of substance as held by Vogt and others:

The two fundamental forms of substance, ponderable matter and ether, are not dead and only moved by extrinsic force; but they are endowed with sensation and will (though, naturally, of the lowest grade); they experience an inclination for condensation, a dislike of strain; they strive after the one, and struggle against the other.

Less like a revival of the dreams of the alchemists is the very probable hypothesis of Schneider, that sentiency begins with the formation of certain combinations — that feeling is evolved from the non-feeling just as organic being has been evolved from inorganic substance. But all these monist ideas enter into surprising combination with the Buddhist teaching about matter as integrated Karma; and for that reason they are well worth citing in this relation. To Buddhist conception all matter is sentient

— the sentiency varying according to condition: "even rocks and stones," a Japanese Buddhist text declares, "can worship Buddha." In the German monism of Professor Haeckel's school, the particular qualities and affinities of the atom represent feeling and inclination, "a soul of the simplest kind"; in Buddhism these qualities are made by Karma — that is to say, they represent tendencies formed in previous states of existence. The hypotheses appear to be very similar. But there is one immense, all-important difference, between the Occidental and the Oriental monism. The former would attribute the qualities of the atom merely to a sort of heredity — to the persistency of tendencies developed under chance influences operating throughout an incalculable past. The latter declares the history of the atom to be purely moral! All matter, according to Buddhism, represents aggregated sentiency, making, by its inherent tendencies, toward conditions of pain or pleasure, evil or good. "Pure actions," writes the author of "Outlines of the Mahâyâna Philosophy," "bring forth the Pure Lands of all the quarters of the universe; while impure deeds produce the Impure Lands." That is to say, the matter integrated by the force of moral acts goes to the making of blissful worlds; and the matter formed by the force of immoral acts goes to the making of miserable worlds. All substance, like all mind, has its Karma; planets, like men, are shaped by the creative power of acts and thoughts; and every atom goes to its appointed place, sooner or later, according to the moral or immoral quality of the tendencies that inform it. Your good or bad thought or deed will not only affect your next rebirth, but will likewise affect in some sort the nature of worlds yet unevolved, wherein, after innumerable cycles, you may have to live again. Of course, this tremendous idea has no counterpart in modern evolutional philosophy. Mr. Spencer's position is well known; but I must quote him for the purpose of emphasizing the contrast between Buddhist and scientific thought:

> ... We have no ethics of nebular condensation, or of sidereal movement, or of planetary evolution; the conception is not relevant to inorganic matter. Nor, when we turn to organized things, do we find that it has any relation to the phenomena of plant-life; though we ascribe to plants superiorities and inferiorities, leading to successes and failures in the struggle for existence, we do not associate with them pra se or blame. It is only with the rise of sentiency in the animal world that the subject-matter of ethics originates.[1]

On the contrary, it will be seen, Buddhism actually teaches what we may call, to borrow Mr. Spencer's phrase, "the ethics of nebular condensation" — though to Buddhist astronomy, the scientific meaning of the term "nebular condensation" was never known. Of course the hypothesis is beyond the power of human intelligence to prove or

[1] *Principles of Ethics*, vol. II, § 326.

to disprove. But it is interesting, for it proclaims a purely moral order of the cosmos, and attaches almost infinite consequence to the least of human acts. Had the old Buddhist metaphysicians been acquainted with the facts of modern chemistry, they might have applied their doctrine, with appalling success, to the interpretation of those facts. They might have explained the dance of atoms, the affinities of molecules, the vibrations of ether, in the most fascinating and terrifying way by their theory of Karma. . . . Here is a universe of suggestion — most weird suggestion — for anybody able and willing to dare the experiment of making a new religion, or at least a new and tremendous system of Alchemy, based upon the notion of a moral order in the inorganic world!

But the metaphysics of Karma in the higher Buddhism include much that is harder to understand than any alchemical hypothesis of atom-combinations. As taught by popular Buddhism, the doctrine of rebirth is simple enough — signifying no more than transmigration: you have lived millions of times in the past, and you are likely to live again millions of times in the future — all the conditions of each rebirth depending upon past conduct. The common notion is that after a certain period of bodiless sojourn in this world, the spirit is guided somehow to the place of its next incarnation. The people, of course, believe in souls. But there is nothing of all this in the higher doctrine, which denies transmigration, denies the existence of the soul, denies personality. There is no Self to be reborn; there is no transmigration — and yet there is rebirth! There is no real "I" that suffers or is glad — and yet there is new suffering to be borne or new happiness to be gained! What we call the Self — the personal consciousness — dissolves at the death of the body; but the Karma, formed during life, then brings about the integration of a new body and a new consciousness. You suffer in this existence because of acts done in a previous existence — yet the author of those acts was not identical with your present self! Are you, then, responsible for the faults of another person?

The Buddhist metaphysician would answer thus: "The form of your question is wrong, because it assumes the existence of personality — and there is no personality. There is really no such individual as the 'you' of the inquiry. The suffering is indeed the result of errors committed in some anterior existence or existences; but there is no responsibility for the acts of another person, since there is no personality. The 'I' that was and the 'I' that is represent in the chain of transitory being aggregations momentarily created by acts and thoughts; and the pain belongs to the aggregates as condition resulting from quality."

All this sounds extremely obscure: to understand the real theory we must put away the notion of personality, which is a very difficult thing to do. Successive births do not mean transmigration in the common sense of that word, but only the self-propagation of Karma: the perpetual multiplying of certain conditions by a kind of ghostly gemmation — if I may borrow a biological term. The Buddhist illustration, however, is that of flame communicated from one lamp-wick to another: a hundred lamps may thus be lighted from one flame, and the hundred flames will all be different, though the origin of all was the same. Within the hollow flame of each transitory life is enclosed a part of the only Reality; but this is not a soul that transmigrates. Nothing passes from birth to birth but Karma — character or condition.

One will naturally ask how can such a doctrine exert any moral influence whatever? If the future being shaped by my Karma is to be in nowise identical with my present self — if the future consciousness evolved by *my* Karma is to be essentially another consciousness — how can I force myself to feel anxious about the sufferings of that unborn person? "Again your question is wrong," a Buddhist would answer: "to understand the doctrine you must get rid of the notion of individuality, and think, not of persons, but of successive states of feeling and consciousness, each of which buds out of the other — a chain of existences interdependently united." . . . I may attempt another illustration. Every individual, as we understand the term, is continually changing. All the structures of the body are constantly undergoing waste and repair; and the body that you have at this hour is not, as to substance, the same body that you had ten years ago. Physically you are not the same person: yet you suffer the same pains, and feel the same pleasures, and find your powers limited by the same conditions. Whatever disintegrations and reconstructions of tissue have taken place within you, you have the same physical and mental peculiarities that you had ten years ago. Doubtless the cells of your brain have been decomposed and recomposed: yet you experience the same emotions, recall the same memories, and think the same thoughts. Everywhere the fresh substance has assumed the qualities and tendencies of the substance replaced. This persistence of condition is like Karma. The transmission of tendency remains, though the aggregate is changed. . . .

These few glimpses into the fantastic world of Buddhist metaphysics will suffice, I trust, to convince any intelligent reader that the higher Buddhism (to which belongs the much-discussed and little-comprehended doctrine of Nirvana) could never have been the religion of millions almost incapable of forming abstract ideas — the religion of a population even yet in a comparatively early stage of religious evolution. It was never understood by the people at all, nor is it ever taught to them to-day.

It is a religion of metaphysicians, a religion of
scholars, a religion so difficult to be understood,
even by persons of some philosophical training,
that it might well be mistaken for a system of universal negation. Yet the reader should now be able
to perceive that, because a man disbelieves in a
personal God, in an immortal soul, and in any con-
tinuation of personality after death, it does not
follow that we are justified in declaring him an
irreligious person — especially if he happen to be
an Oriental. The Japanese scholar who believes in
the moral order of the universe, the ethical responsibility of the present to all the future, the immeasurable consequence of every thought and deed, the
ultimate disparition of evil, and the power of attainment to conditions of infinite memory and infinite
vision — cannot be termed either an atheist or a
materialist, except by bigotry and ignorance. Profound as may be the difference between his religion
and our own, in respect of symbols and modes of
thought, the moral conclusions reached in either
case are very much the same.

NIRVANA

A STUDY IN SYNTHETIC BUDDHISM

I

It is not possible, O Subhûti, that this treatise of the Law should be heard by beings of little faith — by those who believe in Self, in beings, in living beings, and in persons.   *The Diamond-Cutter*

THERE still widely prevails in Europe and America the idea that Nirvana signifies, to Buddhist minds, neither more nor less than absolute nothingness — complete annihilation. This idea is erroneous. But it is erroneous only because it contains half of a truth. This half of a truth has no value or interest, or even intelligibility, unless joined with the other half. And of the other half no suspicion yet exists in the average Western mind.

Nirvana, indeed, signifies an extinction. But if by this extinction of individual being we understand soul-death, our conception of Nirvana is wrong. Or if we take Nirvana to mean such reabsorption of the finite into the infinite as that predicted by Indian pantheism, again our idea is foreign to Buddhism.

Nevertheless, if we declare that Nirvana means the extinction of individual sensation, emotion, thought — the final disintegration of conscious personality — the annihilation of everything that can be included under the term "I" — then we rightly express one side of the Buddhist teaching.

50

NIRVANA

The apparent contradiction of the foregoing statements is due only to our Occidental notion of Self. Self to us signifies feelings, ideas, memory, volition; and it can scarcely occur to any person not familiar with German idealism even to imagine that consciousness might not be Self. The Buddhist, on the contrary, declares all that we call Self to be false. He defines the Ego as a mere temporary aggregate of sensations, impulses, ideas, created by the physical and mental experiences of the race — all related to the perishable body, and all doomed to dissolve with it. What to Western reasoning seems the most indubitable of realities, Buddhist reasoning pronounces the greatest of all illusions, and even the source of all sorrow and sin.

The mind, the thoughts, and all the senses are subject to the law of life and death. With knowledge of Self and the laws of birth and death, there is no grasping, and no sense-perception. Knowing one's self and knowing how the senses act, there is no room for the idea of "I," or the ground for framing it. The thought of "Self" gives rise to all sorrows — binding the world as with fetters; but having found there is no "I" that can be bound, then all these bonds are severed.[1]

The above text suggests very plainly that the consciousness is not the Real Self, and that the mind dies with the body. Any reader unfamiliar with Buddhist thought may well ask, "What, then, is the meaning of the doctrine of Karma, the doctrine of moral progression, the doctrine of the consequence

[1] *Fo-Sho-Hing-Tsan-King.*

of acts?" Indeed, to try to study, only with the ontological ideas of the West, even such translations of the Buddhist Sutras as those given in the "Sacred Books of the East," is to be at every page confronted by seemingly hopeless riddles and contradictions. We find a doctrine of rebirth; but the existence of a soul is denied. We are told that the misfortunes of this life are punishments of faults committed in a previous life; yet personal transmigration does not take place. We find the statement that beings are reindividualized; yet both individuality and personality are called illusions. I doubt whether anybody not acquainted with the deeper forms of Buddhist belief could possibly understand the following extracts which I have made from the first volume of "The Questions of King Milinda":

The King said: "Nagasena, is there any one who after death is not reindividualized?" Nagasena answered: "A sinful being is reindividualized; a sinless one is not" (p. 50).

"Is there, Nagasena, such a thing as the soul?" "There is no such thing as soul" (pp. 86-89). [The same statement is repeated in a later chapter (p. 111), with a qualification: "*In the highest sense*, O King, there is no such thing."]

"Is there any being, Nagasena, who transmigrates from this body to another?" "No: there is not" (p. 112).

"Where there is no transmigration, Nagasena, can there be rebirth?" "Yes: there can."

"Does he, Nagasena, who is about to be reborn, know that he will be reborn?" "Yes: he knows it, O King" (p. 113).

NIRVANA

Naturally the Western reader may ask — "How can there be reindividualization without a soul? How can there be rebirth without transmigration? How can there be personal foreknowledge of rebirth without personality?" But the answers to such questions will not be found in the work cited.

It would be wrong to suppose that the citations given offer any exceptional difficulty. As to the doctrine of the annihilation of Self, the testimony of nearly all those Buddhist texts now accessible to English readers is overwhelming. Perhaps the Sutra of the Great Decease furnishes the most remarkable evidence contained in the "Sacred Books of the East." In its account of the Eight Stages of Deliverance leading to Nirvana, it explicitly describes what we should be justified in calling, from our Western point of view, the process of absolute annihilation. We are told that in the first of these eight stages the Buddhist seeker after truth still retains the ideas of form — subjective and objective. In the second stage he loses the subjective idea of form, and views forms as external phenomena only. In the third stage the sense of the approaching perception of larger truth comes to him. In the fourth stage he passes beyond all ideas of form, ideas of resistance, and ideas of distinction; and there remains to him only the idea of infinite space. In the fifth stage the idea of infinite space vanishes, and the thought comes: *It is all infinite reason.* [Here is the uttermost limit, many might suppose, of panthe-

53

istic idealism; but it is only the half way resting-place on the path which the Buddhist thinker must pursue.] In the sixth stage the thought comes, "*Nothing at all exists.*" In the seventh stage the idea of nothingness itself vanishes. In the eighth stage all sensations and ideas cease to exist. And *after* this comes Nirvana.

The same sutra, in recounting the death of the Buddha, represents him as rapidly passing through the first, second, third, and fourth stages of meditation to enter into "that state of mind to which the Infinity of Space alone is present" and thence into "that state of mind to which the Infinity of Thought alone is present"; and thence into "that state of mind to which nothing at all is specially present"; and thence into "that state of mind between consciousness and unconsciousness"; and thence into "that state of mind in which the consciousness both of sensations and of ideas has wholly passed away."

For the reader who has made any serious attempt to obtain a general idea of Buddhism, such citations are scarcely necessary; since the fundamental doctrine of the concatenation of cause and effect contains the same denial of the reality of Self and suggests the same enigmas. Illusion produces action or Karma; Karma, self-consciousness; self-consciousness, individuality; individuality, the senses; the senses, contact; contact, feeling; feeling, desire; desire, union; union, conception; conception, birth; birth, sorrow and decrepitude and death. Doubtless the reader knows the doctrine of the destruction of the twelve Nidanas; and it is needless here to repeat it at length. But he may be reminded of the teaching that by the cessation of contact feeling is destroyed; by that of feeling, individuality; and by that of individuality, *self-consciousness*.

Evidently, without a preliminary solution of the riddles offered by such texts, any effort to learn the meaning of Nirvana is hopeless. Before being able to comprehend the true meaning of those sutras now made familiar to English readers by translation, it is necessary to understand that the common Occidental ideas of God and Soul, of matter, of spirit, have no existence in Buddhist philosophy; their places being occupied by concepts having no real counterparts in Western religious thought. Above all, it is necessary that the reader should expel from his mind the theological idea of Soul. The texts already quoted should have made it clear that in Buddhist philosophy there is no personal transmigration, and no individual permanent Soul.

II

O Bhagavat, the idea of a self is no idea; and the idea of a being, or a living person, or a person, is no idea. And why? Because the blessed Buddhas are freed from all ideas. *The Diamond-Cutter*

AND now let us try to understand what it is that dies, and what it is that is reborn; what it is that commits faults and what it is that suffers penalties; what passes from states of woe to states of bliss;

what enters into Nirvana after the destruction of self-consciousness; what survives "extinction" and has power to return out of Nirvana; what experiences the Four Infinite Feelings after all finite feeling has been annihilated.

It is not the sentient and conscious Self that enters Nirvana. The Ego is only a temporary aggregate of countless illusions, a phantom-shell, a bubble sure to break. It is a creation of Karma — or rather, as a Buddhist friend insists, it *is* Karma. To comprehend the statement fully, the reader should know that, in this Oriental philosophy, acts and thoughts are forces of integrating themselves into material and mental phenomena — into what we call objective and subjective appearances. The very earth we tread upon — the mountains and forests, the rivers and seas, the world and its moon, the visible universe in short — *is the integration of acts and thoughts*, is Karma, or, at least, Being conditioned by Karma.[1]

---

[1] "The aggregate actions of all sentient beings give birth to the varieties of mountains, rivers, countries, etc. . . . . Their eyes, nostrils, ears, tongues, bodies — as well as their gardens, woods, farms, residences, servants, and maids — men imagine to be their own possessions; but they are, in truth, only results produced by innumerable actions." (KURODA, *Outlines of the Mahayana*.)

"Grass, trees, earth — all these shall become Buddha." (CHŪ-IN-KYŌ.)

"Even swords and things of metal are manifestations of spirit: within them exist all virtues [*or* "power"] in their fullest development and perfection." (HIZŌ-HO-YAKU.)

"When called sentient or non-sentient, matter is Law-Body [*or* "spiritual body"]." (CHISHŌ-HISHŌ.)

NIRVANA

The Karma-Ego we call Self is mind and is body;
— both perpetually decay; both are perpetually
renewed. From the unknown beginning, this double
phenomenon, objective and subjective, has been
alternately dissolved and integrated: each integration is a birth; each dissolution a death. There is no
other birth or death but the birth and death of
Karma in some form or condition. But at each rebirth the reintegration is never the reintegration of
the identical phenomenon, but of another to which
it gives rise — as growth begets growth, as motion
produces motion. So that the phantom-self changes
not only as to form and condition, but as to actual
personality with every reëmbodiment. There is one
Reality; but there is no permanent individual, no
constant personality: there is only phantom-self,
and phantom succeeds to phantom, as undulation
to undulation, over the ghostly Sea of Birth and
Death. And even as the storming of a sea is a motion of undulation, not of translation — even as it
is the form of the wave only, not the wave itself, that
travels — so in the passing of lives there is only the
rising and the vanishing of forms — forms mental,
forms material. The fathomless Reality does not

"The Apparent Doctrine treats of the four great elements [earth, fire,
water, air] as non-sentient. But in the Hidden Doctrine these are said to
be the Sammya-Shin [Samya-Kaya], or Body-Accordant of the Nyōrai
[Tathâgata]." (SOKU-SHIN-JŌ-BUTSU-GI.)

"When every phase of our mind shall be in accord with the mind of
Buddha, . . . then there will not be even one particle of dust that does
not enter into Buddhahood." (ENGAKU-SHŌ.)

pass. "All forms," it is written in the "Kongō-hannya-haramitsu-Kyō," [1] "are unreal: he who rises above all forms is the Buddha." But what can remain to rise above all forms after the total dis-integration of body and the final dissolution of mind?

Unconsciously dwelling behind the false con-sciousness of imperfect man — beyond sensation, perception, thought — wrapped in the envelope of what we call soul (which in truth is only a thickly woven veil of illusion), is the eternal and divine, the Absolute Reality: not a soul, not a personality, but the All-Self without selfishness — the Muga no Taiga — the Buddha enwombed in Karma. Within every phantom-self dwells this divine: yet the in-numerable are but one. Within every creature in-carnate sleeps the Infinite Intelligence unevolved, hidden, unfelt, unknown — yet destined from all the eternities to waken at last, to rend away the ghostly web of sensuous mind, to break forever its chrysalis of flesh, and pass to the supreme conquest of Space and Time. Wherefore it is written in the "Kegon-Kyō" ("Avatamsaka-Sutra"):

Child of Buddha, there is not even one living being that has not the wisdom of the Tathâgata. It is only because of their vain thoughts and affections that all beings are not conscious of this.... I will teach them the holy Way; — I will make them forsake their foolish thoughts, and cause them to see that the vast and deep intelligence which dwells within them is not different from the wis-dom of the very Buddha.

[1] *Vagra-pragñâ pâramita-Sutra.*

NIRVANA

Here we may pause to consider the correspondence between these fundamental Buddhist theories and the concepts of Western science. It will be evident that the Buddhist denial of the reality of the apparitional world is not a denial of the reality of phenomena as phenomena, nor a denial of the forces producing phenomena objectively or subjectively. For the negation of Karma as Karma would involve the negation of the entire Buddhist system. The true declaration is, that what we perceive is never reality in itself, and that even the Ego that perceives is an unstable plexus of aggregates of feelings which are themselves unstable and in the nature of illusions. This position is scientifically strong — perhaps impregnable. Of substance in itself we certainly know nothing: we are conscious of the universe as a vast play of forces only; and, even while we discern the general relative meaning of laws expressed in the action of those forces, all that which is Non-Ego is revealed to us merely through the vibrations of a nervous structure never exactly the same in any two human beings. Yet through such varying and imperfect perception we are sufficiently assured of the impermanency of all forms — of all aggregates objective or subjective.

The test of reality is persistence; and the Buddhist, finding in the visible universe only a perpetual flux of phenomena, declares the material aggregate unreal because non-persistent — unreal, at least, as a bubble, a cloud, or a mirage. Again, relation is the

59

universal form of thought; but since relation is impermanent, how can thought be persistent? ... Judged from these points of view, Buddhist doctrine is not Anti-Realism, but a veritable Transfigured Realism, finding just expression in the exact words of Herbert Spencer:

Every feeling and thought being but transitory; — an entire life made up of such feelings and thoughts being also but transitory; — nay, the objects amid which life is passed, though less transitory, being severally in the course of losing their individualities, whether quickly or slowly — *we learn that the one thing permanent is the Unknowable Reality hidden under all these changing shapes.*

Likewise, the teaching of Buddhism, that what we call Self is an impermanent aggregate — a sensuous illusion — will prove, if patiently analyzed, scarcely possible for any serious thinker to deny. Mind, as known to the scientific psychologist, is composed of feelings and the relations between feelings; and feelings are composed of units of simple sensation which are physiologically coincident with minute nervous shocks. All the sense-organs are fundamentally alike, being evolutional modifications of the same morphological elements; — and all the senses are modifications of touch. Or, to use the simplest possible language, the organs of sense — sight, smell, taste, even hearing — have been alike developed from the skin! Even the human brain itself, by the modern testimony of histology and embryology, "is, at its first beginning, merely an infolding

of the epidermic layer"; and thought, physiologically and evolutionally, is thus a modification of
touch. Certain vibrations, acting through the visual
apparatus, cause within the brain those motions
which are followed by the sensations of light and
color; — other vibrations, acting upon the auditory
mechanism, give rise to the sensation of sound; —
other vibrations, setting up changes in specialized
tissue, produce sensations of taste, smell, touch.
All our knowledge is derived and developed, directly
or indirectly, from physical sensation — from touch.
Of course this is no ultimate explanation, because
nobody can tell us *what feels the touch*. "Everything
physical," well said Schopenhauer, "is at the same
time metaphysical." But science fully justifies the
Buddhist position that what we call Self is a bundle
of sensations, emotions, sentiments, ideas, memories, all relating to the *physical* experiences of the
race and the individual, and that our wish for immortality is a wish for the eternity of this merely
sensuous and selfish consciousness. And science even
supports the Buddhist denial of the permanence
of the sensuous Ego. "Psychology," says Wundt,
"proves that not only our sense-perceptions, but
the memorial images that renew them, depend for
their origin upon the functionings of the organs of
sense and movement.... A continuance of this
sensuous consciousness must appear to her irreconcilable with the facts of her experience. And surely
we may well doubt whether such continuance is an

ethical requisite: more, whether the fulfillment of the wish for it, if possible, were not an intolerable destiny."

III

O Subhûti, if I had had an idea of a being, of a living being, or of a person, I should also have had an idea of malevolence. . . . A gift should not be given by any one who believes in form, sound, smell, taste, or anything that can be touched.

The Diamond-Cutter

THE doctrine of the impermanency of the conscious Ego is not only the most remarkable in Buddhist philosophy: it is also, morally, one of the most important. Perhaps the ethical value of this teaching has never yet been fairly estimated by any Western thinker. How much of human unhappiness has been caused, directly and indirectly, by opposite beliefs — by the delusion of stability — by the delusion that distinctions of character, condition, class, creed, are settled by immutable law — and the delusion of a changeless, immortal, sentient soul, destined, by divine caprice, to eternities of bliss or eternities of fire! Doubtless the ideas of a deity moved by everlasting hate — of soul as a permanent, changeless entity destined to changeless states — of sin as unatonable and of penalty as never-ending — were not without value in former savage stages of social development. But in the course of our future evolution they must be utterly got rid of; and it may be hoped that the contact of Western with Oriental thought will have for one happy result the acceleration of their decay. While even the feelings which they have developed linger with us, there can be no true spirit of tolerance, no sense of human brotherhood, no wakening of universal love.

Buddhism, on the other hand, recognizing no permanency, no finite stabilities, no distinctions of character or class or race, except as passing phenomena — nay, no difference even between gods and men — has been essentially the religion of tolerance. Demon and angel are but varying manifestations of the same Karma; — hell and heaven mere temporary halting-places upon the journey to eternal peace. For all beings there is but one law — immutable and divine: the law by which the lowest *must* rise to the place of the highest — the law by which the worst *must* become the best — the law by which the vilest *must* become a Buddha. In such a system there is no room for prejudice and for hatred. Ignorance alone is the source of wrong and pain; and all ignorance must finally be dissipated in infinite light *through the decomposition of Self*.

Certainly while we still try to cling to the old theories of permanent personality, and of a single incarnation only for each individual, we can find no moral meaning in the universe as it exists. Modern knowledge can discover no justice in the cosmic process; — the very most it can offer us by way of ethical encouragement is that the unknowable forces are not forces of pure malevolence. "Neither moral nor immoral," to quote Huxley, "but simply un-moral." Evolutional science cannot be made to accord with the notion of indissoluble personality; and if we accept its teaching of mental growth and inheritance, we must also accept its teaching of in-dividual dissolution and of the cosmos as inexplicable. It assures us, indeed, that the higher faculties of man have been developed through struggle and pain, and will long continue to be so developed; but it also assures us that evolution is inevitably followed by dissolution — that the highest point of development is the point likewise from which retrogression begins. And if we are each and all mere perishable forms of being — doomed to pass away like plants and trees — what consolation can we find in the assurance that we are suffering for the benefit of the future? How can it concern us whether humanity become more or less happy in another myriad ages, if there remains nothing for us but to live and die in comparative misery? Or, to repeat the irony of Huxley, "what compensation does the Eohippus get for his sor-rows in the fact that, some millions of years after-wards, one of his descendants wins the Derby?"

But the cosmic process may assume quite another aspect if we can persuade ourselves, like the Bud-dhist, that all being is Unity; that personality is but a delusion hiding reality; that all distinctions of "I" and "thou" are ghostly films spun out of perishable sensation; that even Time and Place as revealed to our petty senses are phantasms; that the past and the present and the future are veritably One. Suppose the winner of the Derby quite well able to remember having been the Eohippus? Suppose the being, once man, able to look back through all veils of death and birth, through all evolutions of evolution, even to the moment of the first faint growth of sentiency out of non-sentiency; — able to remember, like the Buddha of the Jatakas, all the experiences of his myriad incarnations, and to relate them like fairy-tales for the sake of another Ananda?

We have seen that it is not the Self but the Non-Self — the one reality underlying all phenomena — which passes from form to form. The striving for Nirvana is a struggle perpetual between false and true, light and darkness, the sensual and the supersensual; and the ultimate victory can be gained only by the total decomposition of the mental and the physical individuality. Not one conquest of self can suffice: millions of selves must be overcome. For the false Ego is a compound of countless ages — possesses a vitality enduring beyond universes. At each breaking and shedding of the chrysalis a new chrysalis appears — more tenuous, perhaps more diaphanous, but woven of like sensuous material — a mental and physical texture spun by Karma from the inherited illusions, passions, desires, pains and pleasures, of innumerable lives. But what is it that feels? — the phantom or the reality?

All phenomena of *Self*-consciousness belong to the false self — but only as a physiologist might say that sensation is a product of the sensiferous apparatus, which would not explain sensation. No more in Buddhism than in physiological psychology is there any real teaching of *two* feeling entities. In Buddhism the only entity is the Absolute; and to that entity the false self stands in the relation of a medium through which right perception is deflected and distorted — in which and because of which sentiency and impulse become possible. The unconditioned Absolute is above all relations: it has nothing of what we call pain or pleasure; it knows no difference of "I" and "thou" — no distinction of place or time. But while conditioned by the illusion of personality, it is aware of pain or pleasure, as a dreamer perceives unrealities without being conscious of their unreality. Pleasures and pains and all the feelings relating to self-consciousness are hallucinations. The false self exists only as a state of sleep exists; and sentiency and desire, and all the sorrows and passions of being, exist only as illusions of that sleep.

But here we reach a point at which science and Buddhism diverge. Modern psychology recognizes no feelings not evolutionally developed through the experiences of the race and the individual; but Buddhism asserts the existence of feelings which are immortal and divine. It declares that in this Karma-state the greater part of our sensations, perceptions, ideas, thoughts, are related only to the phantom self; — that our mental life is little more than a flow of feelings and desires belonging to selfishness; — that our loves and hates, and hopes and fears, and pleasures and pains, are illusions; [1] — but it also declares there are higher feelings, more or less latent within us, according to our degree of knowledge, which have nothing to do with the false self, and which are eternal.

Though science pronounces the ultimate nature of pleasures and pains to be inscrutable, it partly confirms the Buddhist teaching of their impermanent character. Both appear to belong rather to secondary than to primary elements of feeling, and both to be evolutions — forms of sensation developed, through billions of life-experiences, out of primal conditions in which there can have been neither real pleasure nor real pain, but only the vaguest dull sentiency. The higher the evolution the more pain, and the larger the volume of all sensation. After the state of equilibration has been reached, the volume of feeling will begin to diminish. The finer pleasures and the keener pains must first become extinct; then by gradual stages the less complex feelings, according to their complexity; till at last, in all the refrigerating planet, there will survive not even the simplest sensation possible to the lowest form of life.

But, according to the Buddhist, the highest moral feelings survive races and suns and universes. The

[1] "Pleasures and pains have their origin from touch; where there is no touch, they do not arise." (*Atthakavagga*, 11.)

purely unselfish feelings, impossible to grosser natures, belong to the Absolute. In generous natures the divine becomes sentient — quickens within the shell of illusion, as a child quickens in the womb (whence illusion itself is called The Womb of the Tathâgata). In yet higher natures the feelings which are not of self find room for powerful manifestation — shine through the phantom-Ego as light through a vase. Such are purely unselfish love, larger than individual being — supreme compassion — perfect benevolence: they are not of man, but of the Buddha within the man. And as these expand, all the feelings of self begin to thin and weaken. The condition of the phantom-Ego simultaneously purifies: all those opacities which darkened the reality of Mind within the mirage of mind begin to illumine; and the sense of the infinite, like a thrilling of light, passes through the dream of personality into the awakening divine.[1]

But in the case of the average seeker after truth, this refinement and ultimate decomposition of self can be effected only with lentor inexpressible. The phantom-individuality, though enduring only for the space of a single lifetime, shapes out of the sum of its innate qualities, and out of the sum of its own

[1] "To reach the state of the perfect and everlasting happiness is the highest Nirvana; for then all mental phenomena — such as desires, etc. — are annihilated. And as such mental phenomena are annihilated, there appears the true nature of true mind with all its innumerable functions and miraculous actions." (KURODA, *Outlines of the Mahâyâna.*)

particular acts and thoughts, the new combination which succeeds it — a fresh individuality — another prison of illusion for the Self-without-selfishness.[1] As name and form, the false self dissolves; but its impulses live on and recombine; and the final destruction of those impulses — the total extinction of their ghostly vitality — may require a protraction of effort through billions of centuries. Perpetually from the ashes of burnt-out passions subtler passions are born — perpetually from the graves of illusions new illusions arise. The most powerful of human passions is the last to yield: it persists far into super-human conditions. Even when its grosser forms have passed away, its tendencies still lurk in those feelings originally derived from it or interwoven with it — the sensation of beauty, for example, and the delight of the mind in graceful things. On earth these are classed among the higher feelings. But in a supramundane state their indulgence is fraught with peril: a touch or a look may cause the broken fetters of sensual bondage to reform. Beyond all worlds of sex there are strange zones in which thoughts and memories become tangible and visible objective facts — in which emotional fancies are materialized — in which the least unworthy wish may prove creative.

It may be said, in Western religious phraseology,

[1] It is on the subject of this propagation and perpetuation of characters that the doctrine of Karma is in partial agreement with the modern scientific teaching of the hereditary transmission of tendencies.

that throughout the greater part of this vast pilgrimage, and in all the zones of desire, the temptations increase according to the spiritual strength of resistance. With every successive ascent there is a further expansion of the possibilities of enjoyment, an augmentation of power, a heightening of sensation. Immense the reward of self-conquest; but whosoever strives for that reward strives after emptiness. One must not desire heaven as a state of pleasure; it has been written, "Erroneous thoughts as to the joys of heaven are still entwined by the fast cords of lust." One must not wish to become a god or an angel. "Whatsoever brother, O Bhikkus" — the teacher said — "may have adopted the religious life thinking, to himself, 'By this morality I shall become an angel,' his mind does not incline to zeal, perseverance, exertion." Perhaps the most vivid exposition of the duty of the winner of happiness is that given in the Sutra of the Great King of Glory. This great king, coming into possession of all imaginable wealth and power, abstains from enjoyments, despises splendors, refuses the caresses of a queen dowered with "the beauty of the gods," and bids her demand of him, out of her own lips, that he forsake her. She, with dutiful sweetness, but not without natural tears, obeys him; and he passes at once out of existence. Every such refusal of the prizes gained by virtue helps to cause a still more fortunate birth in a still loftier state of being. But no state should be desired; and it is only after the wish for Nirvana itself has ceased that Nirvana can be attained.

And now we may venture for a little while into the most fantastic region of Buddhist ontology — since, without some definite notion of the course of psychical evolution therein described, the suggestive worth of the system cannot be fairly judged. Certainly I am asking the reader to consider a theory about what is beyond the uttermost limit of possible human knowledge. But as much of the Buddhist doctrine as can be studied and tested within the limit of human knowledge is found to accord with scientific opinion better than does any other religious hypothesis; and some of the Buddhist teachings prove to be incomprehensible anticipations of modern scientific discovery — can it, therefore, seem unreasonable to claim that even the pure fancies of a faith so much older than our own, and so much more capable of being reconciled with the widest expansions of nineteenth-century thought, deserve at least respectful consideration?

IV

Non existence is only the entrance to the Great Vehicle.
Daibon-Kyōi

And in which way is it, Siha, that one speaking truly could say of me: "The Samana Gotama maintains annihilation; — he teaches the doctrine of annihilation"? I proclaim, Siha, the annihilation of lust, of ill-will, of delusion; I proclaim the annihilation of the manifold conditions (of heart) which are evil and not good.   *Mahavagga*, VI, 31. 7

"NIN mité, hō toké" (see first the person, then preach

the law) is a Japanese proverb signifying that Buddhism should be taught according to the capacity of the pupil. And the great systems of Buddhist doctrine are actually divided into progressive stages (five usually), to be studied in succession, or otherwise, according to the intellectual ability of the learner. Also there are many varieties of special doctrine held by the different sects and sub-sects — so that, to make any satisfactory outline of Buddhist ontology, it is necessary to shape a synthesis of the more important and non-conflicting among these many tenets. I need scarcely say that popular Buddhism does not include concepts such as we have been examining. The people hold to the simpler creed of a veritable transmigration of souls. The people understand Karma only as the law that makes the punishment or reward of faults committed in previous lives. The people do not trouble themselves about Nehan or Nirvana;[1] but they think much about heaven (Gokuraku), which the members of many sects believe can be attained immediately after this life by the spirits of the good. The followers of the greatest and richest of the modern sects — the Shinshū — hold that, by the invocation of Amida, a righteous person can pass at once after

[1] Scarcely a day passes that I do not hear such words uttered as ingwa, gokuraku, goshō — or other words referring to Karma, heaven, future life, past life, etc. But I have never heard a man or woman of the people use the word "Nehan"; and whenever I have ventured to question such about Nirvana, I found that its philosophical meaning was unknown. On the other hand, the Japanese scholar speaks of Nehan as the reality — of heaven, either as a temporary condition or as a parable.

death to the great Paradise of the West — the Paradise of the Lotus-Flower-Birth. I am taking no account of popular beliefs in this little study, nor of doctrines peculiar to any one sect only.

But there are many differences in the higher teaching as to the attainment of Nirvana. Some authorities hold that the supreme happiness can be won, or at least seen, even on this earth; while others declare that the present world is too corrupt to allow of a perfect life, and that only by winning, through good deeds, the privilege of rebirth into a better world, can men hope for opportunity to practice that holiness which leads to the highest bliss. The latter opinion, which posits the superior conditions of being in other worlds, better expresses the general thought of contemporary Buddhism in Japan.

The conditions of human and of animal being belong to what are termed the Worlds of Desire (Yoku-Kai) — which are four in number. Below these are the states of torment or hells (Jigoku), about which many curious things are written; but neither the Yoku-Kai nor the Jigoku need be considered in relation to the purpose of this little essay. We have only to do with the course of spiritual progress from the world of men up to Nirvana — assuming, with modern Buddhism, that the pilgrimage through death and birth must continue, for the majority of mankind at least, even after the attainment of the highest conditions possible upon this globe. The way rises from terrestrial conditions to other and superior worlds — passing first through the Six Heavens of Desire (Yoku-Ten); — thence through the Seventeen Heavens of Form (Shiki-Kai); — and lastly through the Four Heavens of Formlessness (Mushiki-Kai), beyond which lies Nirvana.

The requirements of physical life — the need of food, rest, and sexual relations — continue to be felt in the Heavens of Desire — which would seem to be higher physical worlds rather than what we commonly understand by the expression "heavens." Indeed, the conditions in some of them are such as might be supposed to exist in planets more favored than our own — in larger spheres warmed by a more genial sun. And some Buddhist texts actually place them in remote constellations — declaring that the Path leads from star to star, from galaxy to galaxy, from universe to universe, up to the Limit of Existence.[1]

In the first of the heavens of this zone, called the Heaven of the Four Kings (Shi-Tennō-Ten), life lasts five times longer than life on this earth according to number of years, and each year there is equal to fifty terrestrial years. But its inhabitants eat and drink, and marry and give in marriage, much after the fashion of mankind. In the succeeding heaven

[1] This astronomical localization of higher conditions of being, or of other "Buddha-fields," may provoke a smile; but it suggests undeniable possibilities. There is no absurdity in supposing that potentialities of life and growth and development really pass, with nebular diffusion and concentration, from expired systems to new systems. Indeed, not to suppose this, in our present state of knowledge, is scarcely possible for the rational mind.

(Sanjiu-san-Ten), the duration of life is doubled, while all other conditions are correspondingly improved; and the grosser forms of passion disappear. The union of the sexes persists, but in a manner curiously similar to that which a certain Father of the Christian Church wished might become possible — a simple embrace producing a new being. In the third heaven (called Emma-Ten), where longevity is again doubled, the slightest touch may create life. In the fourth, or Heaven of Contentment (Tochita-Ten), longevity is further increased. In the fifth, or Heaven of the Transmutation of Pleasure (Keraku-Ten), strange new powers are gained. Subjective pleasures become changed at will into objective pleasures; — thoughts as well as wishes become creative forces; — and even the act of seeing may cause conception and birth. In the sixth heaven (Také-jizai-Ten), the powers obtained in the fifth heaven are further developed; and the subjective pleasures transmuted into objective can be presented to others, or shared with others — like material gifts. But the look of an instant — one glance of the eye — may generate a new Karma.

The Yoku-Kai are all heavens of sensuous life — heavens such as might answer to the dreams of artists and lovers and poets. But those who are able to traverse them without falling (and a fall, be it observed, is not difficult) pass into the Supersensual Zone, first entering the Heavens of Luminous Observation of Existence and of Calm Meditation upon

Existence (Ujin-ushi-shōryo, or Kakkwan). These are in number three — each higher than the preceding — and are named The Heaven of Sanctity, The Heaven of Higher Sanctity, and The Heaven of Great Sanctity. After these come the heavens called the Heavens of Luminous Observation of Non-Existence and of Calm Meditation upon Non-Existence (Mūjin-mushi-shōryo). These also are three; and the names of them in their order signify, Lesser Light, Light Unfathomable, and Light Making Sound, or, Light-Sonorous. Here there is attained the highest degree of supersensuous joy possible to temporary conditions. Above are the states named Riki-shōryo, or the Heavens of the Meditation of the Abandonment of Joy. The names of these states in their ascending order are, Lesser Purity, Purity Unfathomable, and Purity Supreme. In them neither joy nor pain, nor forceful feeling of any sort exist: there is a mild negative pleasure only — the pleasure of heavenly Equanimity.[1] Higher than these heavens are the eight spheres of Calm Meditation upon the Abandonment of all Joy and Pleasure (Riki-raku-shōryo). They are called The Cloudless, Holiness-Manifest, Vast Results, Empty of Name, Void of Heat, Fair-Appearing, Vision-Per-

---

[1] One is reminded by this conception of Mr. Spencer's beautiful definition of Equanimity: "Equanimity may be compared to white light, which, though composed of numerous colors, is colorless; while pleasurable and painful moods of mind may be compared to the modifications of light that result from increasing the proportions of some rays, and decreasing the proportions of others." (*Principles of Psychology.*)

fecting, and The Limit of Form. Herein pleasure and pain, and name and form, pass utterly away. But there remain ideas and thoughts.

He who can pass through these supersensual realms enters at once into the Mushiki-Kai — the spheres of Formlessness. These are four. In the first state of the Mushiki-Kai, all sense of individuality is lost: even the thought of name and form becomes extinct, and there survives only the idea of Infinite Space, or Emptiness. In the second state of the Mushiki-Kai, this idea of space vanishes; and its place is filled by the Idea of Infinite Reason. But this idea of reason is anthropomorphic: it is an illusion; and it fades out in the third state of the Mushiki-Kai, which is called the "State-of-Nothing-to-take-hold-of," or Mū-sho-ū-shō-jō. Here is only the Idea of Infinite Nothingness. But even this condition has been reached by the aid of the action of the personal mind. This action ceases: then the fourth state of the Mushiki-Kai is reached — the Hisō-hihisō-shō, or the state of "neither-namelessness-nor-not-namelessness." Something of personal mentality continues to float vaguely here — the very uttermost expiring vibration of Karma — the last vanishing haze of being. It melts; — and the immeasurable revelation comes. The dreaming Buddha, freed from the last ghostly bond of Self, rises at once into the "infinite bliss" of Nirvana.[1]

---

[1] The expression "infinite bliss" as synonymous with Nirvana is taken from the *Questions of King Milinda*.

But every being does not pass through all the states above enumerated: the power to rise swiftly or slowly depends upon the acquisition of merit as well as upon the character of the Karma to be overcome. Some beings pass to Nirvana immediately after the present life; some after a single new birth; some after two or three births; while many rise directly from this world into one of the Supersensuous Heavens. All such are called Chō — the Leapers, — of whom the highest class reach Nirvana at once after their death as men or women. There are two great divisions of Chō — the Fu-Kwan, or Never-Returning-Ones,[1] and the Kwan, Returning Ones, or *revenants*. Sometimes the return may be in the nature of a prolonged retrogression; and, according to a Buddhist legend of the origin of the world, the first men were beings who had fallen from the Kwō-on-Ten, or Heaven of Sonorous Light. A remarkable fact about the whole theory of progression is that the progression is not conceived of (except in very rare cases) as an advance in straight lines, but as an advance by undulations — a psychical rhythm of motion. This is exemplified by the curious Buddhist classification of the different short courses by which the Kwan or *revenants* may hope to reach Nirvana. These short courses are divided into Even and Uneven; — the

[1] In the Sutra of the Great Decease we find the instance of a woman reaching this condition: "The Sister Nanda, O Ananda, by the destruction of the five bonds that bind people to this world, has become an inhabitant of the highest heaven — there to pass entirely away — thence never to return."

former includes an equal number of heavenly and of earthly rebirths; while in the latter class the heavenly and the earthly intermediate rebirths are not equal in number. There are four kinds of these intermediate stages. A Japanese friend has drawn for me the accompanying diagrams, which explain the subject clearly. Fantastic this may be called; but it harmonizes with the truth that all progress is necessarily rhythmical.

Though all beings do not pass through every stage of the great journey, all beings who attain to the highest enlightenment, by any course whatever, acquire certain faculties not belonging to particular conditions of birth, but only to particular conditions of psychical development. These are, the Roku-Jindzū (Abhidjñâ), or Six Supernatural Powers:[1] (1) Shin-Kyō-Tsū, the power of passing anywhither through any obstacles — through solid walls, for example; (2) Tengen-Tsū, the power of infinite vision; (3) Tenni-Tsū, the power of infinite hearing; (4) Tashin-Tsū, the power of knowing the thoughts of all other beings; (5) Shuku-jū-Tsū, the power of remembering former births; (6) Rojin-Tsū, infinite wisdom with the power of entering at will into Nirvana. The Roku-Jindzū first begin to develop in the

[1] Different Buddhist systems give different enumerations of these mysterious powers whereof the Chinese names literally signify: (1) Calm-Meditation-outward-pouring-no-obstacle-wisdom: (2) Heaven-Eye-no-obstacle-wisdom; (3) Heaven-Ear-no-obstacle-wisdom; (4) Other-minds-no-obstacle-wisdom; (5) Former-States-no-obstacle-wisdom; (6) Leak-Extinction-no-obstacle-wisdom.

GLEANINGS IN BUDDHA-FIELDS

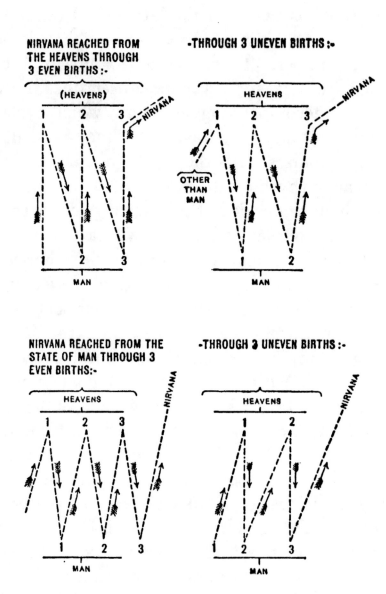

NIRVANA

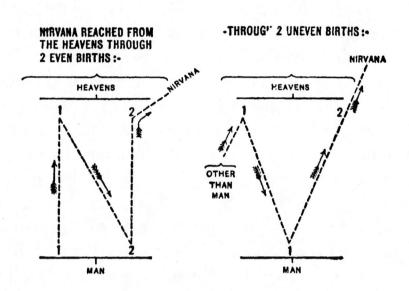

NIRVANA REACHED FROM THE HEAVENS THROUGH 2 EVEN BIRTHS :-

-THROUGH 2 UNEVEN BIRTHS :-

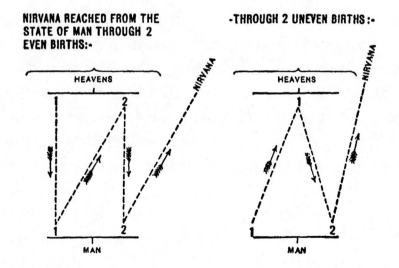

NIRVANA REACHED FROM THE STATE OF MAN THROUGH 2 EVEN BIRTHS:-

-THROUGH 2 UNEVEN BIRTHS :-

state of Shōmon (Sravaka), and expand in the higher conditions of Engaku (Pratyeka-Buddha) and of Bosatsu (Bodhisattva or Mahâsattva). The powers of the Shōmon may be exerted over two thousand worlds; those of the Engaku or Bosatsu, over three thousand; — but the powers of Buddhahood extend over the total cosmos. In the first state of holiness, for example, comes the memory of a certain number of former births, together with the capacity to foresee a corresponding number of future births; — in the next higher state the number of births remembered increases; — and in the state of Bosatsu all former births are visible to memory. But the Buddha sees not only all of his own former births, but likewise all births that ever have been or can be — and all the thoughts and acts, past, present, or future, of all past, present, or future beings. . . . Now these dreams of supernatural power merit attention because of the ethical teaching in regard to them — the same which is woven through every Buddhist hypothesis, rational or unthinkable — the teaching of self-abnegation. The Supernatural Powers must never be used for personal pleasure, but only for the highest beneficence — the propagation of doctrine, the saving of men. Any exercise of them for lesser ends might result in their loss — would certainly signify retrogression in the path.[1] To show them

[1] Beings who have reached the state of Engaku or of Bosatsu are not supposed capable of retrogression, or of any serious error; but it is otherwise in lower spiritual states.

for the purpose of exciting admiration or wonder were to juggle wickedly with what is divine; and the Teacher himself is recorded to have once severely rebuked a needless display of them by a disciple.[1]

This giving up not only of one life, but of countless lives — not only of one world, but of innumerable worlds — not only of natural but also of supernatural pleasures — not only of selfhood but of godhood — is certainly not for the miserable privilege of ceasing to be, but for a privilege infinitely outweighing all that even paradise can give. Nirvana is no cessation, but an emancipation. It means only the passing of conditioned being into unconditioned being — the fading of all mental and physical phantoms into the light of Formless Omnipotence and Omniscience. But the Buddhist hypothesis holds some suggestion of the persistence of that which has once been able to remember all births and states of limited being, — the persistence of the identity of the Buddhas even in Nirvana, notwithstanding the teaching that all Buddhas are one. How reconcile this doctrine of monism with the assurance of various texts that the being who enters Nirvana can, when so desirous, reassume an earthly personality? There are some very remarkable texts on this subject in the Sutra of the Lotus of the Good Law: those for instance in which the Tathâgata Prabhûtarâtna is pictured as sitting *"perfectly extinct upon his throne,"* and speaking before a vast assembly to

[1] See a curious legend in the Vinaya texts — *Kullavagga*, v, 8, 2.

which he has been introduced as "the great Seer who, *although perfectly extinct for many kôtis of æons,* now comes to hear the Law." These texts themselves offer us the riddle of multiplicity in unity; for the Tathâgata Prabhûtarâtna and the myriads of other extinct Buddhas who appear simultaneously, are said to have been all incarnations of but a single Buddha.

A reconciliation is offered by the hypothesis of what might be called a *pluristic monism* — a sole reality composed of groups of consciousness, at once independent and yet interdependent — or, to speak of pure mind in terms of matter, *an atomic spiritual ultimate.* This hypothesis, though not doctrinably enunciated in Buddhist texts, is distinctly implied both by text and commentary. The Absolute of Buddhism is one as ether is one. Ether is conceivable only as a composition of units.[1] The Absolute

---

[1] This position, it will be observed, is very dissimilar from that of Hartmann, who holds that "all plurality of individuation belongs to the sphere of phenomenality" (vol. II, page 233 of English translation). One is rather reminded of the thought of Galton that human beings "may contribute more or less unconsciously to the manifestation of a far higher life than our own — somewhat as the individual cells of one of the more complex animals contribute to the manifestation of its higher order of personality." (*Hereditary Genius,* p. 361.) Another thought of Galton's, expressed on the same page of the work just quoted from, is still more strongly suggestive of the Buddhist concept: "We must not permit ourselves to consider each human or other personality as something supernaturally added to the stock of nature, but rather as a segregation of what already existed, under a new shape, and as a regular consequence of previous conditions. . . . Neither must we be misled by the word 'individuality.' . . . We may look upon each individual as something not wholly detached from its parent source, — as a wave that

is conceivable only (according to any attempt at a synthesis of the Japanese doctrines) as composed of Buddhas. But here the student finds himself voyaging farther, perhaps, beyond the bar of the thinkable than Western philosophers have ever ventured. All are One; — each by union becomes equal with All! We are not only bidden to imagine the ultimate reality as composed of units of conscious being — but to believe each unit permanently equal to every other *and infinite in potentiality*.[1] The central reality of every living creature is a pure Buddha: the visible form and thinking self, which encell it, being but Karma. With some degree of truth it might be

has been lifted and shaped by normal conditions in an unknown and illimitable ocean."

The reader should remember that the Buddhist hypothesis does not imply either individuality or personality in Nirvana, but simple entity — not a spiritual *body*, in our meaning of the term, but only a divine consciousness. "Heart," in the sense of divine mind, is a term used in some Japanese texts to describe such entity. In the *Dai-Nichi Kyō Sŏ* (Commentary on the Dai-Nichi Sutra), for example, is the statement: "When all seeds of Karma-life are entirely burnt out and annihilated, then the *vacuum-pure* Bodhi-heart is reached." (I may observe that Buddhist metaphysicians use the term "vacuum-bodies" to describe one of the high conditions of entity.) The following, from the fifty-first volume of the work called *Daizō-hō-sū* will also be found interesting: "By experience the Tathâgata possesses all forms — forms for multitude numberless as the dust-grains of the universe. . . . The Tathâgata gets himself born in such places as he desires, or in accord with the desire of others, and there saves [literally, "carries over" — that is, over the Sea of Birth and Death] all sentient beings. Wheresoever his will finds an abiding point, there is he embodied: this is called Will-Birth Body. . . . The Buddha makes Law his body, and remains pure as empty space: this is called Law-Body."

[1] Half of this Buddhist thought is really embodied in Tennyson's line —
"Boundless inward, in the atom; boundless outward, in the Whole."

said that Buddhism substitutes for our theory of a universe of physical atoms the hypothesis of a universe of psychical units. Not that it necessarily denies our theory of physical atoms, but that it assumes a position which might be thus expressed in words: "What you call atoms are really combinations, unstable aggregates, essentially impermanent, and therefore essentially unreal. Atoms are but Karma." And this position is suggestive. We know nothing whatever of the ultimate nature of substance and motion: but we have scientific evidence that the known has been evolved from the unknown; that the atoms of our elements *are* combinations; and that what we call matter and force are but different manifestations of a single and infinite Unknown Reality.

There are wonderful Buddhist pictures which at first sight appear to have been made, like other Japanese pictures, with bold free sweeps of a skilled brush, but which, when closely examined, prove to have been executed in a much more marvelous manner. The figures, the features, the robes, the aureoles — also the scenery, the colors, the effects of mist or cloud — all, even to the tiniest detail of tone or line, have been produced by groupings of microscopic Chinese characters — tinted according to position, and more or less thickly massed according to need of light or shade. In brief, these pictures are composed entirely out of texts of Sutras: they are mosaics of minute ideographs — each ideograph a combination of strokes, and the symbol at once of a sound and of an idea.

Is our universe so composed? — an endless phantasmagory made only by combinations of combinations of combinations of combinations of units finding quality and form through unimaginable affinities; — now thickly massed in solid glooms; now palpitating in tremulosities of light and color; always and everywhere grouped by some stupendous art into one vast mosaic of polarities; — yet each unit in itself a complexity inconceivable, and each in itself also a symbol only, a character, a single ideograph of the undecipherable text of the Infinite Riddle? . . . Ask the chemists and the mathematicians.

V

. . . All beings that have life shall lay
Aside their complex form, — that aggregation
Of *mental* and material qualities
That gives them, or in heaven or on earth,
Their fleeting individuality.

The Book of the Great Decease

In every teleological system there are conceptions which cannot bear the test of modern psychological analysis, and in the foregoing unfilled outline of a great religious hypothesis there will doubtless be recognized some "ghosts of beliefs haunting those mazes of verbal propositions in which metaphysicians habitually lose themselves." But truths will be perceived also — grand recognitions of the law of ethical evolution, of the price of progress, and of our relation to the changeless Reality abiding beyond all change.

The Buddhist estimate of the enormity of that opposition to moral progress which humanity must overcome is fully sustained by our scientific knowledge of the past and perception of the future. Mental and moral advance has thus far been effected only through constant struggle against inheritances older than reason or moral feeling — against the instincts and the appetites of primitive brute life. And the Buddhist teaching, that the average man can hope to leave his worse nature behind him only after the lapse of millions of future lives, is much more of a truth than of a theory. Only through millions of births have we been able to reach even this our present imperfect state; and the dark bequests of our darkest past are still strong enough betimes to prevail over reason and ethical feeling. Every future forward pace upon the moral path will have to be taken against the massed effort of millions of ghostly wills. For those past selves which priest and poet have told us to use as steps to higher things are not dead, nor even likely to die for a thousand generations to come: they are too much alive; — they have still power to clutch the climbing feet — sometimes even to fling back the climber into the primeval slime.

Again, in its legend of the Heavens of Desire — progress through which depends upon the ability of triumphant virtue to refuse what it has won —

NIRVANA

Buddhism gives us a wonder-story full of evolutional truth. The difficulties of moral self-elevation do not disappear with the amelioration of material social conditions; — in our own day they rather increase. As life becomes more complex, more multiform, so likewise do the obstacles to ethical advance — so likewise do the results of thoughts and acts. The expansion of intellectual power, the refinement of sensibility, the enlargement of the sympathies, the intensive quickening of the sense of beauty — all multiply ethical dangers just as certainly as they multiply ethical opportunities. The highest material results of civilization, and the increase of possibilities of pleasure, exact an exercise of self-mastery and a power of ethical balance, needless and impossible in older and lower states of existence.

The Buddhist doctrine of impermanency is the doctrine also of modern science: either might be uttered in the words of the other. "Natural knowledge," wrote Huxley in one of his latest and finest essays, "tends more and more to the conclusion that 'all the choir of heaven and furniture of the earth' are the transitory forms of parcels of cosmic substance wending along the road of evolution from nebulous potentiality — through endless growths of sun and planet and satellite — through all varieties of matter — through infinite diversities of life and thought — possibly through modes of being of which we neither have a conception nor are competent to form any — back to the indefinable latency from which they arose. Thus the most obvious attribute of the Cosmos is its impermanency." [1]

And, finally, it may be said that Buddhism not only presents remarkable accordance with nineteenth century thought in regard to the instability of all integrations, the ethical signification of heredity, the lesson of mental evolution, the duty of moral progress, but it also agrees with science in repudiating equally our doctrines of materialism and of spiritualism, our theory of a Creator and of special creation, and our belief in the immortality of the soul. Yet, in spite of this repudiation of the very foundations of Occidental religion, it has been able to give us the revelation of larger religious possibilities — the suggestions of a universal scientific creed nobler than any which has ever existed. Precisely in that period of our own intellectual evolution when faith in a personal God is passing away — when the belief in an individual soul is becoming impossible — when the most religious minds shrink from everything that we have been calling religion — when the universal doubt is an ever-growing weight upon ethical aspiration — light is offered from the East. There we find ourselves in presence of an older and a vaster faith — holding no gross anthropomorphic conceptions of the immeasurable Reality, and denying the existence of soul, but nevertheless inculcating a system of morals superior to any other, and maintaining a hope which no possible

[1] *Evolution and Ethics.*

90

future form of positive knowledge can destroy. Re-enforced by the teaching of science, the teaching of this more ancient faith is that for thousands of years we have been thinking inside-out and upside-down. The only reality is One; — all that we have taken for Substance is only Shadow; — the physical is the unreal; — *and the outer-man is the ghost.*

DUST

Let the Bodhisattva look upon all things as having the nature of space, — as permanently equal to space; without essence, without substantiality.

SADDHARMA-PUNDARÎKA

I HAVE wandered to the verge of the town; and the street I followed has roughened into a country road, and begins to curve away through rice-fields toward a hamlet at the foot of the hills. Between town and rice-fields a vague unoccupied stretch of land makes a favorite playground for children. There are trees, and spaces of grass to roll on, and many butterflies, and plenty of little stones. I stop to look at the children.

By the roadside some are amusing themselves with wet clay, making tiny models of mountains and rivers and rice-fields; tiny mud villages, also — imitations of peasants' huts — and little mud temples, and mud gardens with ponds and humped bridges and imitations of stone-lanterns (tōrō); likewise miniature cemeteries, with bits of broken stone for monuments. And they play at funerals, — burying corpses of butterflies and semi (cicadæ), and pretending to repeat Buddhist sutras over the grave. To-morrow they will not dare to do this; for to-morrow will be the first day of the festival of the Dead. During that festival it is strictly forbidden to molest insects, especially semi, some of which have on their heads little red characters said to be names of Souls.

Children in all countries play at death. Before the sense of personal identity comes, death cannot be seriously considered; and childhood thinks in this regard more correctly, perhaps, than self-conscious maturity. Of course, if these little ones were told, some bright morning, that a playfellow had gone away forever — gone away to be reborn elsewhere — there would be a very real though vague sense of loss, and much wiping of eyes with many-colored sleeves; but presently the loss would be forgotten and the playing resumed. The idea of ceasing to exist could not possibly enter a child-mind: the butterflies and birds, the flowers, the foliage, the sweet summer itself, only play at dying; — they seem to go, but they all come back again after the snow is gone. The real sorrow and fear of death arise in us only through slow accumulation of experience with doubt and pain; and these little boys and girls, being Japanese and Buddhists, will never, in any event, feel about death just as you or I do. They will find reason to fear it for somebody else's sake, but not for their own, because they will learn that they have died millions of times already, and have forgotten the trouble of it, much as one forgets the pain of successive toothaches. In the strangely penetrant light of their creed, teaching the ghostliness of all substance, granite or gossamer — just as those lately found X-rays make visible the ghostliness of flesh — this their present world, with its bigger mountains and rivers and rice-fields, will not appear to them much more real than the mud landscapes which they made in childhood. And much more real it probably is not.

At which thought I am conscious of a sudden soft shock, a familiar shock, and know myself seized by the idea of Substance as Non-Reality.

This sense of the voidness of things comes only when the temperature of the air is so equably related to the temperature of life that I can forget having a body. Cold compels painful notions of solidity; cold sharpens the delusion of personality; cold quickens egotism; cold numbs thought, and shrivels up the little wings of dreams.

To-day is one of those warm, hushed days when it is possible to think of things as they are — when ocean, peak, and plain seem no more real than the arching of blue emptiness above them. All is mirage — my physical self, and the sunlit road, and the slow rippling of the grain under a sleepy wind, and the thatched roofs beyond the haze of the rice-fields, and the blue crumpling of the naked hills behind everything. I have the double sensation of being myself a ghost and of being haunted — haunted by the prodigious luminous Spectre of the World.

There are men and women working in those fields.

DUST

Colored moving shadows they are; and the earth under them — out of which they rose, and back to which they will go — is equally shadow. Only the Forces behind the shadow, that make and unmake, are real — therefore viewless.

Somewhat as Night devours all lesser shadow will this phantasmal earth swallow us at last, and itself thereafter vanish away. But the little shadows and the Shadow-Eater must as certainly reappear — must rematerialize somewhere and somehow. This ground beneath me is old as the Milky Way. Call it what you please — clay, soil, dust: its names are but symbols of human sensations having nothing in common with it. Really it is nameless and un- namable, being a mass of energies, tendencies, in- finite possibilities; for it was made by the beating of that shoreless Sea of Birth and Death whose surges billow unseen out of eternal Night to burst in foam of stars. Lifeless it is not: it feeds upon life, and visi- ble life grows out of it. Dust it is of Karma, waiting to enter into novel combinations — dust of elder Being in that state between birth and birth which the Buddhist calls Chū-U. It is made of forces, and of nothing else; and those forces are not of this planet only, but of vanished spheres innumerable.

Is there aught visible, tangible, measurable, that has never been mixed with sentiency? — atom that has never vibrated to pleasure or to pain? — air that has never been cry or speech? — drop that has

95

never been a tear? Assuredly this dust has felt. It has been everything we know; also much that we cannot know. It has been nebula and star, planet and moon, times unspeakable. Deity also it has been, — the Sun-God of worlds that circled and worshiped in other æons. "Remember, Man, thou art but dust!" — a saying profound only as materialism, which stops short at surfaces. For what is dust?

Remember, Dust, thou hast been Sun, and Sun thou shalt become again! . . . Thou hast been Light, Life, Love; — and into all these, by ceaseless cosmic magic, thou shalt many times be turned again!

For this Cosmic Apparition is more than evolution alternating with dissolution: it is infinite metempsychosis; it is perpetual palingenesis. Those old predictions of a bodily resurrection were not falsehoods; they were rather foreshadowings of a truth vaster than all myths and deeper than all religions.

Suns yield up their ghosts of flame; but out of their graves new suns rush into being. Corpses of worlds pass all to some solar funeral pyre; but out of their own ashes they are born again. This earth must die; her seas shall be Saharas. But those seas once existed in the sun; and their dead tides, revived by fire, will pour their thunder upon the coasts of another world. Transmigration — transmutation: these are not fables! What is impossible? Not the dreams of alchemists and poets; — dross may indeed be changed to gold, the jewel to the living eye, the flower into flesh. What is impossible? If seas can pass from world to sun, from sun to world again, what of the dust of dead selves — dust of memory and thought? Resurrection there is — but a resurrection more stupendous than any dreamed of by Western creeds. Dead emotions will revive as surely as dead suns and moons. Only, so far as we can just now discern, there will be no return of identical individualities. The reapparition will always be a recombination of the preëxisting, a readjustment of affinities, a reintegration of being informed with the experience of anterior being. The Cosmos is a Karma.

Merely by reason of illusion and folly do we shrink from the notion of self-instability. For what is our individuality? Most certainly it is not individuality at all: it is multiplicity incalculable. What is the human body? A form built up out of billions of living entities, an impermanent agglomeration of individuals called cells. And the human soul? A composite of quintillions of souls. We are, each and all, infinite compounds of fragments of anterior lives. And the universal process that continually dissolves and continually constructs personality has always been going on, and is even at this moment going on, in every one of us. What being ever had a totally new feeling, an absolutely new idea? All our emotions and thoughts and wishes, however changing and growing through the varying seasons of life, are only compositions and recompositions of the sensation and ideas and desires of other folk, mostly of dead people — millions of billions of dead people. Cells and souls are themselves recombinations, present aggregations of past knittings of forces, — forces about which nothing is known save that they belong to the Shadow-Makers of universes.

Whether you (by *you* I mean any other agglomeration of souls) really wish for immortality as an agglomeration, I cannot tell. But I confess that "my mind to me a kingdom is" — not! Rather it is a fantastical republic, daily troubled by more revolutions than ever occurred in South America; and the nominal government, supposed to be rational, declares that an eternity of such anarchy is not desirable. I have souls wanting to soar in air, and souls wanting to swim in water (sea-water, I think), and souls wanting to live in woods or on mountain tops. I have souls longing for the tumult of great cities, and souls longing to dwell in tropical solitude; — souls, also, in various stages of naked savagery; — souls demanding nomad freedom without tribute; — souls conservative, delicate, loyal to empire and to feudal tradition, and souls that are Nihilists, deserving Siberia; — sleepless souls, hating inaction, and hermit souls, dwelling in such meditative isolation that only at intervals of years can I feel them moving about; — souls that have faith in fetiches; — polytheistic souls; — souls proclaiming Islam; —

and souls mediæval, loving cloister shadow and incense and glimmer of tapers and the awful altitude of Gothic glooms. Coöperation among all these is not to be thought of: always there is trouble — revolt, confusion, civil war. The majority detest this state of things: multitudes would gladly emigrate. And the wiser minority feel that they need never hope for better conditions until after the total demolition of the existing social structure.

I an individual — an individual soul! Nay, I am a population — a population unthinkable for multitude, even by groups of a thousand millions! Generations of generations I am, æons of æons! Countless times the concourse now making me has been scattered, and mixed with other scatterings. Of what concern, then, the next disintegration? Perhaps, after trillions of ages of burning in different dynasties of suns, the very best of me may come together again.

If one could only imagine some explanation of the Why! The questions of the Whence and the Whither are much less troublesome, since the Present assures us, even though vaguely, of Future and Past. But the Why!

The cooing voice of a little girl dissolves my reverie. She is trying to teach a child brother how to make the Chinese character for Man — I mean

Man with a big M. First she draws in the dust a stroke sloping downwards from right to left, so:

then she draws another curving downwards from left to right, thus:

joining the two so as to form the perfect ji, or character, hito, meaning a person of either sex, or mankind:

Then she tries to impress the idea of this shape on the baby memory by help of a practical illustration — probably learned at school. She breaks a slip of wood in two pieces, and manages to balance the pieces against each other at about the same angle as that made by the two strokes of the character. "Now see," she says: "each stands only by help of the other. One by itself cannot stand. Therefore the ji is like mankind. Without help one person cannot live in this world; but by getting help and giving help everybody can live. If nobody helped anybody, all people would fall down and die."

This explanation is not philologically exact; the two strokes evolutionally standing for a pair of legs — all that survives in the modern ideograph of the whole man figured in the primitive picture-writing. But the pretty moral fancy is much more important than the scientific fact. It is also one charming example of that old-fashioned method of teaching which invested every form and every incident with ethical signification. Besides, as a mere item of moral information, it contains the essence of all earthly religion, and the best part of all earthly philosophy. A world-priestess she is, this dear little maid, with her dove's voice and her innocent gospel of one letter! Verily in that gospel lies the only possible present answer to ultimate problems. Were its whole meaning universally felt — were its whole suggestion of the spiritual and material law of love and help universally obeyed — forthwith, according to the Idealists, this seemingly solid visible world would vanish away like smoke! For it has been written that in whatsoever time all human minds accord in thought and will with the mind of the Teacher, *there shall not remain even one particle of dust that does not enter into Buddhahood.*

WITHIN THE CIRCLE

NEITHER personal pain nor personal pleasure can be really expressed in words. It is never possible to communicate them in their original form. It is only possible, by vivid portrayal of the circumstances or conditions causing them, to awaken in sympathetic minds some kindred qualities of feeling. But if the circumstances causing the pain or the pleasure be totally foreign to common human experience, then no representation of them can make fully known the sensations which they evoked. Hopeless, therefore, any attempt to tell the real pain of seeing my former births. I can say only that no combination of suffering possible to *individual* being could be likened to such pain — the pain of countless lives interwoven. It seemed as if every nerve of me had been prolonged into some monstrous web of sentiency spun back through a million years — and as if the whole of that measureless woof and warp, over all its shivering threads, were pouring into my consciousness, out of the abysmal past, some ghastliness without name — some horror too vast for human brain to hold. For, as I looked backward, I became double, quadruple, octuple; — I multiplied by arithmetical progression; — I became hundreds and thousands — and feared with the terror of thousands — and despaired with the anguish of thousands — and shuddered with the agony of thousands; yet knew the pleasure of none. All joys, all delights appeared but mists or mockeries: only the pain and the fear were real — and always, always growing. Then in the moment when sentiency itself seemed bursting into dissolution, one divine touch ended the frightful vision, and brought again to me the simple consciousness of the single present. Oh! how unspeakably delicious that sudden shrinking back out of multiplicity into unity! — that immense, immeasurable collapse of Self into the blind oblivious numbness of individuality!

"To others also," said the voice of the divine one who had thus saved me — "to others in the like state it has been permitted to see something of their prëexistence. But no one of them ever could endure to look far. Power to see all former births belongs only to those eternally released from the bonds of Self. Such exist outside of illusion — outside of form and name; and pain cannot come nigh them.

"But to you, remaining in illusion, not even the Buddha could give power to look back more than a little way.

"Still you are bewitched by the follies of art and of poetry and of music — the delusions of color and form — the delusions of sensuous speech, the delusions of sensuous sound.

"Still that apparition called Nature — which is but another name for emptiness and shadow — deceives and charms you, and fills you with dreams of longing for the things of sense.

"But he who truly wishes to know, must not love this phantom Nature — must not find delight in the radiance of a clear sky — nor in the sight of the sea — nor in the sound of the flowing of rivers — nor in the forms of peaks and woods and valleys — nor in the colors of them.

"He who truly wishes to know must not find delight in contemplating the works and the deeds of men, nor in hearing their converse, nor in observing the puppet-play of their passions and of their emotions. All this is but a weaving of smoke — a shimmering of vapors — an impermanency — a phantasmagory.

"For the pleasures that men term lofty or noble or sublime are but larger sensualisms, subtler falsities: venomous fair-seeming flowerings of selfishness — all rooted in the elder slime of appetites and desires. To joy in the radiance of a cloudless day — to see the mountains shift their tintings to the wheeling of the sun — to watch the passing of waves, the fading of sunsets — to find charm in the blossoming of plants or trees: all this is of the senses. Not less truly of the senses is the pleasure of observing actions called great or beautiful or heroic — since it is one with the pleasure of imagining those things for which men miserably strive in this miserable world: brief love and fame and honor — all of which are empty as passing foam.

"Sky, sun, and sea; — the peaks, the woods, the plains; — all splendors and forms and colors — are spectres. The feelings and the thoughts and the acts of men — whether deemed high or low, noble or ignoble — all things imagined or done for any save the eternal purpose, are but dreams born of dreams and begetting hollowness. To the clear of sight, all feelings of self — all love and hate, joy and pain, hope and regret, are alike shadows; — youth and age, beauty and horror, sweetness and foulness, are not different; — death and life are one and the same; and Space and Time exist but as the stage and the order of the perpetual Shadow-play.

"All that exists in Time must perish. To the Awakened there is no Time or Space or Change — no night or day — no heat or cold — no moon or season — no present, past, or future. Form and the names of form are alike nothingness: Knowledge only is real; and unto whomsoever gains it, the universe becomes a ghost. But it is written: 'He who hath overcome Time in the past and the future must be of exceedingly pure understanding.'

"Such understanding is not yours. Still to your eyes the shadow seems the substance — and darkness, light — and voidness, beauty. And therefore to see your former births could give you only pain."

I asked:
"Had I found strength to look back to the begin-

ning — back to the verge of Time — could I have read the Secret of the universe?"

"Nay," was answer made. "Only by Infinite Vision can the Secret be read. Could you have looked back incomparably further than your power permitted, then the Past would have become for you the Future. And could you have endured even yet more, the Future would have orbed back for you into the Present."

"Yet why?" I murmured, marveling. . . . "What is the Circle?"

"Circle there is none," was the response; — "Circle there is none but the great phantom-whirl of birth and death to which, by their own thoughts and deeds, the ignorant remain condemned. But this has being only in Time; and Time itself is illusion."

BY FORCE OF KARMA

"The face of the beloved and the face of the risen sun cannot be looked at."   JAPANESE PROVERB

I

MODERN science assures us that the passion of first love, so far as the individual may be concerned, is "absolutely antecedent to all relative experience whatever." [1] In other words, that which might well seem to be the most strictly personal of all feelings, is not an individual matter at all. Philosophy discovered the same fact long ago, and never theorized more attractively than when trying to explain the mystery of the passion. Science, so far, has severely limited itself to a few suggestions on the subject. This seems a pity, because the metaphysicians could at no time give properly detailed explanations — whether teaching that the first sight of the beloved quickens in the soul of the lover some dormant prenatal remembrance of divine truth, or that the illusion is made by spirits unborn seeking incarnation. But science and philosophy both agree as to one all-important fact — that the lovers themselves have no choice, that they are merely the subjects of an influence. Science is even the more positive on this point: it states quite plainly that the dead, not the

[1] Herbert Spencer, *Principles of Psychology:* "The Feelings."

107

living, are responsible. There would seem to be some sort of ghostly remembrance in first loves. It is true that science, unlike Buddhism, does not declare that under particular conditions we may begin to recollect our former lives. That pyschology which is based upon physiology even denies the possibility of memory-inheritance in this individual sense. But it allows that something more powerful, though more indefinite, is inherited — the sum of ancestral memories incalculable — the sum of countless billions of trillions of experiences. Thus can it interpret our most enigmatical sensations — our conflicting impulses — our strangest intuitions; all those seemingly irrational attractions or repulsions — all those vague sadnesses or joys, never to be accounted for by individual experience. But it has not yet found leisure to discourse much to us about first love — although first love, in its relation to the world invisible, is the very weirdest of all human feelings, and the most mysterious.

In our Occident the riddle runs thus. To the growing youth, whose life is normal and vigorous, there comes a sort of atavistic period in which he begins to feel for the feebler sex that primitive contempt created by mere consciousness of physical superiority. But it is just at the time when the society of girls has grown least interesting to him that he suddenly becomes insane. There crosses his life-path a maiden never seen before — but little different from other daughters of men — not at all wonderful to common vision. At the same instant, with a single surging shock, the blood rushes to his heart; and all his senses are bewitched. Thereafter, till the madness ends, his life belongs wholly to that new-found being, of whom he yet knows nothing, except that the sun's light seems more beautiful when it touches her. From that glamour no mortal science can disenthrall him. But whose the witchcraft? Is it any power in the living idol? No, psychology tells us that it is the power of the dead within the idolater. The dead cast the spell. Theirs the shock in the lover's heart; theirs the electric shiver that tingled through his veins at the first touch of one girl's hand.

But why they should want *her*, rather than any other, is the deeper part of the riddle. The solution offered by the great German pessimist will not harmonize well with scientific psychology. The choice of the dead, evolutionally considered, would be a choice based upon remembrance rather than on prescience. And the enigma is not cheerful.

There is, indeed, the romantic possibility that they want her because there survives in her, as in some composite photograph, the suggestion of each and all who loved them in the past. But there is the possibility also that they want her because there reappears in her something of the multitudinous charm of all the women they loved in vain.

Assuming the more nightmarish theory, we should believe that passion, though buried again and again, can neither die nor rest. They who have vainly loved only seem to die; they really live on in generations of hearts, that their desire may be fulfilled. They wait, perhaps through centuries, for the reincarnation of shapes beloved — forever weaving into the dreams of youth their vapory composite of memories. Hence the ideals unattainable — the haunting of troubled souls by the Woman-never-to be-known.

In the Far East thoughts are otherwise; and what I am about to write concerns the interpretation of the Lord Buddha.

II

A PRIEST died recently under very peculiar circumstances. He was the priest of a temple, belonging to one of the older Buddhist sects, in a village near Ōsaka. (You can see that temple from the Kwan-Setsu Railway, as you go by train to Kyōto.)

He was young, earnest, and extremely handsome — very much too handsome for a priest, the women said. He looked like one of those beautiful figures of Amida made by the great Buddhist statuaries of other days.

The men of his parish thought him a pure and learned priest, in which they were right. The women did not think about his virtue or his learning only: he possessed the unfortunate power to attract them, independently of his own will, as a mere man. He was admired by them, and even by women of other parishes also, in ways not holy; and their admiration interfered with his studies and disturbed his meditations. They found irreproachable pretexts for visiting the temple at all hours, just to look at him and talk to him; asking questions which it was his duty to answer, and making religious offerings which he could not well refuse. Some would ask questions, not of a religious kind, that caused him to blush. He was by nature too gentle to protect himself by severe speech, even when forward girls from the city said things that country-girls never would have said — things that made him tell the speakers to leave his presence. And the more he shrank from the admiration of the timid, or the adulation of the unabashed, the more the persecution increased, till it became the torment of his life.[1]

His parents had long been dead; he had no worldly ties: he loved only his calling, and the studies belonging to it; and he did not wish to think of foolish and forbidden things. His extraordinary beauty — the beauty of a living idol — was only a misfortune. Wealth was offered him under conditions that he could not even discuss. Girls threw themselves at his feet, and prayed him in vain to love them. Love-letters were constantly being sent to him, letters which never brought a reply. Some were written in that classical enigmatic style which speaks of "the

[1] Actors in Japan often exercise a similar fascination upon sensitive girls of the lower classes, and often take cruel advantage of the power so gained. It is very rarely, indeed, that such fascination can be exerted by a priest.

Rock-Pillow of Meeting," and "waves on the shadow of a face," and "streams that part to re-unite." Others were artless and frankly tender, full of the pathos of a girl's first confession of love.

For a long time such letters left the young priest as unmoved, to outward appearance, as any image of that Buddha in whose likeness he seemed to have been made. But, as a matter of fact, he was not a Buddha, but only a weak man; and his position was trying.

One evening there came to the temple a little boy who gave him a letter, whispered the name of the sender, and ran away in the dark. According to the subsequent testimony of an acolyte, the priest read the letter, restored it to its envelope, and placed it on the matting, beside his kneeling cushion. After remaining motionless for a long time, as if buried in thought, he sought his writing-box, wrote a letter himself, addressed it to his spiritual superior, and left it upon the writing-stand. Then he consulted the clock, and a railway time-table in Japanese. The hour was early; the night windy and dark. He prostrated himself for a moment in prayer before the altar; then hurried out into the blackness, and reached the railway exactly in time to kneel down in the middle of the track, facing the roar and rush of the express from Kobé. And, in another moment, those who had worshiped the strange beauty of the man would have shrieked to see, even by lantern-light, all that remained of his poor earthliness, smearing the iron way.

KOKORO

The letter written to his superior was found. It contained a bare statement to the effect that, feeling his spiritual strength departing from him, he had resolved to die in order that he might not sin.

The other letter was still lying where he had left it on the floor — a letter written in that woman-language of which every syllable is a little caress of humility. Like all such letters (they are never sent through the post) it contained no date, no name, no initial, and its envelope bore no address. Into our incomparably harsher English speech it might be imperfectly rendered as follows:

To take such freedom may be to assume overmuch; yet I feel that I must speak to you, and therefore send this letter. As for my lowly self, I have to say only that when first seeing you in the period of the Festival of the Further Shore, I began to think; and that since then I have not, even for a moment, been able to forget. More and more each day I sink into that ever-growing thought of you; and when I sleep I dream; and when, awaking and seeing you not, I remember there was no truth in my thoughts of the night, I can do nothing but weep. Forgive me that, having been born into this world a woman, I should utter my wish for the exceeding favor of being found not hateful to one so high. Foolish and without delicacy I may seem in allowing my heart to be thus tortured by the thought of one so far above me. But only because knowing that I cannot restrain my heart, out of the depth of it I have suffered these poor words to come, that I may write them with my unskillful brush, and send them to you. I pray that you will deem me worthy of pity; I beseech that you will not send me cruel words in return. Compassionate me, seeing that this is but the overflowing of my humble feelings; deign to divine and justly to judge — be it only with the least of kindliness — this heart that, in its great distress alone, so ventures to address you. Each moment I shall hope and wait for some gladdening answer.

Concerning all things fortunate, felicitation.

To-day —
from the honorably-known,
to the longed-for, beloved, august one,
this letter goes.

III

I CALLED upon a Japanese friend, a Buddhist scholar, to ask some questions about the religious aspects of the incident. Even as a confession of human weakness, that suicide appeared to me a heroism.

It did not so appear to my friend. He spoke words of rebuke. He reminded me that one who even suggested suicide as a means of escape from sin had been pronounced by the Buddha a spiritual outcast — unfit to live with holy men. As for the dead priest, he had been one of those whom the Teacher called fools. Only a fool could imagine that by destroying his own body he was destroying also within himself the sources of sin.

"But," I protested, "this man's life was pure. . . . Suppose he sought death that he might not, unwittingly, cause others to commit sin?"

My friend smiled ironically. Then he said:

"There was once a lady of Japan, nobly born and very beautiful, who wanted to become a nun. She

114

went to a certain temple, and made her wish known. But the high-priest said to her, 'You are still very young. You have lived the life of courts. To the eyes of worldly men you are beautiful; and, because of your face, temptations to return to the pleasures of the world will be devised for you. Also this wish of yours may be due to some momentary sorrow. Therefore, I cannot now consent to your request.' But she still pleaded so earnestly, that he deemed it best to leave her abruptly. There was a large hibachi — a brazier of glowing charcoal — in the room where she found herself alone. She heated the iron tongs of the brazier till they were red, and with them horribly pierced and seamed her face, destroying her beauty forever. Then the priest, alarmed by the smell of the burning, returned in haste, and was very much grieved by what he saw. But she pleaded again, without any trembling in her voice: 'Because I was beautiful, you refused to take me. Will you take me now?' She was accepted into the Order, and became a holy nun.... Well, which was the wiser, that woman, or the priest you wanted to praise?"

"But was it the duty of the priest," I asked, "to disfigure his face?"

"Certainly not! Even the woman's action would have been very unworthy if done only as a protection against temptation. Self-mutilation of any sort is forbidden by the law of Buddha; and she transgressed. But as she burned her face only that she might be able to enter at once upon the Path, and not because afraid of being unable by her own will to resist sin, her fault was a minor fault. On the other hand, the priest who took his own life committed a very great offense. He should have tried to convert those who tempted him. This he was too weak to do. If he felt it impossible to keep from sinning as a priest, then it would have been better for him to return to the world, and there try to follow the law for such as do not belong to the Order."

"According to Buddhism, therefore, he has obtained no merit?" I queried.

"It is not easy to imagine that he has. Only by those ignorant of the Law can his action be commended."

"And by those knowing the Law, what will be thought of the results, the karma of his act?"

My friend mused a little; then he said, thoughtfully:

"The whole truth of that suicide we cannot fully know. Perhaps it was not the first time."

"Do you mean that in some former life also he may have tried to escape from sin by destroying his own body?"

"Yes. Or in many former lives."

"What of his future lives?"

"Only a Buddha could answer that with certain knowledge."

"But what is the teaching?"

"You forget that it is not possible for us to know what was in the mind of that man."

"Suppose that he sought death only to escape from sinning?"

"Then he will have to face the like temptation again and again, and all the sorrow of it, and all the pain, even for a thousand times a thousand times, until he shall have learned to master himself. There is no escape through death from the supreme necessity of self-conquest."

After parting with my friend, his words continued to haunt me; and they haunt me still. They forced new thoughts about some theories hazarded in the first part of this paper. I have not yet been able to assure myself that his weird interpretation of the amatory mystery is any less worthy of consideration than our Western interpretations. I have been wondering whether the loves that lead to death might not mean much more than the ghostly hunger of buried passions. Might they not signify also the inevitable penalty of long-forgotten sins?

THE IDEA OF PREËXISTENCE

If a Bikkhu should desire, O brethren, to call to mind his various temporary states in days gone by — such as one birth, two births, three, four, five, ten, twenty, thirty, fifty, one hundred, or one thousand, or one hundred thousand births — in all their modes and all their details, let him be devoted to quietude of heart — let him look through things, let him be much alone. AKANKHEYYA SUTTA

I

WERE I to ask any reflecting Occidental, who had passed some years in the real living atmosphere of Buddhism, what fundamental idea especially differentiates Oriental modes of thinking from our own, I am sure he would answer: "The Idea of Preëxistence." It is this idea, more than any other, which permeates the whole mental being of the Far East. It is universal as the wash of air: it colors every emotion; it influences, directly or indirectly, almost every act. Its symbols are perpetually visible, even in details of artistic decoration; and hourly, by day or night, some echoes of its language float uninvited to the ear. The utterances of the people — their household sayings, their proverbs, their pious or profane exclamations, their confessions of sorrow, hope, joy, or despair — are all informed with it. It qualifies equally the expression of hate or the speech of affection; and the term "ingwa," or "innen" — meaning karma as inevitable retribution — comes

118

naturally to every lip as an interpretation, as a consolation, or as a reproach. The peasant toiling up
some steep road, and feeling the weight of his hand-
cart straining every muscle, murmurs patiently:
"Since this is ingwa, it must be suffered." Servants
disputing, ask each other, "By reason of what ingwa
must I now dwell with such a one as you?" The incapable or vicious man is reproached with his ingwa;
and the misfortunes of the wise or the virtuous are
explained by the same Buddhist word. The law-
breaker confesses his crime, saying: "That which I
did I knew to be wicked when doing; but my ingwa
was stronger than my heart." Separated lovers seek
death under the belief that their union in this life is
banned by the results of their sins in a former one;
and the victim of an injustice tries to allay his natural anger by the self-assurance that he is expiat-
ing some forgotten fault which had to be expiated in
the eternal order of things. . . . So likewise even the
commonest references to a spiritual future imply the
general creed of a spiritual past. The mother warns
her little ones at play about the effect of wrong-do-
ing upon their future births, as the children of other
parents. The pilgrim or the street-beggar accepts
your alms with the prayer that your next birth may
be fortunate. The aged inkyō, whose sight and hearing begin to fail, talks cheerily of the impending
change that is to provide him with a fresh young
body. And the expressions "Yakusoku," signifying
the Buddhist idea of necessity; "mae no yo," the

last life; "akirame," resignation, recur as frequently in Japanese common parlance as do the words "right" and "wrong" in English popular speech.

After long dwelling in this psychological medium, you find that it has penetrated your own thought, and has effected therein various changes. All concepts of life implied by the idea of preëxistence — all those beliefs which, however sympathetically studied, must at first have seemed more than strange to you — finally lose that curious or fantastic character with which novelty once invested them, and present themselves under a perfectly normal aspect. They explain so many things so well as even to look rational; and quite rational some assuredly are when measured by the scientific thought of the nineteenth century. But to judge them fairly, it is first necessary to sweep the mind clear of all Western ideas of metempsychosis. For there is no resemblance between the old Occidental conceptions of soul — the Pythagorean or the Platonic, for example — and the Buddhist conception; and it is precisely because of this unlikeness that the Japanese beliefs prove themselves reasonable. The profound difference between old-fashioned Western thought and Eastern thought in this regard is, that for the Buddhist the conventional soul — the single, tenuous, tremulous, transparent inner man, or ghost — does not exist. The Oriental Ego is not individual. Nor is it even a definitely numbered multiple like the Gnostic soul. It is an aggregate or composite of inconceivable complexity — the concentrated sum of the creative thinking of previous lives beyond all reckoning.

II

THE interpretative power of Buddhism, and the singular accord of its theories with the facts of modern science, appear especially in that domain of psychology whereof Herbert Spencer has been the greatest of all explorers. No small part of our psychological life is composed of feelings which Western theology never could explain. Such are those which cause the still speechless infant to cry at the sight of certain faces, or to smile at the sight of others. Such are those instantaneous likes or dislikes experienced on meeting strangers, those repulsions or attractions called "first impressions," which intelligent children are prone to announce with alarming frankness, despite all assurance that "people must not be judged by appearances": a doctrine no child in his heart believes. To call these feelings instinctive or intuitive, in the theological meaning of instinct or intuition, explains nothing at all — merely cuts off inquiry into the mystery of life, just like the special creation hypothesis. The idea that a personal impulse or emotion might be more than individual, except through demoniacal possession, still seems to old-fashioned orthodoxy a monstrous heresy. Yet it is now certain that most of our deeper feelings are super-individual — both those which we classify as passional, and those which we call sublime The individuality of the amatory passion is absolutely denied by science; and what is true of love at first sight is also true of hate: both are super-individual. So likewise are those vague impulses to wander which come and go with spring, and those vague depressions experienced in autumn — survivals, perhaps, from an epoch in which human migration followed the course of the seasons, or even from an era preceding the apparition of man. Super-individual also those emotions felt by one who, after having passed the greater part of a life on plain or prairies, first looks upon a range of snow-capped peaks; or the sensations of some dweller in the interior of a continent when he first beholds the ocean, and hears its eternal thunder. The delight, always toned with awe, which the sight of a stupendous landscape evokes; or that speechless admiration, mingled with melancholy inexpressible, which the splendor of a tropical sunset creates — never can be interpreted by individual experience. Psychological analysis has indeed shown these emotions to be prodigiously complex, and interwoven with personal experiences of many kinds; but in either case the deeper wave of feeling is never individual: it is a surging up from that ancestral sea of life out of which we came. To the same psychological category possibly belongs likewise a peculiar feeling which troubled men's minds long before the time of Cicero, and troubles them even more betimes in our own generation —

the feeling of having already seen a place really
visited for the first time. Some strange air of fa-
miliarity about the streets of a foreign town, or the
forms of a foreign landscape, comes to the mind with
a sort of soft weird shock, and leaves one vainly ran-
sacking memory for interpretations. Occasionally,
beyond question, similar sensations are actually
produced by the revival or recombination of former
relations in consciousness; but there would seem to
be many which remain wholly mysterious when we
attempt to explain them by individual experience.

Even in the most common of our sensations there
are enigmas never to be solved by those holding the
absurd doctrine that all feeling and cognition belong
to individual experience, and that the mind of the
child newly born is a *tabula rasa*. The pleasure excited by the perfume of a flower, by certain shades
of color, by certain tones of music; the involuntary
loathing or fear aroused by the first sight of dangerous or venomous life; even the nameless terror of
dreams — are all inexplicable upon the old-fashioned soul-hypothesis. How deeply reaching into
the life of the race some of these sensations are, such
as the pleasure in odors and in colors, Grant Allen
has most effectively suggested in his "Physiological
Æsthetics," and in his charming treatise on the
Color-Sense. But long before these were written,
his teacher, the greatest of all psychologists, had
clearly proven that the experience-hypothesis was
utterly inadequate to account for many classes of

psychological phenomena. "If possible," observes Herbert Spencer, "it is even more at fault in respect to the emotions than to the cognitions. The doctrine that all the desires, all the sentiments, are generated by the experiences of the individual, is so glaringly at variance with facts that I cannot but wonder how any one should ever have ventured to entertain it." It was Mr. Spencer, also, who showed us that words like "instinct," "intuition," have no true signification in the old sense; they must hereafter be used in a very different one. Instinct, in the language of modern psychology, means "organized memory," and memory itself is "incipient instinct" — the sum of impressions to be inherited by the next succeeding individual in the chain of life. Thus science recognizes inherited memory: not in the ghostly signification of a remembering of the details of former lives, but as a minute addition to psychological life accompanied by minute changes in the structure of the inherited nervous system. "The human brain is an organized register of infinitely numerous experiences received during the evolution of life, or rather, during the evolution of that series of organisms through which the human organism has been reached. The effects of the most uniform and frequent of these experiences have been successively bequeathed, principal and interest; and have slowly amounted to that high intelligence which lies latent in the brain of the infant — which the infant in after-life exercises and perhaps strengthens or further

complicates — and which, with minute additions, it
bequeaths to future generations." [1] Thus we have
solid physiological ground for the idea of preëxistence and the idea of a multiple Ego. It is incontro-
vertible that in every individual brain is locked up
the inherited memory of the absolutely inconceivable multitude of experiences received by all the
brains of which it is the descendant. But this
scientific assurance of self in the past is uttered in no
materialistic sense. Science is the destroyer of materialism: it has proven matter incomprehensible;
and it confesses the mystery of mind insoluble, even
while obliged to postulate an ultimate unit of sensation. Out of the units of simple sensation, older than
we by millions of years, have undoubtedly been
built up all the emotions and faculties of man. Here
Science, in accord with Buddhism, avows the Ego
composite, and, like Buddhism, explains the psychical riddles of the present by the psychical experiences of the past.

III

To many persons it must seem that the idea of Soul
as an infinite multiple would render impossible any
idea of religion in the Western sense; and those unable to rid themselves of old theological conceptions
doubtless imagine that even in Buddhist countries,
and despite the evidence of Buddhist texts, the
faith of the common people is really based upon the

[1] *Principles of Psychology:* "The Feelings."

idea of the soul as a single entity. But Japan furnishes remarkable proof to the contrary. The uneducated common people, the poorest country-folk who have never studied Buddhist metaphysics, believe the self composite. What is even more remarkable is that in the primitive faith, Shintō, a kindred doctrine exists; and various forms of the belief seem to characterize the thought of the Chinese and of the Koreans. All these peoples of the Far East seem to consider the soul compound, whether in the Buddhist sense, or in the primitive sense represented by Shintō (a sort of ghostly multiplying by fission), or in the fantastic sense elaborated by Chinese astrology. In Japan I have fully satisfied myself that the belief is universal. It is not necessary to quote here from the Buddhist texts, because the common or popular beliefs, and not the philosophy of a creed, can alone furnish evidence that religious fervor is compatible and consistent with the notion of a composite soul. Certainly the Japanese peasant does not think the psychical Self nearly so complex a thing as Buddhist philosophy considers it, or as Western science proves it to be. *But he thinks of himself as multiple.* The struggle within him between impulses good and evil he explains as a conflict between the various ghostly wills that make up his Ego; and his spiritual hope is to disengage his better self or selves from his worse selves — Nirvana, or the supreme bliss, being attainable only through the survival of the best within him. Thus his religion appears to be founded upon a natural perception of psychical evolution not nearly so remote from scientific thought as are those conventional notions of soul held by our common people at home. Of course his ideas on these abstract subjects are vague and unsystematized; but their general character and tendencies are unmistakable; and there can be no question whatever as to the earnestness of his faith, or as to the influence of that faith upon his ethical life.

Wherever belief survives among the educated classes, the same ideas obtain definition and synthesis. I may cite, in example, two selections from compositions, written by students aged respectively twenty-three and twenty-six. I might as easily cite a score; but the following will sufficiently indicate what I mean:

Nothing is more foolish than to declare the immortality of the soul. The soul is a compound; and though its elements be eternal, we know they can never twice combine in exactly the same way. All compound things must change their character and their conditions.

Human life is composite. A combination of energies make the soul. When a man dies his soul may either remain unchanged, or be changed according to that which it combines with. Some philosophers say the soul is immortal; some, that it is mortal. They are both right. The soul is mortal or immortal according to the change of the combinations composing it. The elementary energies from which the soul is formed are, indeed, eternal; but the nature of the soul is determined by the character of the combinations into which those energies enter.

THE IDEA OF PREËXISTENCE

Now the ideas expressed in these compositions will appear to the Western reader, at first view, unmistakably atheistic. Yet they are really compatible with the sincerest and deepest faith. It is the use of the English word "soul," not understood at all as we understand it, which creates the false impression. "Soul," in the sense used by the young writers, means an almost infinite combination of both good and evil tendencies — a compound doomed to disintegration not only by the very fact of its being a compound, but also by the eternal law of spiritual progress.

IV

THAT the idea, which has been for thousands of years so vast a factor in Oriental thought-life, should have failed to develop itself in the West till within our own day, is sufficiently explained by Western theology. Still, it would not be correct to say that theology succeeded in rendering the notion of preëxistence absolutely repellent to Occidental minds. Though Christian doctrine, holding each soul specially created out of nothing to fit each new body, permitted no avowed beliefs in preëxistence, popular common sense recognized a contradiction of dogma in the phenomena of heredity. In the same way, while theology decided animals to be mere automata, moved by a sort of incomprehensible machinery called instinct, the people generally recognized that animals had reasoning powers. The theories of instinct and of intuition held even a generation ago seem utterly barbarous to-day. They were commonly felt to be useless as interpretations; but as dogmas they served to check speculation and to prevent heresy. Wordsworth's "Fidelity" and his marvelously overrated "Intimations of Immortality" bear witness to the extreme timidity and crudeness of Western notions on these subjects even at the beginning of the century. The love of the dog for his master is indeed "great beyond all human estimate," but for reasons Wordsworth never dreamed about; and although the fresh sensations of childhood are certainly intimations of something much more wonderful than Wordsworth's denominational idea of immortality, his famous stanza concerning them has been very justly condemned by Mr. John Morley as nonsense. Before the decay of theology, no rational ideas of psychological inheritance, of the true nature of instinct, or of the unity of life, could possibly have forced their way to general recognition.

But with the acceptance of the doctrine of evolution, old forms of thought crumbled; new ideas everywhere arose to take the place of worn-out dogmas; and we now have the spectacle of a general intellectual movement in directions strangely parallel with Oriental philosophy. The unprecedented rapidity and multiformity of scientific progress during the last fifty years could not have failed to provoke an equally unprecedented intellectual quickening among the non-scientific. That the highest and most complex organisms have been developed from the lowest and simplest; that a single physical basis of life is the substance of the whole living world; that no line of separation can be drawn between the animal and vegetable; that the difference between life and non-life is only a difference of degree, not of kind; that matter is not less incomprehensible than mind, while both are but varying manifestations of one and the same unknown reality — these have already become the commonplaces of the new philosophy. After the first recognition even by theology of physical evolution, it was easy to predict that the recognition of psychical evolution could not be indefinitely delayed; for the barrier erected by old dogma to keep men from looking backward had been broken down. And to-day for the student of scientific psychology the idea of preëxistence passes out of the realm of theory into the realm of fact, proving the Buddhist explanation of the universal mystery quite as plausible as any other. "None but very hasty thinkers," wrote the late Professor Huxley, "will reject it on the ground of inherent absurdity. Like the doctrine of evolution itself, that of transmigration has its roots in the world of reality; and it may claim such support as the great argument from analogy is capable of supplying." [1]

Now this support, as given by Professor Huxley, is singularly strong. It offers us no glimpse of a sin-

[1] *Evolution and Ethics*, p. 61 (ed. 1894).

gle soul flitting from darkness to light, from death to rebirth, through myriads of millions of years; but it leaves the main idea of preëxistence almost exactly in the form enunciated by the Buddha himself. In the Oriental doctrine, the psychical personality, like the individual body, is an aggregate doomed to disintegration. By psychical personality I mean here that which distinguishes mind from mind — the "me" from the "you": that which we call self. To Buddhism this is a temporary composite of illusions. What makes it is the karma. What reincarnates is the karma — the sum-total of the acts and thoughts of countless anterior existences — each one of which, as an integer in some great spiritual system of addition and subtraction, may affect all the rest. Like a magnetism, the karma is transmitted from form to form, from phenomenon to phenomenon, determining conditions by combinations. The ultimate mystery of the concentrative and creative effects of karma the Buddhist acknowledges to be inscrutable; but the cohesion of effects he declares to be produced by tanhā, the desire of life, corresponding to what Schopenhauer called the "will" to live. Now we find in Herbert Spencer's "Biology" a curious parallel for this idea. He explains the transmission of tendencies, and their variations, by a theory of polarities — polarities of the physiological unit. Between this theory of polarities and the Buddhist theory of tanhā, the difference is much less striking than the resemblance. Karma or heredity, tanhā or polarity, are inexplicable as to their ultimate nature: Buddhism and Science are here at one. The fact worthy of attention is that both recognize the same phenomena under different names.

v

THE prodigious complexity of the methods by which Science has arrived at conclusions so strangely in harmony with the ancient thought of the East, may suggest the doubt whether those conclusions could ever be made clearly comprehensible to the mass of Western minds. Certainly it would seem that just as the real doctrines of Buddhism can be taught to the majority of believers through forms only, so the philosophy of science can be communicated to the masses through suggestion only — suggestion of such facts, or arrangements of fact, as must appeal to any naturally intelligent mind. But the history of scientific progress assures the efficiency of this method; and there is no strong reason for the supposition that, because the processes of the higher science remain above the mental reach of the unscientific classes, the conclusions of that science will not be generally accepted. The dimensions and weights of planets; the distances and the composition of stars; the law of gravitation; the signification of heat, light, and color; the nature of sound, and a host of other scientific discoveries, are familiar to thousands quite ignorant of the details of the methods by which such knowledge was obtained. Again we have evidence that every great progressive movement of science during the century has been followed by considerable modifications of popular beliefs. Already the churches, though clinging still to the hypothesis of a specially created soul, have accepted the main doctrine of physical evolution; and neither fixity of belief nor intellectual retrogression can be rationally expected in the immediate future. Further changes of religious ideas are to be looked for; and it is even likely that they will be effected rapidly rather than slowly. Their exact nature, indeed, cannot be predicted; but existing intellectual tendencies imply that the doctrine of psychological evolution must be accepted, though not at once so as to set any final limit to ontological speculation; and that the whole conception of the Ego will be eventually transformed through the consequently developed idea of preëxistence.

VI

MORE detailed consideration of these probabilities may be ventured. They will not, perhaps, be acknowledged as probabilities by persons who regard science as a destroyer rather than a modifier. But such thinkers forget that religious feeling is something infinitely more profound than dogma; that it survives all gods and all forms of creed; and that it only widens and deepens and gathers power with intellectual expansion. That as mere doctrine religion will ultimately pass away is a conclusion to which the study of evolution leads; but that religion as feeling, or even as faith in the unknown power shaping equally a brain or a constellation, can ever utterly die, is not at present conceivable. Science wars only upon erroneous interpretations of phenomena; it only magnifies the cosmic mystery, and proves that everything, however minute, is infinitely wonderful and incomprehensible. And it is this indubitable tendency of science to broaden beliefs and to magnify cosmic emotion which justifies the supposition that future modifications of Western religious ideas will be totally unlike any modifications effected in the past; that the Occidental conception of Self will orb into something akin to the Oriental conception of Self; and that all present petty metaphysical notions of personality and individuality as realities *per se* will be annihilated. Already the growing popular comprehension of the facts of heredity, as science teaches them, indicates the path by which some, at least, of these modifications will be reached. In the coming contest over the great question of psychological evolution, common intelligence will follow Science along the line of least resistance; and that line will doubtless be the study of heredity, since the phenomena to be considered, however in themselves uninterpretable, are familiar to general experience, and afford partial answers to countless old enigmas. It is thus quite possible to imagine a coming form of Western religion supported by the whole power of synthetic philosophy; differing from Buddhism mainly in the greater exactness of its conceptions; holding the soul as a composite; and teaching a new spiritual law resembling the doctrine of karma.

An objection to this idea will, however, immediately present itself to many minds. Such a modification of belief, it will be averred, would signify the sudden conquest and transformation of feelings by ideas. "The world," says Herbert Spencer, "is not governed by ideas, but by feelings, to which ideas serve only as guides." How are the notions of a change, such as that supposed, to be reconciled with common knowledge of existing religious sentiment in the West, and the force of religious emotionalism?

Were the ideas of preëxistence and of the soul as multiple really antagonistic to Western religious sentiment, no satisfactory answer could be made. But are they so antagonistic? The idea of preëxistence certainly is not; the Occidental mind is already prepared for it. It is true that the notion of Self as a composite, destined to dissolution, may seem little better than the materialistic idea of annihilation — at least to those still unable to divest themselves of the old habits of thought. Nevertheless, impartial reflection will show that there is no emotional reason for dreading the disintegration of the Ego. Actually, though unwittingly, it is for this very disintegration that Christians and Buddhists alike perpetually pray. Who has not often wished to rid himself of the worse parts of his nature, of tendencies to folly or to wrong, of impulses to say or do unkind things — of all that lower inheritance which still clings about the higher man, and weighs down his finest aspirations? Yet that of which we so earnestly desire the separation, the elimination, the death, is not less surely a part of psychological inheritance, of veritable Self, than are those younger and larger faculties which help to the realization of noble ideals. Rather than an end to be feared, the dissolution of Self is the one object of all objects to which our efforts should be turned. What no new philosophy can forbid us to hope is that the best elements of Self will thrill on to seek loftier affinities, to enter into grander and yet grander combinations, till the supreme revelation comes, and we discern, through infinite vision — through the vanishing of all Self — the Absolute Reality.

For while we know that even the so-called elements themselves are evolving, we have no proof that anything utterly dies. That we are is the certainty that we have been and will be. We have survived countless evolutions, countless universes. We know that through the Cosmos all is law. No chance decides what units shall form the planetary core, or what shall feel the sun; what shall be locked in granite and basalt, or shall multiply in plant and in animal. So far as reason can venture to infer from analogy, the cosmical history of every ultimate unit, psychological or physical, is determined just as surely and as exactly as in the Buddhist doctrine of karma.

KOKORO

VII

THE influence of Science will not be the only factor in the modification of Western religious beliefs: Oriental philosophy will certainly furnish another. Sanscrit, Chinese, and Pali scholarship, and the tireless labor of philologists in all parts of the East, are rapidly familiarizing Europe and America with all the great forms of Oriental thought; Buddhism is being studied with interest throughout the Occident; and the results of these studies are yearly showing themselves more and more definitely in the mental products of the highest culture. The schools of philosophy are not more visibly affected than the literature of the period. Proof that a reconsideration of the problem of the Ego is everywhere forcing itself upon Occidental minds, may be found not only in the thoughtful prose of the time, but even in its poetry and its romance. Ideas impossible a generation ago are changing current thought, destroying old tastes, and developing higher feelings. Creative art, working under larger inspiration, is telling what absolutely novel and exquisite sensations, what hitherto unimaginable pathos, what marvelous deepening of emotional power, may be gained in literature with the recognition of the idea of preëxistence. Even in fiction we learn that we have been living in a hemisphere only; that we have been thinking but half-thoughts; that we need a new faith to join past with future over the great parallel of the present, and so to round out our emotional world into a perfect sphere. The clear conviction that the self is multiple, however paradoxical the statement seem, is the absolutely necessary step to the vaster conviction that the many are One, that life is unity, that there is no finite, but only infinite. Until that blind pride which imagines Self unique shall have been broken down, and the *feeling* of self and of self-ishness shall have been utterly decomposed, the knowledge of the Ego as infinite — as the very Cosmos — never can be reached.

Doubtless the simple emotional conviction that we have been in the past will be developed long before the intellectual conviction that the Ego as one is a fiction of selfishness. But the composite nature of Self must at last be acknowledged, though its mystery remain. Science postulates a hypothetical psychological unit as well as a hypothetical physiological unit; but either postulated entity defies the uttermost power of mathematical estimate — seems to resolve itself into pure ghostliness. The chemist, for working purposes, must imagine an ultimate atom; but the fact of which the imagined atom is the symbol may be a force centre only — nay, a void, a vortex, an emptiness, as in Buddhist concept. "Form is emptiness, and emptiness is form. What is form, that is emptiness; what is emptiness, that is form. Perception and conception, name and knowledge — all these are emptiness."

KOKORO

For science and for Buddhism alike the cosmos resolves itself into a vast phantasmagoria — a mere play of unknown and immeasurable forces. Buddhist faith, however, answers the questions "Whence?" and "Whither?" in its own fashion — and predicts in every great cycle of evolution a period of spiritual expansion in which the memory of former births returns, and all the future simultaneously opens before the vision unveiled — even to the heaven of heavens. Science here remains dumb. But her silence is the Silence of the Gnostics — Sigé, the Daughter of Depth and the Mother of Spirit.

What we may allow ourselves to believe, with the full consent of Science, is that marvelous revelations await us. Within recent time new senses and powers have been developed — the sense of music, the ever-growing faculties of the mathematician. Reasonably it may be expected that still higher unimaginable faculties will be evolved in our descendants. Again it is known that certain mental capacities, undoubtedly inherited, develop in old age only; and the average life of the human race is steadily lengthening. With increased longevity there surely may come into sudden being, through the unfolding of the larger future brain, powers not less wonderful than the ability to remember former births. The dreams of Buddhism can scarcely be surpassed, because they touch the infinite; but who can presume to say they never will be realized?

THE IDEA OF PREËXISTENCE

NOTE

It may be necessary to remind some of those kind enough to read the foregoing that the words "soul," "self," "ego," "transmigration," "heredity," although freely used by me, convey meanings entirely foreign to Buddhist philosophy. "Soul," in the English sense of the word, does not exist for the Buddhist. "Self" is an illusion, or rather a plexus of illusions. "Transmigration," as the passing of soul from one body to another, is expressly denied in Buddhist texts of unquestionable authority. It will therefore be evident that the real analogy which does exist between the doctrine of karma and the scientific facts of heredity is far from complete. Karma signifies the survival, not of the same composite individuality, but of its tendencies, which recombine to form a new composite individuality. The new being does not necessarily take even a human form: the karma does not descend from parent to child; it is independent of the line of heredity, although physical conditions of life seem to depend upon karma. The karma-being of a beggar may have rebirth in the body of a king; that of a king in the body of a beggar; yet the conditions of either reincarnation have been predetermined by the influence of karma.

It will be asked, What then is the spiritual element in each being that continues unchanged — the spiritual kernel, so to speak, within the shell of karma — the power that makes for righteousness? If soul and body alike are temporary composites, and the karma (itself temporary) the only source of personality, what is the worth or meaning of Buddhist doctrine? What is it that suffers by karma; what is it that lies within the illusion — that makes progress — that attains Nirvana? Is it not a *self*? Not in our sense of the word. The reality of what we call self is denied by Buddhism. That which forms and dissolves the karma; that which makes for righteousness; that which reaches Nirvana, is not our Ego in our Western sense of the word. Then what is it? It is the divine in each being. It is called in Japanese Muga-no-taiga — the Great Self-without-selfishness. There is no other true self. The self wrapped in illusion is called Nyōrai-zō (Tathâgata-gharba) — the Buddha yet unborn, as one in a womb. The Infinite exists potentially in every being. That is the Reality. The other self is a falsity — a lie — a mirage. The doctrine of extinction refers only to the extinction of illusions; and those sensations and feelings and thoughts, which belong to this life of the flesh alone, are the illusions which make the complex illusive self. By the total decomposition of this false self — as by a tearing away of veils, the Infinite Vision comes. There is no "soul": the Infinite All-Soul is the only eternal principle in any being; all the rest is dream.

What remains in Nirvana? According to one school of Buddhism potential identity in the infinite — so that a Buddha, after having reached Nirvana, can return to earth. According to another, identity more than potential, yet not in our sense "personal." A Japanese friend says: "I take a piece of gold, and say it is one. But this means that it produces on my visual organs a single impression. Really in the multitude of atoms composing it each atom is nevertheless distinct and separate, and independent of every other atom. In Buddhahood even so are untied psychical atoms innumerable. They are one as to condition; yet each has its own independent existence."

But in Japan the primitive religion has so affected the common class of Buddhist beliefs that it is not incorrect to speak of the Japanese "idea of self." It is only necessary that the popular Shintō idea be simultaneously considered. In Shintō we have the plainest possible evidence of the conception of soul. But this soul is a composite —

not a mere "bundle of sensations, perceptions, and voli-
tions," like the karma-being, but a number of souls
united to form one ghostly personality. A dead man's
ghost may appear as one or as many. It can separate its
units, each of which remains capable of a special independent action. Such separation, however, appears to be
temporary, the various souls of the composite naturally
cohering even after death, and reuniting after any voluntary separation. The vast mass of the Japanese people
are both Buddhists and Shintōists; but the primitive beliefs concerning the self are certainly the most powerful,
and in the blending of the two faiths remain distinctly
recognizable. They have probably supplied to common
imagination a natural and easy explanation of the difficulties of the karma-doctrine, though to what extent I am
not prepared to say. Be it also observed that in the primitive as well as in the Buddhist form of belief the self is not
a principle transmitted from parent to offspring — not
an inheritance always dependent upon physiological descent.

These facts will indicate how wide is the difference between Eastern ideas and our own upon the subject of the
preceding essay. They will also show that any general
consideration of the real analogies existing between this
strange combination of Far-Eastern beliefs and the scientific thought of the nineteenth century could scarcely
be made intelligible by strict philosophical accuracy
in the use of terms relating to the idea of self. Indeed,
there are no European words capable of rendering the
exact meaning of the Buddhist terms belonging to Buddhist idealism.

Perhaps it may be regarded as illegitimate to wander
from that position so tersely enunciated by Professor
Huxley in his essay on "Sensation and the Sensiferous
Organs": "In ultimate analysis it appears that a sensa-

tion is the equivalent in terms of consciousness for a mode of motion of the matter of the sensorium. But if inquiry is pushed a stage further, and the question is asked, What, then, do we know about matter and motion? there is but one reply possible: All we know about motion is that it is a name for certain changes in the relations of our visual, tactile, and muscular sensations; and all we know about matter is that it is the hypothetical substance of physical phenomena, *the assumption of which is as pure a piece of metaphysical speculation as is that of a substance of mind.*" But metaphysical speculation certainly will not cease because of scientific recognition that ultimate truth is beyond the utmost possible range of human knowledge. Rather, for that very reason, it will continue. Perhaps it will never wholly cease. Without it there can be no further modification of religious beliefs, and without modifications there can be no religious progress in harmony with scientific thought. Therefore, metaphysical speculation seems to me not only justifiable, but necessary.

Whether we accept or deny a *substance* of mind; whether we imagine thought produced by the play of some unknown element through the cells of the brain, as music is made by the play of wind through the strings of a harp; whether we regard the motion itself as a special mode of vibration inherent in and peculiar to the units of the cerebral structure — still the mystery is infinite, and still Buddhism remains a noble moral working-hypothesis, in deep accord with the aspirations of mankind and with the laws of ethical progression. Whether we believe or disbelieve in the reality of that which is called the material universe, still the ethical significance of the inexplicable laws of heredity — of the transmission of both racial and personal tendencies in the unspecialized reproductive cell — remains to justify the doctrine of karma. Whatever be that which makes consciousness, its relation to all the past and to all the future is unquestionable. Nor can the doctrine of Nirvana ever cease to command the profound respect of the impartial thinker. Science has found evidence that known substance is not less a product of evolution than mind — that all our so-called "elements" have been evolved out of "one primary undifferentiated form of matter." And this evidence is startlingly suggestive of some underlying truth in the Buddhist doctrine of emanation and illusion — the evolution of all forms from the Formless, of all material phenomena from immaterial Unity — and the ultimate return of all into "that state which is empty of lusts, of malice, of dullness — that state in which the excitements of individuality are known no more, and which is therefore designated THE VOID SUPREME."

A PILGRIMAGE TO ENOSHIMA

I

KAMAKURA.

A long, straggling country village, between low wooded hills, with a canal passing through it. Old Japanese cottages, dingy, neutral-tinted, with roofs of thatch, very steeply sloping above their wooden walls and paper shōji. Green patches on all the roof-slopes, some sort of grass; and on the very summits, on the ridges, luxurious growths of yane-shōbu,[1] the roof-plant, bearing pretty purple flowers. In the lukewarm air a mingling of Japanese odors, smells of saké, smells of seaweed soup, smells of daikon, the strong native radish; and dominating all, a sweet, thick, heavy scent of incense — incense from the shrines of gods.

Akira has hired two jinrikisha for our pilgrimage; a speckless azure sky arches the world; and the land lies glorified in a joy of sunshine. And yet a sense of melancholy, of desolation unspeakable, weighs upon me as we roll along the bank of the tiny stream, between the mouldering lines of wretched little homes with grass growing on their roofs. For this mouldering hamlet represents all that remains of the million-peopled streets of Yoritomo's capital,

[1] Yane, "roof"; shōbu, "sweet-flag" (*Acorus calamus*).

145

the mighty city of the Shōgunate, the ancient seat of feudal power, whither came the envoys of Kublai Khan demanding tribute, to lose their heads for their temerity. And only some of the unnumbered temples of the once magnificent city now remain, saved from the conflagrations of the fifteenth and sixteenth centuries, doubtless because built in high places, or because isolated from the maze of burning streets by vast courts and groves. Here still dwell the ancient gods in the great silence of their decaying temples, without worshipers, without revenues, surrounded by desolations of rice-fields, where the chanting of frogs replaces the sea-like murmur of the city that was and is not.

II

THE first great temple — En-gaku-ji — invites us to cross the canal by a little bridge facing its outward gate — a roofed gate with fine Chinese lines, but without carving. Passing it, we ascend a long, imposing succession of broad steps, leading up through a magnificent grove to a terrace, where we reach the second gate. This gate is a surprise; a stupendous structure of two stories, with huge sweeping curves of roof and enormous gables — antique, Chinese, magnificent. It is more than four hundred years old, but seems scarcely affected by the wearing of the centuries. The whole of the ponderous and complicated upper structure is sustained upon an open-work of round, plain pillars and cross-beams; the vast eaves are full of bird-nests; and the storm of twittering from the roofs is like a rushing of water. Immense the work is, and imposing in its aspect of settled power; but, in its way, it has great severity: there are no carvings, no gargoyles, no dragons; and yet the maze of projecting timbers below the eaves will both excite and delude expectation, so strangely does it suggest the grotesqueries and fantasticalities of another art. You look everywhere for the heads of lions, elephants, dragons, and see only the four-angled ends of beams, and feel rather astonished than disappointed. The majesty of the edifice could not have been strengthened by any such carving.

After the gate another long series of wide steps, and more trees, millennial, thick-shadowing, and then the terrace of the temple itself, with two beautiful stone lanterns (tōrō) at its entrance. The architecture of the temple resembles that of the gate, although on a lesser scale. Over the doors is a tablet with Chinese characters, signifying, "Great, Pure, Clear, Shining Treasure." But a heavy framework of wooden bars closes the sanctuary, and there is no one to let us in. Peering between the bars I see, in a sort of twilight, first a pavement of squares of marble, then an aisle of massive wooden pillars upholding the dim lofty roof, and at the farther end, between the pillars, Shaka, colossal, black-visaged, gold-robed, enthroned upon a giant lotus fully forty feet in circumference. At his right hand some white mysterious figure stands, holding an incense-box; at his left, another white figure is praying with clasped hands. Both are of superhuman stature. But it is too dark within the edifice to discern who they may be — whether disciples of the Buddha, or divinities, or figures of saints.

Beyond this temple extends an immense grove of trees — ancient cedars and pines — with splendid bamboos thickly planted between them, rising perpendicularly as masts to mix their plumes with the foliage of the giants: the effect is tropical, magnificent. Through this shadowing, a flight of broad stone steps slant up gently to some yet older shrine. And ascending them we reach another portal, smaller than the imposing Chinese structure through which we already passed, but wonderful, weird, full of dragons, dragons of a form which sculptors no longer carve, which they have even forgotten how to make, winged dragons rising from a storm-whirl of waters or thereinto descending. The dragon upon the panel of the left gate has her mouth closed; the jaws of the dragon on the panel of the right gate are open and menacing. Female and male they are, like the lions of Buddha. And the whirls of the eddying water, and the crests of the billowing, stand out from the panel in astonishing boldness of relief, in loops and curlings of gray wood time-seasoned to the hardness of stone.

The little temple beyond contains no celebrated image, but a shari only, or relic of Buddha, brought from India. And I cannot see it, having no time to wait until the absent keeper of the shari can be found.

III

"Now we shall go to look at the big bell," says Akira.

We turn to the left as we descend, along a path cut between hills faced for the height of seven or eight feet with protection-walls made green by moss; and reach a flight of extraordinarily dilapidated steps, with grass springing between their every joint and break — steps so worn down and displaced by countless feet that they have become ruins, painful and even dangerous to mount. We reach the summit, however, without mishap, and find ourselves before a little temple, on the steps of which an old priest awaits us, with smiling bow of welcome. We return his salutation; but ere entering the temple turn to look at the tsurigane on the right — the famous bell.

Under a lofty open shed, with a tilted Chinese roof, the great bell is hung. I should judge it to be fully nine feet high, and about five feet in diameter, with lips about eight inches thick. The shape of it is not like that of our bells, which broaden toward the lips; this has the same diameter through all its height, and it is covered with Buddhist texts cut into the smooth metal of it. It is rung by means of a heavy swinging beam, suspended from the roof by chains, and moved like a battering-ram. There are loops of palm-fibre rope attached to this beam to pull it by; and when you pull hard enough, so as to give it a good swing, it strikes a moulding like a lotus-flower on the side of the bell. This it must have done many hundred times; for the square, flat end of it, though showing the grain of a very dense wood, has been battered into a convex disk with ragged protruding edges, like the surface of a long-used printer's mallet.

A priest makes a sign to me to ring the bell. I first touch the great lips with my hand very lightly; and a musical murmur comes from them. Then I set the beam swinging strongly; and a sound deep as thunder, rich as the bass of a mighty organ — a sound enormous, extraordinary, yet beautiful — rolls over the hills and away. Then swiftly follows another and lesser and sweeter billowing of tone; then another; then an eddying of waves of echoes. Only once was it struck, the astounding bell; yet it continues to sob and moan for at least ten minutes!

And the age of this bell is six hundred and fifty years.[1]

[1] At the time this paper was written, nearly three years ago, I had not seen the mighty bells at Kyōto and at Nara.

The largest bell in Japan is suspended in the grounds of the grand Jōdo temple of Chion-in, at Kyōto. Visitors are not allowed to sound it. It was cast in 1633. It weighs seventy-four tons, and requires, they say, twenty-five men to ring it properly. Next in size ranks the bell of the Daibutsu temple in Kyōto, which visitors are allowed to ring on payment of a small sum. It was cast in 1615, and weighs sixty-three tons. The wonderful bell of Tōdaiji, at Nara, although ranking only third, is perhaps the most interesting of all. It is thirteen feet six inches

In the little temple near by, the priest shows us a series of curious paintings, representing the six hundredth anniversary of the casting of the bell. (For this is a sacred bell, and the spirit of a god is believed to dwell within it.) Otherwise the temple has little of interest. There are some kakemono representing Iyeyasu and his retainers; and on either side of the door, separating the inner from the outward sanctuary, there are life-size images of Japanese warriors in antique costume. On the altars of the inner shrine are small images, grouped upon a miniature landscape-work of painted wood — the Jiugo-Dōji, or Fifteen Youths — the Sons of the Goddess Benten. There are gohei before the shrine, and a mirror upon it; emblems of Shintō. The sanctuary has changed hands in the great transfer of Buddhist temples to the state religion.

In nearly every celebrated temple little Japanese prints are sold, containing the history of the shrine, and its miraculous legends. I find several such things on sale at the door of the temple, and in one of them, ornamented with a curious engraving of the bell, I discover, with Akira's aid, the following traditions.

IV

In the twelfth year of Bummei, this bell rang itself. And one who laughed on being told of the miracle,

high, and nine feet in diameter; and its inferiority to the Kyōto bells is not in visible dimensions so much as in weight and thickness. It weighs thirty-seven tons. It was cast in 733, and is therefore eleven hundred and sixty years old. Visitors pay one cent to sound it once.

met with misfortune; and another, who believed, thereafter prospered, and obtained all his desires.

Now, in that time there died in the village of Tamanawa a sick man whose name was Ono-no-Kimi; and Ono-no-Kimi descended to the region of the dead, and went before the Judgment-Seat of Emma-Ō. And Emma, Judge of Souls, said to him, "You come too soon! The measure of life allotted you in the Shaba-world has not yet been exhausted. Go back at once." But Ono-no-Kimi pleaded, saying, "How may I go back, not knowing my way through the darkness?" And Emma answered him, "You can find your way back by listening to the sound of the bell of En-gaku-ji, which is heard in the Nan-en-budi world, going south." And Ono-no-Kimi went south, and heard the bell, and found his way through the darknesses, and revived in the Shaba-world.

Also in those days there appeared in many provinces a Buddhist priest of giant stature, whom none remembered to have seen before, and whose name no man knew, traveling through the land, and everywhere exhorting the people to pray before the bell of En-gaku-ji. And it was at last discovered that the giant pilgrim was the holy bell itself, transformed by supernatural power into the form of a priest. And after these things had happened, many prayed before the bell, and obtained their wishes.

V

"Oн! there is something still to see," my guide exclaims as we reach the great Chinese gate again; and he leads the way across the grounds by another path to a little hill, previously hidden from view by trees. The face of the hill, a mass of soft stone perhaps one hundred feet high, is hollowed out into chambers, full of images. These look like burial-caves; and the images seem funereal monuments. There are two stories of chambers — three above, two below; and the former are connected with the latter by a narrow interior stairway cut through the living rock. And all around the dripping walls of these chambers on pedestals are gray slabs, shaped exactly like the haka in Buddhist cemeteries, and chiseled with figures of divinities in high relief. All have glory-disks: some are naïve and sincere like the work of our own mediæval image-makers. Several are not unfamiliar. I have seen before, in the cemetery of Kuboyama, this kneeling woman with countless shadowy hands; and this figure tiara-coiffed, slumbering with one knee raised, and cheek pillowed upon the left hand — the placid and pathetic symbol of the perpetual rest. Others, like Madonnas, hold lotus-flowers, and their feet rest upon the coils of a serpent. I cannot see them all, for the rock roof of one chamber has fallen in; and a sunbeam entering the ruin reveals a host of inaccessible sculptures half buried in rubbish.

But no! — this grotto-work is not for the dead; and these are not haka, as I imagined, but only images of the Goddess of Mercy. These chambers are chapels; and these sculptures are the En-gaku-ji-no-hyaku-Kwannon, "the Hundred Kwannons of En-gaku-ji." And I see in the upper chamber above the stairs a granite tablet in a rock-niche, chiseled with an inscription in Sanscrit transliterated into Chinese characters, "Adoration to the great merciful Kwan-ze-on, who looketh down above the sound of prayer."[1]

VI

ENTERING the grounds of the next temple, the Temple of Ken-chō-ji, through the "Gate of the Forest of Contemplative Words," and the "Gate of the Great Mountain of Wealth," one might almost fancy one's self reëntering, by some queer mistake, the grounds of En-gaku-ji. For the third gate before us, and the imposing temple beyond it, constructed upon the same models as those of the structures previously visited, were also the work of the same architect. Passing this third gate — colossal, severe, superb — we come to a fountain of bronze before the temple doors, an immense and beautiful lotus-leaf of

[1] In Sanscrit, "Avalokitesvara." The Japanese Kwannon, or Kwan-ze-on, is identical in origin with the Chinese virgin-goddess Kwanyin adopted by Buddhism as an incarnation of the Indian Avalokitesvara. (See Eitel's *Handbook of Chinese Buddhism*.) But the Japanese Kwannon has lost all Chinese characteristics — has become artistically an idealization of all that is sweet and beautiful in the woman of Japan.

metal, forming a broad shallow basin kept full to the brim by a jet in its midst.

This temple also is paved with black and white square slabs, and we can enter it with our shoes. Outside it is plain and solemn as that of En-gaku-ji; but the interior offers a more extraordinary spectacle of faded splendor. In lieu of the black Shaka throned against a background of flamelets, is a colossal Jizō-Sama, with a nimbus of fire — a single gilded circle large as a wagon-wheel, breaking into fire-tongues at three points. He is seated upon an enormous lotus of tarnished gold — over the lofty edge of which the skirt of his robe trails down. Behind him, standing on ascending tiers of golden steps, are glimmering hosts of miniature figures of him, reflections, multiplications of him, ranged there by ranks of hundreds — the Thousand Jizō. From the ceiling above him droop the dingy splendors of a sort of daïs-work, a streaming circle of pendants like a fringe, shimmering faintly through the webbed dust of centuries. And the ceiling itself must once have been a marvel; all beamed in caissons, each caisson containing, upon a gold ground, the painted figure of a flying bird. Formerly the eight great pillars supporting the roof were also covered with gilding; but only a few traces of it linger still upon their worm-pierced surfaces, and about the bases of their capitals. And there are wonderful friezes above the doors, from which all color has long since faded away, marvelous gray old carvings in relief; floating figures of tennin, or heavenly spirits playing upon flutes and biwa.

There is a chamber separated by a heavy wooden screen from the aisle on the right; and the priest in charge of the building slides the screen aside, and bids us enter. In this chamber is a drum elevated upon a brazen stand — the hugest I ever saw, fully eighteen feet in circumference. Beside it hangs a big bell, covered with Buddhist texts. I am sorry to learn that it is prohibited to sound the great drum. There is nothing else to see except some dingy paper lanterns figured with the swastika — the sacred Buddhist symbol called by the Japanese manji.

VII

AKIRA tells me that in the book called Jizō-kyō-Kosui, this legend is related of the great statue of Jizō in this same ancient temple of Ken-chō-ji.

Formerly there lived at Kamakura the wife of a Rōnin[1] named Soga Sadayoshi. She lived by feeding silkworms and gathering the silk. She used often to visit the temple of Ken-chō-ji; and one very cold day that she went there, she thought that the image of Jizō looked like one suffering from cold; and she resolved to make a cap to keep the god's head warm — such a cap as the people of the country wear in cold weather. And she went home and made the

[1] Let the reader consult Mitford's admirable *Tales of Old Japan* for the full meaning of the term "Rōnin."

cap and covered the god's head with it, saying, "Would I were rich enough to give thee a warm covering for all thine august body; but, alas! I am poor, and even this which I offer thee is unworthy of thy divine acceptance."

Now this woman very suddenly died in the fiftieth year of her age, in the twelfth month of the fifth year of the period called Chisho. But her body remained warm for three days, so that her relatives would not suffer her to be taken to the burning-ground. And on the evening of the third day she came to life again.

Then she related that on the day of her death she had gone before the Judgment-Seat of Emma, King and Judge of the Dead. And Emma, seeing her, became wroth, and said to her: "You have been a wicked woman, and have scorned the teaching of the Buddha. All your life you have passed in destroying the lives of silkworms by putting them into heated water. Now you shall go to the Kwakkto-Jigoku, and there burn until your sins shall be expiated." Forthwith she was seized and dragged by demons to a great pot filled with molten metal, and thrown into the pot, and she cried out horribly. And suddenly Jizō-Sama descended into the molten metal beside her, and the metal became like a flowing of oil and ceased to burn; and Jizō put his arms about her and lifted her out. And he went with her before King Emma, and asked that she should be pardoned for his sake, forasmuch as she had become related to him by one act of goodness. So she found pardon, and returned to the Shaba-world.

"Akira," I ask, "it cannot then be lawful, according to Buddhism, for any one to wear silk?"

"Assuredly not," replies Akira; "and by the law of Buddha priests are expressly forbidden to wear silk. Nevertheless," he adds with that quiet smile of his, in which I am beginning to discern suggestions of sarcasm, "nearly all the priests wear silk."

VIII

AKIRA also tells me this:

It is related in the seventh volume of the book Kamakurashi that there was formerly at Kamakura a temple called Emmei-ji, in which there was enshrined a famous statue of Jizō, called Hadaka-Jizō, or Naked Jizō. The statue was indeed naked, but clothes were put upon it; and it stood upright with its feet upon a chessboard. Now, when pilgrims came to the temple and paid a certain fee, the priest of the temple would remove the clothes of the statue; and then all could see that, though the face was the face of Jizō, the body was the body of a woman.

Now this was the origin of the famous image of Hadaka-Jizō standing upon the chessboard. On one occasion the great prince Taira-no-Tokyori was playing chess with his wife in the presence of many guests. And he made her agree, after they had played several games, that whosoever should lose the next game would have to stand naked on the chessboard. And in the next game they played his wife lost. And she prayed to Jizō to save her from the shame of appearing naked. And Jizō came in answer to her prayer and stood upon the chessboard, and disrobed himself, and changed his body suddenly into the body of a woman.

IX

As we travel on, the road curves and narrows between higher elevations, and becomes more sombre. "Oi! mate!" my Buddhist guide calls softly to the runners; and our two vehicles halt in a band of sunshine, descending, through an opening in the foliage of immense trees, over a flight of ancient mossy steps. "Here," says my friend, "is the temple of the King of Death; it is called Emma-Dō; and it is a temple of the Zen sect — Zen-Oji. And it is more than seven hundred years old, and there is a famous statue in it."

We ascend to a small, narrow court in which the edifice stands. At the head of the steps, to the right, is a stone tablet, very old, with characters cut at least an inch deep into the granite of it, Chinese characters signifying, "This is the Temple of Emma, King."

The temple resembles outwardly and inwardly the others we have visited, and, like those of Shaka and of the colossal Jizō of Kamakura, has a paved floor, so that we are not obliged to remove our shoes

159

on entering. Everything is worn, dim, vaguely gray; there is a pungent scent of mouldiness; the paint has long ago peeled away from the naked wood of the pillars. Throned to right and left against the high walls tower nine grim figures — five on one side, four on the other — wearing strange crowns with trumpet-shapen ornaments; figures hoary with centuries, and so like to the icon of Emma, which I saw at Kuboyama, that I ask, "Are all these Emma?" "Oh, no!" my guide answers; "these are his attendants only — the Jiu-Ō, the Ten Kings." "But there are only nine?" I query. "Nine, and Emma completes the number. You have not yet seen Emma."

Where is he? I see at the farther end of the chamber an altar elevated upon a platform approached by wooden steps; but there is no image, only the usual altar furniture of gilded bronze and lacquerware. Behind the altar I see only a curtain about six feet square — a curtain once dark red, now almost without any definite hue — probably veiling some alcove. A temple guardian approaches, and invites us to ascend the platform. I remove my shoes before mounting upon the matted surface, and follow the guardian behind the altar, in front of the curtain. He makes me a sign to look, and lifts the veil with a long rod. And suddenly, out of the blackness of some mysterious profundity masked by that sombre curtain, there glowers upon me an apparition at the sight of which I involuntarily

GLIMPSES OF UNFAMILIAR JAPAN

start back — a monstrosity exceeding all anticipa-
tion — a Face.[1]

A Face tremendous, menacing, frightful, dull
red, as with the redness of heated iron cooling into
gray. The first shock of the vision is no doubt partly
due to the somewhat theatrical manner in which the
work is suddenly revealed out of darkness by the
lifting of the curtain. But as the surprise passes I
begin to recognize the immense energy of the conception — to look for the secret of the grim artist.
The wonder of the creation is not in the tiger frown,
nor in the violence of the terrific mouth, nor in the
fury and ghastly color of the head as a whole: it is
in the eyes — eyes of nightmare.

x

Now this weird old temple has its legend.

Seven hundred years ago, 't is said, there died the
great image-maker, the great busshi, Unke-Sosei.
And Unke-Sosei signifies "Unke who returned from
the dead." For when he came before Emma, the
Judge of Souls, Emma said to him: "Living, thou
madest no image of me. Go back unto earth and
make one, now that thou hast looked upon me."

[1] There is a delicious Japanese proverb, the full humor of which is
only to be appreciated by one familiar with the artistic representations
of the divinities referred to:
        Karutoki no Jizō-gao,
        Nasutoki no Emma-gao.

    ["Borrowing-time, the face of Jizō;
      Repaying-time, the face of Emma."]

And Unke found himself suddenly restored to the world of men; and they that had known him before, astonished to see him alive again, called him Unke-Sosei. And Unke-Sosei, bearing with him always the memory of the countenance of Emma, wrought this image of him, which still inspires fear in all who behold it; and he made also the images of the grim Jiu-Ō, the Ten Kings obeying Emma, which sit throned about the temple.

I want to buy a picture of Emma, and make my wish known to the temple guardian. Oh, yes, I may buy a picture of Emma, but I must first see the Oni. I follow the guardian out of the temple, down the mossy steps, and across the village highway into a little Japanese cottage, where I take my seat upon the floor. The guardian disappears behind a screen, and presently returns dragging with him the Oni — the image of a demon, naked, blood-red, indescribably ugly. The Oni is about three feet high. He stands in an attitude of menace, brandishing a club. He has a head shaped something like the head of a bull-dog, with brazen eyes; and his feet are like the feet of a lion. Very gravely the guardian turns the grotesquery round and round, that I may admire its every aspect; while a naïf crowd collects before the open door to look at the stranger and the demon.

Then the guardian finds me a rude woodcut of Emma, with a sacred inscription printed upon it;

and as soon as I have paid for it, he proceeds to stamp the paper with the seal of the temple. The seal he keeps in a wonderful lacquered box, covered with many wrappings of soft leather. These having been removed, I inspect the seal — an oblong, vermilion-red polished stone, with the design cut in intaglio upon it. He moistens the surface with red ink, presses it upon the corner of the paper bearing the grim picture, and the authenticity of my strange purchase is established forever.

XI

You do not see the Dai-Butsu as you enter the grounds of his long-vanished temple, and proceed along a paved path across stretches of lawn; great trees hide him. But very suddenly, at a turn, he comes into full view and you start! No matter how many photographs of the colossus you may have already seen, this first vision of the reality is an astonishment. Then you imagine that you are already too near, though the image is at least a hundred yards away. As for me, I retire at once thirty or forty yards back, to get a better view. And the jinrikisha man runs after me, laughing and gesticulating, thinking that I imagine the image alive and am afraid of it.

But, even were that shape alive, none could be afraid of it. The gentleness, the dreamy passionlessness of those features — the immense repose of the whole figure — are full of beauty and charm.

And, contrary to all expectation, the nearer you approach the giant Buddha, the greater this charm becomes. You look up into the solemnly beautiful face — into the half-closed eyes that seem to watch you through their eyelids of bronze as gently as those of a child; and you feel that the image typifies all that is tender and calm in the Soul of the East. Yet you feel also that only Japanese thought could have created it. Its beauty, its dignity, its perfect repose, reflect the higher life of the race that imagined it; and, though doubtless inspired by some Indian model, as the treatment of the hair and various symbolic marks reveal, the art is Japanese.

So mighty and beautiful the work is, that you will not for some time notice the magnificent lotus-plants of bronze, fully fifteen feet high, planted before the figure, on either side of the great tripod in which incense-rods are burning.

Through an orifice in the right side of the enormous lotus-blossom on which the Buddha is seated, you can enter into the statue. The interior contains a little shrine of Kwannon, and a statue of the priest Yuten, and a stone tablet bearing in Chinese characters the sacred formula, Namu Amida Butsu.

A ladder enables the pilgrim to ascend into the interior of the colossus as high as the shoulders, in which are two little windows commanding a wide prospect of the grounds; while a priest, who acts as guide, states the age of the statue to be six hundred and thirty years, and asks for some small contribution to aid in the erection of a new temple to shelter it from the weather.

For this Buddha once had a temple. A tidal wave following an earthquake swept walls and roof away, but left the mighty Amida unmoved, still meditating upon his lotus.

XII

AND we arrive before the far-famed Kamakura temple of Kwannon — Kwannon, who yielded up her right to the Eternal Peace that she might save the souls of men, and renounced Nirvana to suffer with humanity for other myriad million ages — Kwannon, the Goddess of Pity and of Mercy.

I climb three flights of steps leading to the temple, and a young girl, seated at the threshold, rises to greet us. Then she disappears within the temple to summon the guardian priest, a venerable man, white-robed, who makes me a sign to enter.

The temple is large as any that I have yet seen, and, like the others, gray with the wearing of six hundred years. From the roof there hang down votive offerings, inscriptions, and lanterns in multitude, painted with various pleasing colors. Almost opposite to the entrance is a singular statue, a seated figure, of human dimensions and most human aspect, looking upon us with small weird eyes set in a wondrously wrinkled face. This face was originally painted flesh-tint, and the robes of the image pale blue; but now the whole is uniformly gray with age and dust, and its colorlessness harmonizes so well with the senility of the figure that one is almost ready to believe one's self gazing at a living mendicant pilgrim. It is Benzuru, the same personage whose famous image at Asakusa has been made featureless by the wearing touch of countless pilgrim-fingers. To left and right of the entrance are the Ni-Ō, enormously muscled, furious of aspect; their crimson bodies are speckled with a white scum of paper pellets spat at them by worshipers. Above the altar is a small but very pleasing image of Kwannon, with her entire figure relieved against an oblong halo of gold, imitating the flickering of flame.

But this is not the image for which the temple is famed; there is another to be seen upon certain conditions. The old priest presents me with a petition, written in excellent and eloquent English, praying visitors to contribute something to the maintenance of the temple and its pontiff, and appealing to those of another faith to remember that "any belief which can make men kindly and good is worthy of respect." I contribute my mite, and I ask to see the great Kwannon.

Then the old priest lights a lantern, and leads the way, through a low doorway on the left of the altar, into the interior of the temple, into some very lofty darkness. I follow him cautiously awhile, discerning nothing whatever but the flicker of the lantern; then we halt before something which gleams. A

moment, and my eyes, becoming more accustomed
to the darkness, begin to distinguish outlines; the
gleaming object defines itself gradually as a Foot,
an immense golden Foot, and I perceive the hem of
a golden robe undulating over the instep. Now the
other foot appears; the figure is certainly standing.
I can perceive that we are in a narrow but also very
lofty chamber, and that out of some mysterious
blackness overhead ropes are dangling down into
the circle of lantern-light illuminating the golden
feet. The priest lights two more lanterns, and sus-
pends them upon hooks attached to a pair of pendent ropes about a yard apart; then he pulls up
both together slowly. More of the golden robe is
revealed as the lanterns ascend, swinging on their
way; then the outlines of two mighty knees; then
the curving of columnar thighs under chiseled drapery, and, as with the still waving ascent of the lanterns the golden Vision towers ever higher through
the gloom, expectation intensifies. There is no
sound but the sound of the invisible pulleys overhead, which squeak like bats. Now above the golden
girdle, the suggestion of a bosom. Then the glowing of a golden hand uplifted in benediction. Then
another golden hand holding a lotus. And at last a
Face, golden, smiling with eternal youth and infinite
tenderness, the face of Kwannon.

So revealed out of the consecrated darkness, this
ideal of divine feminity — creation of a forgotten
art and time — is more than impressive. I can

scarcely call the emotion which it produces admiration; it is rather reverence.

But the lanterns, which paused awhile at the level of the beautiful face, now ascend still higher, with a fresh squeaking of pulleys. And lo! the tiara of the divinity appears, with strangest symbolism. It is a pyramid of heads, of faces — charming faces of maidens, miniature faces of Kwannon herself.

For this is the Kwannon of the Eleven Faces — Jiu-ichi-men-Kwannon.

XIII

MOST sacred this statue is held; and this is its legend.

In the reign of Emperor Gensei, there lived in the province of Yamato a Buddhist priest, Tokudo Shōnin, who had been in a previous birth Hoki Bosatsu, but had been reborn among common men to save their souls. Now at that time, in a valley in Yamato, Tokudo Shōnin, walking by night, saw a wonderful radiance; and going toward it found that it came from the trunk of a great fallen tree, a kusunoki, or camphor-tree. A delicious perfume came from the tree, and the shining of it was like the shining of the moon. And by these signs Tokudo Shōnin knew that the wood was holy; and he bethought him that he should have the statue of Kwannon carved from it. And he recited a sutra, and repeated the Nenbutsu, praying for inspiration; and even while he prayed there came and stood before him an aged man and an aged woman; and these said to him, "We know that your desire is to have the image of Kwannon-Sama carved from this tree with the help of Heaven; continue therefore, to pray, and we shall carve the statue."

And Tokudo Shōnin did as they bade him; and he saw them easily split the vast trunk into two equal parts, and begin to carve each of the parts into an image. And he saw them so labor for three days; and on the third day the work was done — and he saw the two marvelous statues of Kwannon made perfect before him. And he said to the strangers, "Tell me, I pray you, by what names you are known." Then the old man answered, "I am Kasuga Myōjin." And the woman answered, "I am called Ten-shō-kō-dai-jin; I am the Goddess of the Sun." And as they spoke both became transfigured and ascended to heaven and vanished from the sight of Tokudo Shōnin.[1]

And the Emperor, hearing of these happenings, sent his representative to Yamato to make offerings, and to have a temple built. Also the great priest, Gyōgi-Bosatsu, came and consecrated the images, and dedicated the temple which by order of the Emperor was built. And one of the statues he

[1] This old legend has peculiar interest as an example of the efforts made by Buddhism to absorb the Shintō divinities, as it had already absorbed those of India and of China. These efforts were, to a great extent, successful prior to the disestablishment of Buddhism and the revival of Shintō as the state religion. But in Izumo, and other parts of western Japan, Shintō has always remained dominant, and has even appropriated and amalgamated much belonging to Buddhism.

placed in the temple, enshrining it, and commanding it, "Stay thou here always to save all living
creatures!" But the other statue he cast into the
sea, saying to it, "Go thou whithersoever it is best,
to save all the living."

Now the statue floated to Kamakura. And there
arriving by night it shed a great radiance all about
it as if there were sunshine upon the sea; and the
fishermen of Kamakura were awakened by the
great light; and they went out in boats, and found
the statue floating and brought it to shore. And the
Emperor ordered that a temple should be built for
it, the temple called Shin-haseidera, on the mountain called Kaiko-San, at Kamakura.

XIV

As we leave the temple of Kwannon behind us,
there are no more dwellings visible along the road;
the green slopes to left and right become steeper,
and the shadows of the great trees deepen over us.
But still, at intervals, some flight of venerable
mossy steps, a carven Buddhist gateway, or a lofty
torii, signals the presence of sanctuaries we have
no time to visit: countless crumbling shrines are
all around us, dumb witnesses to the antique splendor and vastness of the dead capital; and everywhere, mingled with perfume of blossoms, hovers
the sweet, resinous smell of Japanese incense. Betimes we pass a scattered multitude of sculptured
stones, like segments of four-sided pillars — old

haka, the forgotten tombs of a long-abandoned
cemetery; or the solitary image of some Buddhist
deity — a dreaming Amida or faintly smiling Kwannon. All are ancient, time-discolored, mutilated; a
few have been weather-worn into unrecognizability.
I halt a moment to contemplate something pathetic,
a group of six images of the charming divinity who
cares for the ghosts of little children — the Roku-
Jizō. Oh, how chipped and scurfed and mossed they
are! Five stand buried almost up to their shoulders
in a heaping of little stones, testifying to the prayers
of generations; and votive yodarekake, infant bibs
of divers colors, have been put about the necks of
these for the love of children lost. But one of the
gentle god's images lies shattered and overthrown
in its own scattered pebble-pile — broken perhaps
by some passing wagon.

XV

THE road slopes before us as we go, sinks down between cliffs steep as the walls of a cañon, and curves.
Suddenly we emerge from the cliffs, and reach the
sea. It is blue like the unclouded sky — a soft
dreamy blue.

And our path turns sharply to the right, and
winds along cliff-summits overlooking a broad
beach of dun-colored sand; and the sea wind blows
deliciously with a sweet saline scent, urging the
lungs to fill themselves to the very utmost; and far
away before me, I perceive a beautiful high green

mass, an island foliage-covered, rising out of the water about a quarter of a mile from the mainland — Enoshima, the holy island, sacred to the Goddess of the Sea, the Goddess of Beauty. I can already distinguish a tiny town, gray-sprinkling its steep slope. Evidently it can be reached to-day on foot, for the tide is out, and has left bare a long broad reach of sand, extending to it, from the opposite village which we are approaching, like a causeway.

At Katase, the little settlement facing the island, we must leave our jinrikisha and walk; the dunes between the village and the beach are too deep to pull the vehicle over. Scores of other jinrikisha are waiting here in the little narrow street for pilgrims who have preceded me. But to-day, I am told, I am the only European who visits the shrine of Benten.

Our two men lead the way over the dunes, and we soon descend upon damp firm sand.

As we near the island the architectural details of the little town define delightfully through the faint sea-haze — curved bluish sweeps of fantastic roofs, angles of airy balconies, high-peaked curious gables, all above a fluttering of queerly shaped banners covered with mysterious lettering. We pass the sand-flats; and the ever-open Portal of the Sea-City, the City of the Dragon-Goddess, is before us, a beautiful torii. All of bronze it is, with shime-nawa of bronze above it, and a brazen tablet inscribed with characters declaring: "This is the

Palace of the Goddess of Enoshima." About the bases of the ponderous pillars are strange designs in *relievo*, eddyings of waves with tortoises struggling in the flow. This is really the gate of the city, facing the shrine of Benten by the land approach; but it is only the third torii of the imposing series through Katase: we did not see the others, having come by way of the coast.

And lo! we are in Enoshima. High before us slopes the single street, a street of broad steps, a street shadowy, full of multi-colored flags and dark blue drapery dashed with white fantasticalities, which are words, fluttered by the sea wind. It is lined with taverns and miniature shops. At every one I must pause to look; and to dare to look at anything in Japan is to want to buy it. So I buy, and buy, and buy!

For verily 't is the City of Mother-of-Pearl, this Enoshima. In every shop, behind the lettered draperies there are miracles of shell-work for sale at absurdly small prices. The glazed cases laid flat upon the matted platforms, the shelved cabinets set against the walls, are all opalescent with nacreous things — extraordinary surprises, incredible ingenuities; strings of mother-of-pearl fish, strings of mother-of-pearl birds, all shimmering with rainbow colors. There are little kittens of mother-of-pearl, and little foxes of mother-of-pearl, and little puppies of mother-of-pearl, and girls' hair-combs, and cigarette-holders, and pipes too beautiful to use. There are little tortoises, not larger than a shilling, made of shells, that, when you touch them, however lightly, begin to move head, legs, and tail, all at the same time, alternately withdrawing or protruding their limbs so much like real tortoises as to give one a shock of surprise. There are storks and birds, and beetles and butterflies, and crabs and lobsters, made so cunningly of shells, that only touch convinces you they are not alive. There are bees of shell, poised on flowers of the same material — poised on wire in such a way that they seem to buzz if moved only with the tip of a feather. There is shell-work jewelry indescribable, things that Japanese girls love, enchantments in mother-of-pearl, hair-pins carven in a hundred forms, brooches, necklaces. And there are photographs of Enoshima.

XVI

THIS curious street ends at another torii, a wooden torii, with a steeper flight of stone steps ascending to it. At the foot of the steps are votive stone lamps and a little well, and a stone tank at which all pilgrims wash their hands and rinse their mouths before approaching the temples of the gods. And hanging beside the tank are bright blue towels, with large white Chinese characters upon them. I ask Akira what these characters signify:

" 'Ho-Keng' is the sound of the characters in the Chinese; but in Japanese the same characters are pronounced 'Kenjitatematsuru,' and signify that those towels are most humbly offered to Benten. They are what you call votive offerings. And there are many kinds of votive offerings made to famous shrines. Some people give towels, some give pictures, some give vases; some offer lanterns of paper, or bronze, or stone. It is common to promise such offerings when making petitions to the gods; and it is usual to promise a torii. The torii may be small or great according to the wealth of him who gives it; the very rich pilgrim may offer to the gods a torii of metal, such as that below, which is the Gate of Enoshima."

"Akira, do the Japanese always keep their vows to the gods?"

Akira smiles a sweet smile, and answers:

"There was a man who promised to build a torii of good metal if his prayers were granted. And he obtained all that he desired. And then he built a torii with three exceedingly small needles."

XVII

ASCENDING the steps, we reach a terrace, overlooking all the city roofs. There are Buddhist lions of stone and stone lanterns, mossed and chipped, on either side the torii; and the background of the terrace is the sacred hill, covered with foliage. To the left is a balustrade of stone, old and green, surrounding a shallow pool covered with scum of water-weed. And on the farther bank above it, out of the bushes, protrudes a strangely shaped stone slab, poised on edge, and covered with Chinese characters. It is a sacred stone, and is believed to have the form of a great frog, gama; wherefore it is called Gama-ishi, the Frog-Stone. Here and there along the edge of the terrace are other graven monuments, one of which is the offering of certain pilgrims who visited the shrine of the Sea-Goddess one hundred times. On the right other flights of steps lead to loftier terraces; and an old man, who sits at the foot of them, making bird-cages of bamboo, offers himself as guide.

We follow him to the next terrace, where there is a school for the children of Enoshima, and another sacred stone, huge and shapeless: Fuku-ishi, the Stone of Good Fortune. In old times pilgrims who rubbed their hands upon it believed they would thereby gain riches; and the stone is polished and worn by the touch of innumerable palms.

More steps and more green-mossed lions and lanterns, and another terrace with a little temple in its midst, the first shrine of Benten. Before it a few stunted palm-trees are growing. There is nothing in the shrine of interest, only Shintō emblems. But there is another well beside it with other votive towels, and there is another mysterious monument, a stone shrine brought from China six hundred years ago. Perhaps it contained some far-famed statue before this place of pilgrimage was given over to the priests of Shintō. There is nothing in it now; the monolith slab forming the back of it has been fractured by the falling of rocks from the cliff above; and the inscription cut therein has been almost effaced by some kind of scum. Akira reads, "Dai-Nippon-goku-Enoshima-no-reiseki-ken . . ."; the rest is undecipherable. He says there is a statue in the neighboring temple, but it is exhibited only once a year, on the fifteenth day of the seventh month.

Leaving the court by a rising path to the left, we proceed along the verge of a cliff overlooking the sea. Perched upon this verge are pretty tea-houses, all widely open to the sea wind, so that, looking through them, over their matted floors and lacquered balconies one sees the ocean as in a picture-frame, and the pale clear horizon specked with snowy sails, and a faint blue-peaked shape also, like a phantom island, the far vapory silhouette of Ōshima. Then we find another torii, and other steps leading to a terrace almost black with shade of enormous evergreen trees, and surrounded on the sea side by another stone balustrade, velveted with moss. On the right more steps, another torii, another terrace; and more mossed green lions and stone lamps; and a monument inscribed with the record of the change whereby Enoshima passed away from Buddhism to become Shintō. Beyond, in the centre of another plateau, the second shrine of Benten.

But there is no Benten! Benten has been hidden away by Shintō hands. The second shrine is void as the first. Nevertheless, in a building to the left of the temple, strange relics are exhibited. Feudal armor; suits of plate and chain-mail; helmets with visors which are demoniac masks of iron; helmets crested with dragons of gold; two-handed swords worthy of giants; and enormous arrows, more than five feet long, with shafts nearly an inch in diameter. One has a crescent head about nine inches from horn to horn, the interior edge of the crescent being sharp as a knife. Such a missile would take off a man's head; and I can scarcely believe Akira's assurance that such ponderous arrows were shot from a bow by hand only. There is a specimen of the writing of Nichiren, the great Buddhist priest — gold characters on a blue ground; and there is, in a lacquered shrine, a gilded dragon said to have been made by that still greater priest and writer and master-wizard, Kōbōdaishi.

A path shaded by overarching trees leads from this plateau to the third shrine. We pass a torii and beyond it come to a stone monument covered with figures of monkeys chiseled in relief. What the signification of this monument is, even our guide cannot explain. Then another torii. It is of wood; but I am told it replaces one of metal, stolen in the night by thieves. Wonderful thieves! that torii must have weighed at least a ton! More stone lanterns; then an immense court, on the very summit of the mountain, and there, in its midst, the third and chief temple of Benten. And before the temple is a large vacant space surrounded by a fence in such manner as to render the shrine totally inaccessible. Vanity and vexation of spirit!

There is, however, a little haiden, or place of prayer, with nothing in it but a money-box and a bell, before the fence, and facing the temple steps. Here the pilgrims make their offerings and pray. Only a small raised platform covered with a Chinese roof supported upon four plain posts, the back of the structure being closed by a lattice about breast high. From this praying-station we can look into the temple of Benten, and see that Benten is not there.

But I perceive that the ceiling is arranged in caissons; and in a central caisson I discover a very curious painting — a foreshortened Tortoise, gazing down at me. And while I am looking at it I hear Akira and the guide laughing; and the latter exclaims, "Benten-Sama!"

A beautiful little damask snake is undulating up the lattice-work, poking its head through betimes to look at us. It does not seem in the least afraid, nor has it much reason to be, seeing that its kind are deemed the servants and confidants of Benten. Sometimes the great goddess herself assumes the serpent-form; perhaps she has come to see us.

Near by is a singular stone, set on a pedestal in the court. It has the form of the body of a tortoise, and markings like those of the creature's shell; and it is held a sacred thing, and is called the Tortoise-stone. But I fear exceedingly that in all this place we shall find nothing save stones and serpents!

XVIII

Now we are going to visit the Dragon cavern, not so called, Akira says, because the Dragon of Benten ever dwelt therein, but because the shape of the cavern is the shape of a dragon. The path descends toward the opposite side of the island, and suddenly breaks into a flight of steps cut out of the pale hard rock — exceedingly steep, and worn, and slippery, and perilous — overlooking the sea. A vision of low pale rocks, and surf bursting among them, and a tōrō or votive stone lamp in the centre of them — all seen as in a bird's-eye view, over the verge of an awful precipice. I see also deep, round holes in one of the rocks. There used to be a tea-house below; and the wooden pillars supporting it were fitted into those holes.

I descend with caution; the Japanese seldom slip in their straw sandals, but I can only proceed with the aid of the guide. At almost every step I slip. Surely these steps could never have been thus worn away by the straw sandals of pilgrims who came to see only stones and serpents!

At last we reach a plank gallery carried along the face of the cliff above the rocks and pools, and following it round a projection of the cliff enter the sacred cave. The light dims as we advance; and the sea-waves, running after us into the gloom, make a stupefying roar, multiplied by the extraordinary echo. Looking back, I see the mouth of the cavern like a prodigious sharply angled rent in blackness, showing a fragment of azure sky.

We reach a shrine with no deity in it, pay a fee; and lamps being lighted and given to each of us, we proceed to explore a series of underground passages. So black they are that even with the light of three lamps, I can at first see nothing. In a while, however, I can distinguish stone figures in relief — chiseled on slabs like those I saw in the Buddhist graveyard. These are placed at regular intervals along the rock walls. The guide approaches his light to the face of each one, and utters a name, "Daikoku-Sama," "Fudō-Sama," "Kwannon-Sama." Sometimes in lieu of a statue there is an empty shrine only, with a money-box before it; and these void shrines have names of Shintō gods, "Daijingu," "Hachiman," "Inari-Sama." All the statues are black, or seem black in the yellow lamp-light, and sparkle as if frosted. I feel as if I were in some mortuary pit, some subterranean burial-place of dead gods. Interminable the corridor appears; yet there is at last an end — an end with a shrine in it — where the rocky ceiling descends so low that to reach the shrine one must go down on hands and knees. And there is nothing in the shrine. This is the Tail of the Dragon.

We do not return to the light at once, but enter

into other lateral black corridors — the Wings of the Dragon. More sable effigies of dispossessed gods; more empty shrines; more stone faces covered with salt-petre; and more money-boxes, possible only to reach by stooping, where more offerings should be made. And there is no Benten, either of wood or stone.

I am glad to return to the light. Here our guide strips naked, and suddenly leaps head foremost into a black deep swirling current between rocks. Five minutes later he reappears, and clambering out lays at my feet a living, squirming sea-snail and an enormous shrimp. Then he resumes his robe, and we reascend the mountain.

XIX

"And this," the reader may say — "this is all that you went forth to see: a torii, some shells, a small damask snake, some stones?"

It is true. And nevertheless I know that I am be-witched. There is a charm indefinable about the place — that sort of charm which comes with a little ghostly thrill never to be forgotten.

Not of strange sights alone is this charm made, but of numberless subtle sensations and ideas inter-woven and interblended: the sweet sharp scents of grove and sea; the blood-brightening, vivifying touch of the free wind; the dumb appeal of ancient mystic mossy things; vague reverence evoked by knowledge of treading soil called holy for a thousand years; and a sense of sympathy, as a human duty, compelled by the vision of steps of rock worn down into shapelessness by the pilgrim feet of vanished generations.

And other memories ineffaceable: the first sight of the sea-girt City of Pearl through a fairy veil of haze; the windy approach to the lovely island over the velvety soundless · brown stretch of sand; the weird majesty of the giant gate of bronze; the queer, high-sloping, fantastic, quaintly gabled street, flinging down sharp shadows of aerial balconies; the flutter of colored draperies in the sea wind, and of flags with their riddles of lettering; the pearly glimmering of the astonishing shops.

And impressions of the enormous day — the day of the Land of the Gods — a loftier day than ever our summers know; and the glory of the view from those green sacred silent heights between sea and sun; and the remembrance of the sky, a sky spiritual as holiness, a sky with clouds ghost-pure and white as the light itself — seeming, indeed, not clouds but dreams, or souls of Bodhisattvas about to melt forever into some blue Nirvana.

And the romance of Benten, too — the Deity of Beauty, the Divinity of Love, the Goddess of Eloquence. Rightly is she likewise named Goddess of the Sea. For is not the Sea most ancient and most excellent of Speakers — the eternal Poet, chanter of that mystic hymn whose rhythm shakes the world, whose mighty syllables no man may learn?

A PILGRIMAGE TO ENOSHIMA

XX

WE return by another route.

For a while the way winds through a long narrow winding valley between wooded hills: the whole extent of bottom-land is occupied by rice-farms; the air has a humid coolness, and one hears only the chanting of frogs, like a clattering of countless castanets, as the jinrikisha jolts over the rugged elevated paths separating the flooded rice-fields.

As we skirt the foot of a wooded hill upon the right, my Japanese comrade signals to our runners to halt, and himself dismounting, points to the blue-peaked roof of a little temple high-perched on the green slope. "Is it really worth while to climb up there in the sun?" I ask. "Oh, yes!" he answers: "it is the temple of Kishibojin — Kishibojin, the Mother of Demons!"

We ascend a flight of broad stone steps, meet the Buddhist guardian lions at the summit, and enter the little court in which the temple stands. An elderly woman, with a child clinging to her robe, comes from the adjoining building to open the screens for us; and taking off our footgear we enter the temple. Without, the edifice looked old and dingy; but within all is neat and pretty. The June sun, pouring through the open shōji, illuminates an artistic confusion of brasses gracefully shaped and multi-colored things — images, lanterns, paintings, gilded inscriptions, pendent scrolls. There are three altars.

GLIMPSES OF UNFAMILIAR JAPAN

Above the central altar Amida Buddha sits enthroned on his mystic golden lotus in the attitude of the Teacher. On the altar to the right gleams a shrine of five miniature golden steps, where little images stand in rows, tier above tier, some seated, some erect, male and female, attired like goddesses or like daimyō: the Sanjiubanjin, or Thirty Guardians. Below, on the façade of the altar, is the figure of a hero slaying a monster. On the altar to the left is the shrine of the Mother of Demons.

Her story is a legend of horror. For some sin committed in a previous birth, she was born a demon, devouring her own children. But being saved by the teaching of Buddha, she became a divine being, especially loving and protecting infants; and Japanese mothers pray to her for their little ones, and wives pray to her for beautiful boys.

The face of Kishibojin[1] is the face of a comely woman. But her eyes are weird. In her right hand she bears a lotus-blossom; with her left she supports in a fold of her robe, against her half-veiled breast, a naked baby. At the foot of her shrine stands Jizō-Sama, leaning upon his shakujō. But the altar and its images do not form the startling feature of the temple-interior. What impresses the visitor in a totally novel way are the votive offerings. High before the shrine, suspended from strings stretched taut between tall poles of bamboo, are scores, no,

[1] In Sanscrit "Hariti." "Karitei-Bo" is the Japanese name for one form of Kishibojin.

185

hundreds, of pretty tiny dresses — Japanese baby-dresses of many colors. Most are made of poor material, for these are the thank-offerings of very poor simple women, poor country mothers, whose prayers to Kishibojin for the blessing of children have been heard.

And the sight of all those little dresses, each telling so naïvely its story of joy and pain — those tiny kimono shaped and sewn by docile patient fingers of humble mothers — touches irresistibly, like some unexpected revelation of the universal mother-love. And the tenderness of all the simple hearts that have testified thus to faith and thankfulness seems to thrill all about me softly, like a caress of summer wind.

Outside the world appears to have suddenly grown beautiful; the light is sweeter; it seems to me there is a new charm even in the azure of the eternal day.

XXI

THEN, having traversed the valley, we reach a main road so level and so magnificently shaded by huge old trees that I could believe myself in an English lane — a lane in Kent or Surrey, perhaps — but for some exotic detail breaking the illusion at intervals; a torii, towering before temple-steps descending to the highway, or a sign-board lettered with Chinese characters, or the wayside shrine of some unknown god.

GLIMPSES OF UNFAMILIAR JAPAN

All at once I observe by the roadside some unfamiliar sculptures in relief — a row of chiseled slabs protected by a little bamboo shed; and I dismount to look at them, supposing them to be funereal monuments. They are so old that the lines of their sculpturing are half obliterated; their feet are covered with moss, and their visages are half effaced. But I can discern that these are not haka, but six images of one divinity; and my guide knows him — Kōshin, the God of Roads. So chipped and covered with scurf he is, that the upper portion of his form has become indefinably vague; his attributes have been worn away. But below his feet, on several slabs, chiseled cunningly, I can still distinguish the figures of the Three Apes, his messengers. And some pious soul has left before one image an humble votive offering — the picture of a black cock and a white hen, painted upon a wooden shingle. It must have been left here very long ago; the wood has become almost black, and the painting has been damaged by weather and by the droppings of birds. There are no stones piled at the feet of these images, as before the images of Jizō; they seem like things forgotten, crusted over by the neglect of generations — archaic gods who have lost their worshipers.

But my guide tells me, "The Temple of Kōshin is near, in the village of Fujisawa." Assuredly I must visit it.

A PILGRIMAGE TO ENOSHIMA

XXII

THE temple of Kōshin is situated in the middle of the village, in a court opening upon the main street. A very old wooden temple it is, unpainted, dilapidated, gray with the grayness of all forgotten and weather-beaten things. It is some time before the guardian of the temple can be found, to open the doors. For this temple has doors in lieu of shōji — old doors that moan sleepily at being turned upon their hinges. And it is not necessary to remove one's shoes; the floor is matless, covered with dust, and squeaks under the unaccustomed weight of entering feet. All within is crumbling, mouldering, worn; the shrine has no image, only Shintō emblems, some poor paper lanterns whose once bright colors have vanished under a coating of dust, some vague inscriptions. I see the circular frame of a metal mirror; but the mirror itself is gone. Whither? The guardian says, "No priest lives now in this temple; and thieves might come in the night to steal the mirror; so we have hidden it away." I ask about the image of Kōshin. He answers it is exposed but once in every sixty-one years: so I cannot see it; but there are other statues of the god in the temple court.

I go to look at them: a row of images, much like those upon the public highway, but better preserved. One figure of Kōshin, however, is different from the others I have seen — apparently made after some Hindoo model, judging by the Indian coiffure, mitre-shaped and lofty. The god has three eyes; one in the centre of his forehead, opening perpendicularly instead of horizontally. He has six arms. With one hand he supports a monkey; with another he grasps a serpent; and the other hands hold out symbolic things — a wheel, a sword, a rosary, a sceptre. And serpents are coiled about his wrists and about his ankles; and under his feet is a monstrous head, the head of a demon, Amanjako, sometimes called Utatesa ("Sadness"). Upon the pedestal below the Three Apes are carven; and the face of an ape appears also upon the front of the god's tiara.

I see also tablets of stone, graven only with the god's name — votive offerings. And near by, in a tiny wooden shrine, is the figure of the Earth-God, Ken-ro-ji-jin, gray, primeval, vaguely wrought, holding in one hand a spear, in the other a vessel containing something indistinguishable.

XXIII

PERHAPS to uninitiated eyes these many-headed, many-handed gods at first may seem — as they seem always in the sight of Christian bigotry — only monstrous. But when the knowledge of their meaning comes to one who feels the divine in all religions, then they will be found to make appeal to the higher æstheticism, to the sense of moral beauty, with a force never to be divined by minds knowing nothing of the Orient and its thought. To me the image of Kwannon of the Thousand Hands is not less admir-

able than any other representation of human love-
liness idealized bearing her name — the Peerless,
the Majestic, the Peace-Giving, or even White
Sui-Getsu, who sails the moonlit waters in her rosy
boat made of a single lotus-petal; and in the triple-
headed Shaka I discern and revere the mighty
power of that Truth, whereby, as by a conjunction
of suns, the Three Worlds have been illuminated.

But vain to seek to memorize the names and attributes of all the gods; they seem, self-multiplying,
to mock the seeker; Kwannon the Merciful, is revealed as the Hundred Kwannon; the Six Jizō become the Thousand. And as they multiply before
research, they vary and change: less multiform, less
complex, less elusive the moving of waters than the
visions of this Oriental faith. Into it, as into a
fathomless sea, mythology after mythology from
India and China and the farther East has sunk and
been absorbed; and the stranger, peering into its
deeps, finds himself, as in the tale of Undine, contemplating a flood in whose every surge rises and
vanishes a Face — weird or beautiful or terrible —
a most ancient shoreless sea of forms incomprehen-
sibly interchanging and intermingling, but symbol-
izing the protean magic of that infinite Unknown
that shapes and re-shapes forever all cosmic being.

XXIV

I WONDER if I can buy a picture of Kōshin. In most
Japanese temples little pictures of the tutelar deity

are sold to pilgrims, cheap prints on thin paper. But the temple guardian here tells me, with a gesture of despair, that there are no pictures of Kōshin for sale; there is only an old kakemono on which the god is represented. If I would like to see it he will go home and get it for me. I beg him to do me the favor; and he hurries into the street.

While awaiting his return, I continue to examine the queer old statues, with a feeling of mingled melancholy and pleasure. To have studied and loved an ancient faith only through the labors of palæographers and archæologists, and as a something astronomically remote from one's own existence, and then suddenly in after years to find the same faith a part of one's human environment — to feel that its mythology, though senescent, is *alive* all around you — is almost to realize the dream of the Romantics, to have the sensation of returning through twenty centuries into the life of a happier world. For these quaint Gods of Roads and Gods of Earth are really living still, though so worn and mossed and feebly worshiped. In this brief moment, at least, I am really in the Elder World — perhaps just at that epoch of it when the primal faith is growing a little old-fashioned, crumbling slowly before the corrosive influence of a new philosophy; and I know myself a pagan still, loving these simple old gods, these gods of a people's childhood.

And they need some human love, these naïf, innocent, ugly gods. The beautiful divinities will live forever by that sweetness of womanhood idealized in the Buddhist art of them: eternal are Kwannon and Benten; they need no help of man; they will compel reverence when the great temples shall all have become voiceless and priestless as this shrine of Kōshin is. But these kind, queer, artless, mouldering gods, who have given ease to so many troubled minds, who have gladdened so many simple hearts, who have heard so many innocent prayers — how gladly would I prolong their beneficent lives in spite of the so-called "laws of progress" and the irrefutable philosophy of evolution!

The guardian returns, bringing with him a kakemono, very small, very dusty, and so yellow-stained by time that it might be a thousand years old. But I am disappointed as I unroll it; there is only a very common print of the god within — all outline. And while I am looking at it, I become for the first time conscious that a crowd has gathered about me — tanned kindly faced laborers from the fields, and mothers with their babies on their backs, and school-children, and jinrikisha men — all wondering that a stranger should be thus interested in their gods. And although the pressure about me is very, very gentle, like a pressure of tepid water for gentleness, I feel a little embarrassed. I give back the old kakemono to the guardian, make my offering to the god, and take my leave of Kōshin and his good servant.

All the kind oblique eyes follow me as I go. And something like a feeling of remorse seizes me at thus abruptly abandoning the void, dusty, crumbling temple, with its mirrorless altar and its colorless lanterns, and the decaying sculptures of its neglected court, and its kindly guardian whom I see still watching my retreating steps, with the yellow kakemono in his hand. The whistle of a locomotive warns me that I shall just have time to catch the train. For Western civilization has invaded all this primitive peace, with its webs of steel, with its ways of iron. This is not of thy roads, O Kōshin! — the old gods are dying along its ash-strewn verge!

THE ANCIENT CULT

THE real religion of Japan, the religion still professed in one form or other, by the entire nation, is that cult which has been the foundation of all civilized religion, and of all civilized society — ancestor-worship. In the course of thousands of years this original cult has undergone modifications, and has assumed various shapes; but everywhere in Japan its fundamental character remains unchanged. Without including the different Buddhist forms of ancestor-worship, we find three distinct rites of purely Japanese origin, subsequently modified to some degree by Chinese influence and ceremonial. These Japanese forms of the cult are all classed together under the name of "Shintō," which signifies, "The Way of the Gods." It is not an ancient term; and it was first adopted only to distinguish the native religion, or "Way," from the foreign religion of Buddhism called "Butsudō," or "The Way of the Buddha." The three forms of the Shintō worship of ancestors are the Domestic Cult, the Communal Cult, and the State Cult; — or, in other words, the worship of family ancestors, the worship of clan or tribal ancestors, and the worship of imperial ancestors. The first is the religion of the home; the second is the religion of the local divinity, or tutelar god; the third is the national religion. There are various other forms of Shintō worship; but they need not be considered for the present.

Of the three forms of ancester-worship above mentioned, the family-cult is the first in evolutional order — the others being later developments. But, in speaking of the family-cult as the oldest, I do not mean the home-religion as it exists to-day; — neither do I mean by "family" anything corresponding to the term "household." The Japanese family in early times meant very much more than "household": it might include a hundred or a thousand households: it was something like the Greek γένος or the Roman "gens" — the patriarchal family in the largest sense of the term. In prehistoric Japan the domestic cult of the house-ancestor probably did not exist; — the family-rites would appear to have been performed only at the burial-place. But the later domestic cult, having been developed out of the primal family-rite, indirectly represents the most ancient form of the religion, and should therefore be considered first in any study of Japanese social evolution.

The evolutional history of ancestor-worship has been very much the same in all countries; and that of the Japanese cult offers remarkable evidence in support of Herbert Spencer's exposition of the law of religious development. To comprehend this general law, we must, however, go back to the origin of religious beliefs. One should bear in mind that, from a sociological point of view, it is no more correct to speak of the existing ancestor-cult in Japan as "primitive," than it would be to speak of the domestic cult of the Athenians in the time of Pericles as "primitive." No persistent form of ancestor-worship is primitive; and every established domestic cult has been developed out of some irregular and non-domestic family-cult, which, again, must have grown out of still more ancient funeral-rites.

Our knowledge of ancestor-worship, as regards the early European civilizations, cannot be said to extend to the primitive form of the cult. In the case of the Greeks and the Romans, our knowledge of the subject dates from a period at which a domestic religion had long been established; and we have documentary evidence as to the character of that religion. But of the earlier cult that must have preceded the home-worship, we have little testimony; and we can surmise its nature only by study of the natural history of ancestor-worship among peoples not yet arrived at a state of civilization. The true domestic cult begins with a settled civilization. Now when the Japanese race first established itself in Japan, it does not appear to have brought with it any civilization of the kind which we would call settled, nor any well-developed ancestor-cult. The cult certainly existed; but its ceremonies would seem to have been irregularly performed at graves only. The domestic cult proper may not have been established until about the eighth century, when the spirit-tablet is supposed to have been introduced from China. The earliest ancestor-cult, as we shall presently see, *was* developed out of the primitive funeral-rites and propitiatory ceremonies.

The existing family religion is therefore a comparatively modern development; but it is at least as old as the true civilization of the country, and it conserves beliefs and ideas which are indubitably primitive, as well as ideas and beliefs, derived from these. Before treating further of the cult itself, it will be necessary to consider some of these older beliefs.

The earliest ancestor-worship — "the root of all religions," as Herbert Spencer calls it — was probably coeval with the earliest definite belief in ghosts. As soon as men were able to conceive the idea of a shadowy inner self, or double, so soon, doubtless, the propitiatory cult of spirits began. But this earliest ghost-worship must have long preceded that period of mental development in which men first became capable of forming abstract ideas. The primitive ancestor-worshipers could not have formed the notion of a supreme deity; and all evidence existing as to the first forms of their worship tends to show that there primarily existed no difference whatever between the conception of ghosts and the conception of gods. There were, consequently, no definite beliefs in any future state of reward or of punishment — no ideas of any heaven or hell. Even the notion of a shadowy underworld, or Hades, was of much later evolution. At first the dead were thought of only as dwelling in the tombs provided for them — whence they could issue, from time to time, to visit their former habitations, or to make apparition in the dreams of the living. Their real world was the place of burial — the grave, the tumulus. Afterwards there slowly developed the idea of an underworld, connected in some mysterious way with the place of sepulture. Only at a much later time did this dim underworld of imagination expand and divide into regions of ghostly bliss and woe. . . . It is a noteworthy fact that Japanese mythology never evolved the ideas of an Elysium or a Tartarus — never developed the notion of a heaven or a hell. Even to this day Shintō belief represents the pre-Homeric stage of imagination as regards the supernatural.

Among the Indo-European races likewise there appeared to have been at first no difference between gods and ghosts, nor any ranking of gods as greater and lesser. These distinctions were gradually developed. "The spirits of the dead," says Mr. Spencer, "forming, in a primitive tribe, an ideal group the members of which are but little distinguished from one another, will grow more and more distinguished; — and as societies advance, and as traditions, local and general, accumulate and complicate, these once similar human souls, acquiring in the popular mind differences of character and importance, will diverge

— until their original community of nature becomes scarcely recognizable." So in antique Europe, and so in the Far East, were the greater gods of nations evolved from ghost-cults; but those ethics of ancestor-worship which shaped alike the earliest societies of West and East, date from a period before the time of the greater gods — from the period when all the dead were supposed to become gods, with no distinction of rank.

No more than the primitive ancestor-worshipers of Aryan race did the early Japanese think of their dead as ascending to some extra-mundane region of light and bliss, or as descending into some realm of torment. They thought of their dead as still inhabiting this world, or at least as maintaining with it a constant communication. Their earliest sacred records do, indeed, make mention of an underworld, where mysterious Thunder-gods and evil goblins dwelt in corruption; but this vague world of the dead communicated with the world of the living; and the spirit there, though in some sort attached to its decaying envelope, could still receive upon earth the homage and the offerings of men. Before the advent of Buddhism, there was no idea of a heaven or a hell. The ghosts of the departed were thought of as constant presences, needing propitiation, and able in some way to share the pleasures and the pains of the living. They required food and drink and light; and in return for these, they could confer benefits. Their bodies had melted into earth;

but their spirit-power still lingered in the upper world, thrilled its substance, moved in its winds and waters. By death they had acquired mysterious force; — they had become "superior ones," Kami, gods.

That is to say, gods in the oldest Greek and Roman sense. Be it observed that there were no moral distinctions, East or West, in this deification. "All the dead become gods," wrote the great Shintō commentator, Hirata. So likewise, in the thought of the early Greeks and even of the later Romans, all the dead became gods. M. de Coulanges observes, in "La Cité Antique": "This kind of apotheosis was not the privilege of the great alone: no distinction was made. . . . It was not even necessary to have been a virtuous man: the wicked man became a god as well as the good man — only that in this after-existence, he retained the evil inclinations of his former life." Such also was the case in Shintō belief: the good man became a beneficent divinity, the bad man an evil deity — but all alike became Kami. "And since there are bad as well as good gods," wrote Motowori, "it is necessary to propitiate them with offerings of agreeable food, playing the harp, blowing the flute, singing and dancing and whatever is likely to put them in a good humor." The Latins called the maleficent ghosts of the dead, "Larvæ," and called the beneficent or harmless ghosts, "Lares," or "Manes," or "Genii," according to Apuleius. But all alike were gods — dii-manes; and Cicero admonished his readers to render to all dii-manes the rightful worship: "They are men," he declared, "who have departed from this life; — consider them divine beings. . . ."

In Shintō, as in old Greek belief, to die was to enter into the possession of superhuman power — to become capable of conferring benefit or of inflicting misfortune by supernatural means. . . . But yesterday, such or such a man was a common toiler, a person of no importance; — to-day, being dead, he becomes a divine power, and his children pray to him for the prosperity of their undertakings. Thus also we find the personages of Greek tragedy, such as Alcestis, suddenly transformed into divinities by death, and addressed in the language of worship or prayer. But, in despite of their supernatural power, the dead are still dependent upon the living for happiness. Though viewless, save in dreams, they need earthly nourishment and homage — food and drink, and the reverence of their descendants. Each ghost must rely for such comfort upon its living kindred; — only through the devotion of that kindred can it ever find repose. Each ghost must have shelter — a fitting tomb; — each must have offerings. While honorably sheltered and properly nourished, the spirit is pleased, and will aid in maintaining the good-fortune of its propitiators. But if refused the sepulchral home, the funeral rites, the offerings of food and fire and drink, the spirit will suffer from hunger and cold and thirst, and, becoming angered, will act malevolently and contrive misfortune for those by whom it has been neglected. . . . Such were the ideas of the old Greeks regarding the dead; and such were the ideas of the old Japanese.

Although the religion of ghosts was once the religion of our own forefathers — whether of northern or southern Europe — and although practices derived from it, such as the custom of decorating graves with flowers, persist to-day among our most advanced communities — our modes of thought have so changed under the influences of modern civilization that it is difficult for us to imagine how people could ever have supposed that the happiness of the dead depended upon material food. But it is probable that the real belief in ancient European societies was much like the belief as it exists in modern Japan. The dead are not supposed to consume the substance of the food, but only to absorb the invisible essence of it. In the early period of ancestor-worship the food-offerings were large; later on they were made smaller and smaller as the idea grew up that the spirits required but little sustenance of even the most vapory kind. But, however small the offerings, it was essential that they should be made regularly. Upon these shadowy repasts depended the well-being of the dead; and upon the well-being of the dead depended the fortunes of the living. Neither could dispense with the help of the other: the visible and the invisible worlds were forever united by bonds innumerable of mutual necessity; and no single relation of that union could be broken without the direst consequences.

The history of all religious sacrifices can be traced back to this ancient custom of offerings made to ghosts; and the whole Indo-Aryan race had at one time no other religion than this religion of spirits. In fact, every advanced human society has, at some period of its history, passed through the stage of ancestor-worship; but it is to the Far East that we must look to-day in order to find the cult coexisting with an elaborate civilization. Now the Japanese ancestor-cult — though representing the beliefs of a non-Aryan people, and offering in the history of its development various interesting peculiarities — still embodies much that is characteristic of an-cestor-worship in general. There survive in it especially these three beliefs, which underlie all forms of persistent ancestor-worship in all climes and countries:

1. The dead remain in this world — haunting their tombs, and also their former homes, and shar-ing invisibly in the life of their living descendants.

2. All the dead become gods, in the sense of acquiring supernatural power; but they retain the characters which distinguished them during life.

3. The happiness of the dead depends upon the respectful service rendered them by the living; and the happiness of the living depends upon the fulfillment of pious duty to the dead.

To these very early beliefs may be added the following, probably of later development, which at one time must have exercised immense influence:

4. Every event in the world, good or evil — fair seasons or plentiful harvests — flood and famine — tempest and tidal-wave and earthquake — is the work of the dead.

5. All human actions, good or bad, are controlled by the dead.

The first three beliefs survive from the dawn of civilization, or before it — from the time in which the dead were the only gods, without distinctions of power. The latter two would seem rather of the period in which a true mythology — an enormous polytheism — had been developed out of the primitive ghost-worship. There is nothing simple in these beliefs: they are awful, tremendous beliefs; and before Buddhism helped to dissipate them, their pressure upon the mind of a people dwelling in a land of cataclysms, must have been like an endless weight of nightmare. But the elder beliefs, in softened form, are yet a fundamental part of the existing cult. Though Japanese ancestor-worship has undergone many modifications in the past two thousand years, these modifications have not transformed its essential character in relation to conduct; and the whole framework of society rests upon it, as on a moral foundation. The history of Japan is really the history of her religion. No single fact in this connection is more significant than the fact that the ancient Japanese term for government — "matsuri-goto"— signifies literally "matters of worship." Later on we shall find that not only government, but almost everything in Japanese society, derives directly or indirectly from this ancestor-cult; and that in all matters the dead, rather than the living, have been the rulers of the nation and the shapers of its destinies.

THE RELIGION OF THE HOME

THREE stages of ancestor-worship are to be distinguished in the general course of religious and social evolution; and each of these finds illustration in the history of Japanese society. The first stage is that which exists before the establishment of a settled civilization, when there is yet no national ruler, and when the unit of society is the great patriarchal family, with its elders or war-chiefs for lords. Under these conditions, the spirits of the family-ancestors only are worshiped; — each family propitiating its own dead, and recognizing no other form of worship. As the patriarchal families, later on, become grouped into tribal clans, there grows up the custom of tribal sacrifice to the spirits of the clan-rulers; — this cult being superadded to the family-cult, and marking the second stage of ancestor-worship. Finally, with the union of all the clans or tribes under one supreme head, there is developed the custom of propitiating the spirits of national rulers. This third form of the cult becomes the obligatory religion of the country; but it does not replace either of the preceding cults: the three continue to exist together.

Though, in the present state of our knowledge, the evolution in Japan of these three stages of ancestor-worship is but faintly traceable, we can divine tolerably well, from various records, how the permanent forms of the cult were first developed out of the earlier funeral-rites. Between the ancient Japanese funeral customs and those of antique Europe, there was a vast difference — a difference indicating, as regards Japan, a far more primitive social condition. In Greece and in Italy it was an early custom to bury the family dead within the limits of the family estate; and the Greek and Roman laws of property grew out of this practice. Sometimes the dead were buried close to the house. The author of "La Cité Antique" cites, among other ancient texts bearing upon the subject, an interesting invocation from the tragedy of "Helen," by Euripides: "All hail! my father's tomb! I buried thee, Proteus, at the place where men pass out, that I might often greet thee; and so, even as I go out and in, I, thy son Theoclymenus, call upon thee, father! . . ." But in ancient Japan, men fled from the neighborhood of death. It was long the custom to abandon, either temporarily, or permanently, the house in which a death occurred; and we can scarcely suppose that, at any time, it was thought desirable to bury the dead close to the habitation of the surviving members of the household. Some Japanese authorities declare that in the very earliest ages there was no burial, and that corpses were merely conveyed to desolate places, and there abandoned to wild creatures. Be this as it may, we have documentary evidence, of an unmistakable sort, concerning the early funeral-rites as they existed when the custom of burying had become established — rites weird and strange, and having nothing in common with the practices of settled civilization. There is reason to believe that the family-dwelling was at first permanently, not temporarily, abandoned to the dead; and in view of the fact that the dwelling was a wooden hut of very simple structure, there is nothing improbable in the supposition. At all events the corpse was left for a certain period, called the period of mourning, either in the abandoned house where the death occurred, or in a shelter especially built for the purpose; and, during the mourning period, offerings of food and drink were set before the dead, and ceremonies performed without the house. One of these ceremonies consisted in the recital of poems in praise of the dead — which poems were called "shinobigoto." There was music also of flutes and drums, and dancing; and at night a fire was kept burning before the house. After all this had been done for the fixed period of mourning — eight days, according to some authorities, fourteen according to others — the corpse was interred. It is probable that the deserted house may thereafter have become an ancestral temple, or ghost-house — prototype of the Shintō miya.

At an early time — though when we do not know — it certainly became the custom to erect a moya, or "mourning-house" in the event of a death; and the rites were performed at the mourning-house prior to the interment. The manner of burial was very simple: there were yet no tombs in the literal meaning of the term, and no tombstones. Only a mound was thrown up over the graves; and the size of the mound varied according to the rank of the dead.

The custom of deserting the house in which a death took place would accord with the theory of a nomadic ancestry for the Japanese people: it was a practice totally incompatible with a settled civilization like that of the early Greeks and Romans, whose customs in regard to burial presuppose small landholdings in permanent occupation. But there may have been, even in early times, some exceptions to general custom — exceptions made by necessity. To-day, in various parts of the country, and perhaps more particularly in districts remote from temples, it is the custom for farmers to bury their dead upon their own lands.

At regular intervals after burial, ceremonies were performed at the graves; and food and drink were then served to the spirits. When the spirit-tablet had been introduced from China, and a true domestic cult established, the practice of making offerings at the place of burial was not discontinued. It survives to the present time — both in the Shintō and the Buddhist rite; and every spring an Imperial messenger presents at the tomb of the Emperor Jimmu, the same offerings of birds and fish and seaweed, rice and rice-wine, which were made to the spirit of the Founder of the Empire twenty-five hundred years ago. But before the period of Chinese influence the family would seem to have worshiped its dead only before the mortuary house, or at the grave; and the spirits were yet supposed to dwell especially in their tombs, with access to some mysterious subterranean world. They were supposed to need other things besides nourishment; and it was customary to place in the grave various articles for their ghostly use — a sword, for example, in the case of a warrior; a mirror in the case of a woman — together with certain objects, especially prized during life — such as objects of precious metal, and polished stones or gems. . . . At this stage of ancestor-worship, when the spirits are supposed to require shadowy service of a sort corresponding to that exacted during their lifetime in the body, we should expect to hear of human sacrifices as well as of animal sacrifices. At the funerals of great personages such sacrifices were common. Owing to beliefs of which all knowledge has been lost, these sacrifices assumed a character much more cruel than that of the immolations of the Greek Homeric epic. The human victims [1] were buried up to the neck in a circle about the grave, and thus left to perish under the beaks of birds and the teeth of wild beasts. The term applied to this form of immolation — "hitogaki,"

[1] How the horses and other animals were sacrificed, does not clearly appear.

or "human hedge" — implies a considerable number of victims in each case. This custom was abolished, by the Emperor Suinin, about nineteen hundred years ago; and the "Nihongi" declares that it was then an ancient custom. Being grieved by the crying of the victims interred in the funeral mound erected over the grave of his brother, Yamato-hiko-no-mikoto, the Emperor is recorded to have said: "It is a very painful thing to force those whom one has loved in life to follow one in death. Though it be an ancient custom, why follow it, if it is bad? From this time forward take counsel to put a stop to the following of the dead." Nomi-no-Sukuné, a court-noble — now apotheosized as the patron of wrestlers — then suggested the substitution of earth images of men and horses for the living victims; and his suggestion was approved. The "hitogaki" was thus abolished; but compulsory as well as voluntary following of the dead certainly continued for many hundred years after, since we find the Emperor Kōtoku issuing an edict on the subject in the year 646 A.D.:

When a man dies, there have been cases of people sacrificing themselves by strangulation, or of strangling others by way of sacrifice, or of compelling the dead man's horse to be sacrificed, or of burying valuables in the grave in honour of the dead, or of cutting off the hair and stabbing the thighs and [in that condition] pronouncing a eulogy on the dead. Let all such old customs be entirely discontinued.[1]

[1] *Nihongi*; Aston's translation.

As regarded compulsory sacrifice and popular custom, this edict may have had the immediate effect desired; but voluntary human sacrifices were not definitively suppressed. With the rise of the military power there gradually came into existence another custom of junshi, or following one's lord in death — suicide by the sword. It is said to have begun about 1333, when the last of the Hōjō regents, Takatoki, performed suicide, and a number of his retainers took their own lives by harakiri, in order to follow their master. It may be doubted whether this incident really established the practice. But by the sixteenth century junshi had certainly become an honored custom among the samurai. Loyal retainers esteemed it a duty to kill themselves after the death of their lord, in order to attend upon him during his ghostly journey. A thousand years of Buddhist teaching had not therefore sufficed to eradicate all primitive notions of sacrificial duty. The practice continued into the time of the Tokugawa shōgunate, when Iyéyasu made laws to check it. These laws were rigidly applied — the entire family of the suicide being held responsible for a case of junshi: yet the custom cannot be said to have become extinct until considerably after the beginning of the era of Meiji. Even during my own time there have been survivals — some of a very touching kind: suicides performed in hope of being able to serve or aid the spirit of master or husband or parent in the invisible world. Perhaps the strangest case was that of a boy fourteen years old, who killed himself in order to wait upon the spirit of a child, his master's little son.

The peculiar character of the early human sacrifices at graves, the character of the funeral-rites, the abandonment of the house in which death had occurred — all prove that the early ancestor-worship was of a decidedly primitive kind. This is suggested also by the peculiar Shintō horror of death as pollution: even at this day to attend a funeral — unless the funeral be conducted after the Shintō rite — is religious defilement. The ancient legend of Izanagi's descent to the nether world, in search of his lost spouse, illustrates the terrible beliefs that once existed as to goblin-powers presiding over decay. Between the horror of death as corruption, and the apotheosis of the ghost, there is nothing incongruous: we must understand the apotheosis itself as a propitiation. This earliest Way of the Gods was a religion of perpetual fear. Not ordinary homes only were deserted after a death: even the Emperors, during many centuries, were wont to change their capital after the death of a predecessor. But, gradually, out of the primal funeral-rites, a higher cult was evolved. The mourning-house, or moya, became transformed into the Shintō temple, which still retains the shape of the primitive hut. Then under Chinese influence, the ancestral cult became established in the home; and Buddhism at a later day maintained this domestic cult. By degrees the household religion became a religion of tenderness as well as of duty, and changed and softened the thoughts of men about their dead. As early as the eighth century, ancestor-worship appears to have developed the three principal forms under which it still exists; and thereafter the family-cult began to assume a character which offers many resemblances to the domestic religion of the old European civilizations.

Let us now glance at the existing forms of this domestic cult — the universal religion of Japan. In every home there is a shrine devoted to it. If the family profess only the Shintō belief, this shrine, or mitamaya [1] ("august-spirit-dwelling") — tiny model of a Shintō temple — is placed upon a shelf fixed against the wall of some inner chamber, at a height of about six feet from the floor. Such a shelf is called "Mitama-San-no-tana," or "Shelf of the august spirits." In the shrine are placed thin tablets of white wood, inscribed with the names of the household dead. Such tablets are called by a name signifying "spirit-substitutes" (mitama-shiro), or by a probably older name signifying "spirit-sticks." . . . If the family worships its ancestors according to the Buddhist rite, the mortuary tablets are placed in the Buddhist household-shrine, or Butsudan,

---

[1] It is more popularly termed "miya" ("august house") — a name given also to the ordinary Shintō temples.

which usually occupies the upper shelf of an alcove in one of the inner apartments. Buddhist mortuary-tablets (with some exceptions) are called "ihai" — a term signifying "soul-commemoration." They are lacquered and gilded, usually having a carved lotus-flower as pedestal; and they do not, as a rule, bear the real, but only the religious and posthumous name of the dead.

Now it is important to observe that, in either cult, the mortuary tablet actually suggests a miniature tombstone — which is a fact of some evolutional interest, though the evolution itself should be Chinese rather than Japanese. The plain grave-stones in Shintō cemeteries resemble in form the simple wooden ghost-sticks, or spirit-sticks; while the Buddhist monuments in the old-fashioned Buddhist graveyards are shaped like the ihai, of which the form is slightly varied to indicate sex and age, which is also the case with the tombstone.

The number of mortuary tablets in a household shrine does not generally exceed five or six — only grandparents and parents and the recently dead being thus represented but the names of remoter ancestors are inscribed upon scrolls, which are kept in the Butsudan or the mitamaya.

Whatever be the family rite, prayers are repeated and offerings are placed before the ancestral tablets every day. The nature of the offerings and the character of the prayers depend upon the religion of the household; but the essential duties of the cult are everywhere the same. These duties are not to be neglected under any circumstances: their perform-ance in these times is usually entrusted to the elders, or to the women of the household.[1] There is no long ceremony, no imperative rule about prayers, nothing solemn: the food-offerings are selected out of the family cooking; the murmured or whispered invo-cations are short and few. But, trifling as the rites may seem, their performance must never be over-looked. Not to make the offerings is a possibility undreamed of: so long as the family exists they must be made.

To describe the details of the domestic rite would require much space — not because they are compli-cated in themselves, but because they are of a sort unfamiliar to Western experience, and vary accord-ing to the sect of the family. But to consider the details will not be necessary: the important matter

[1] Not, however, upon any public occasion — such as a gathering of relatives at the home for a religious anniversary: at such times the rites are performed by the head of the household.

Speaking of the ancient custom (once prevalent in every Japanese household, and still observed in Shintō homes) of making offerings to the deities of the cooking range and of food, Sir Ernest Satow observes: "The rites in honour of these gods were at first performed by the head of the household; but in after-times the duty came to be delegated to the women of the family" (*Ancient Japanese Rituals*). We may infer that in regard to the ancestral rites likewise, the same transfer of duties occurred at an early time, for obvious reasons of convenience. When the duty devolves upon the elders of the family — grandfather and grand-mother — it is usually the grandmother who attends to the offerings. In the Greek and Roman household the performance of the domestic rites appears to have been obligatory upon the head of the household; but we know that the women took part in them.

is to consider the religion and its beliefs in relation to conduct and character. It should be recognized that no religion is more sincere, no faith more touching than this domestic worship, which regards the dead as continuing to form a part of the household life, and needing still the affection and the respect of their children and kindred. Originating in those dim ages when fear was stronger than love — when the wish to please the ghosts of the departed must have been chiefly inspired by dread of their anger — the cult at last developed into a religion of affection; and this it yet remains. The belief that the dead need affection, that to neglect them is a cruelty, that their happiness depends upon duty, is a belief that has almost cast out the primitive fear of their displeasure. They are not thought of as dead: they are believed to remain among those who loved them. Unseen they guard the home, and watch over the welfare of its inmates: they hover nightly in the glow of the shrine-lamp; and the stirring of its flame is the motion of them. They dwell mostly within their lettered tablets; — sometimes they can animate a tablet — change it into the substance of a human body, and return in that body to active life, in order to succor and console. From their shrine they observe and hear what happens in the house; they share the family joys and sorrows; they delight in the voices and the warmth of the life about them. They want affection; but the morning and the evening greetings of the family are enough to make them happy. They require nourishment; but the vapor of food contents them. They are exacting only as regards the daily fulfillment of duty. They were the givers of life, the givers of wealth, the makers and teachers of the present: they represent the past of the race, and all its sacrifices; — whatever the living possess is from them. Yet how little do they require in return! Scarcely more than to be thanked, as the founders and guardians of the home, in simple words like these: "For aid received, by day and by night, accept, August Ones, our reverential gratitude." . . . To forget or neglect them, to treat them with rude indifference, is the proof of an evil heart; to cause them shame by ill-conduct, to disgrace their name by bad actions, is the supreme crime. They repre-sent the moral experience of the race: whosoever denies that experience denies them also, and falls to the level of the beast, or below it. They represent the unwritten law, the traditions of the commune, the duties of all to all: whosoever offends against these, sins against the dead. And, finally, they represent the mystery of the invisible: to Shintō belief, at least, they are gods.

It is to be remembered, of course, that the Japa-nese word for gods, "Kami," does not imply, any more than did the old Latin term, "dii-manes," ideas like those which have become associated with the modern notion of divinity. The Japanese term might be more closely rendered by some such expression as "the Superiors," "the Higher Ones"; and it was formerly applied to living rulers as well as to deities and ghosts. But it implies considerably more than the idea of a disembodied spirit; for, according to old Shintō teaching the dead became world-rulers. They were the cause of all natural events — of winds, rains, and tides, of buddings and ripenings, of growth and decay, of everything desirable or dreadful. They formed a kind of subtler element — an ancestral ether — universally extending and unceasingly operating. Their powers, when united for any purpose, were resistless; and in time of national peril they were invoked en masse for aid against the foe. . . . Thus, to the eyes of faith, behind each family ghost there extended the measureless shadowy power of countless Kami; and the sense of duty to the ancestor was deepened by dim awe of the forces controlling the world — the whole invisible Vast. To primitive Shintō conception the universe was filled with ghosts; — to later Shintō conception the ghostly condition was not limited by place or time, even in the case of individual spirits. "Although," wrote Hirata, "the home of the spirits is in the Spirit-house, they are equally present wherever they are worshiped — being gods, and therefore ubiquitous."

The Buddhist dead are not called gods, but Buddhas (Hotoké) — which term, of course, expresses a pious hope, rather than a faith. The belief is that

219

they are only on their way to some higher state of existence; and they should not be invoked or worshiped after the manner of the Shintō gods: prayers should be said *for* them, not, as a rule, *to* them.[1] But the vast majority of Japanese Buddhists are also followers of Shintō; and the two faiths, though seemingly incongruous, have long been reconciled in the popular mind. The Buddhist doctrine has therefore modified the ideas attaching to the cult much less deeply than might be supposed.

In all patriarchal societies with a settled civilization, there is evolved, out of the worship of ancestors, a Religion of Filial Piety. Filial piety still remains the supreme virtue among civilized peoples possessing an ancestor-cult. . . . By filial piety must not be understood, however, what is commonly signified by the English term — the devotion of children to parents. We must understand the word "piety" rather in its classic meaning, as the "pietas" of the early Romans — that is to say, as the religious sense of household duty. Reverence for the dead, as well as the sentiment of duty towards the living; the affection of children to parents, and the affection of parents to children; the mutual duties of husband and wife; the duties likewise of sons-in-law and daughters-in-law to the family as a body; the duties of servant to master, and of master to dependent — all these were included under the term. The

[1] Certain Buddhist rituals prove exceptions to this teaching.

family itself was a religion; the ancestral home a temple. And so we find the family and the home to be in Japan, even at the present day. Filial piety in Japan does not mean only the duty of children to parents and grandparents: it means still more, the cult of the ancestors, reverential service to the dead, the gratitude of the present to the past, and the conduct of the individual in relation to the entire household. Hirata therefore declared that all virtues derived from the worship of ancestors; and his words, as translated by Sir Ernest Satow, deserve particular attention:

It is the duty of a subject to be diligent in worshiping his ancestors, whose minister he should consider himself to be. The custom of adoption arose from the natural desire of having some one to perform sacrifices; and this desire ought not to be rendered of no avail by neglect. Devotion to the memory of ancestors is the mainspring of all virtues. No one who discharges his duty to them will ever be disrespectful to the gods or to his living parents. Such a man also will be faithful to his prince, loyal to his friends, and kind and gentle to his wife and children. For the essence of this devotion is indeed filial piety.

From the sociologist's point of view, Hirata is right: it is unquestionably true that the whole system of Far-Eastern ethics derives from the religion of the household. By aid of that cult have been evolved all ideas of duty to the living as well as to the dead — the sentiment of reverence, the sentiment of loyalty, the spirit of self-sacrifice, and the spirit of patriotism. What filial piety signifies as a religious force can best be imagined from the fact that you can buy life in the East! — that it has its price in the market. This religion is the religion of China, and of countries adjacent; and life is for sale in China. It was the filial piety of China that rendered possible the completion of the Panama Railroad, where to strike the soil was to liberate death — where the land devoured laborers by the thousand, until white and black labor could no more be procured in quantity sufficient for the work. But labor could be obtained from China — any amount of labor — at the cost of life; and the cost was paid; and multitudes of men came from the East to toil and die, in order that the price of their lives might be sent to their families. . . . I have no doubt that, were the sacrifice imperatively demanded, life could be as readily bought in Japan — though not, perhaps, so cheaply. Where this religion prevails, the individual is ready to give his life, in a majority of cases, for the family, the home, the ancestors. And the filial piety impelling such sacrifice becomes, by extension, the loyalty that will sacrifice even the family itself for the sake of the lord — or, by yet further extension, the loyalty that prays, like Kusunoki Masashigé, for seven successive lives to lay down on behalf of the sovereign. Out of filial piety, indeed, has been developed the whole moral power that protects the State — the power also that has seldom failed to impose the rightful restraints upon official despotism whenever that despotism grew dangerous to the common weal.

Probably the filial piety that centred about the domestic altars of the ancient West differed in little from that which yet rules the most eastern East. But we miss in Japan the Aryan hearth, the family altar with its perpetual fire. The Japanese home-religion represents, apparently, a much earlier stage of the cult than that which existed within historic time among the Greeks and Romans. The homestead in Old Japan was not a stable institution like the Greek or the Roman home; the custom of burying the family dead upon the family estate never became general; the dwelling itself never assumed a substantial and lasting character. It could not be literally said of the Japanese warrior, as of the Roman, that he fought pro aris et focis. There was neither altar nor sacred fire: the place of these was taken by the spirit-shelf or shrine, with its tiny lamp, kindled afresh each evening; and, in early times, there were no Japanese images of divinities. For Lares and Penates there were only the mortuary-tablets of the ancestors, and certain little tablets bearing names of other gods — tutelar gods. . . . The presence of these frail wooden objects still makes the home; and they may be, of course, transported anywhere.

To apprehend the full meaning of ancestor-wor-

ship as a family religion, a living faith, is now difficult for the Western mind. We are able to imagine
only in the vaguest way how our Aryan forefathers
felt and thought about their dead. But in the living
beliefs of Japan we find much to suggest the nature
of the old Greek piety. Each member of the family
supposes himself, or herself, under perpetual ghostly
surveillance. Spirit-eyes are watching every act;
spirit-ears are listening to every word. Thoughts
too, not less than deeds, are visible to the gaze of the
dead: the heart must be pure, the mind must be
under control, within the presence of the spirits.
Probably the influence of such beliefs, uninter-
ruptedly exerted upon conduct during thousands of
years, did much to form the charming side of Japanese character. Yet there is nothing stern or solemn
in this home-religion to-day — nothing of that rigid
and unvarying discipline supposed by Fustel de
Coulanges to have especially characterized the
Roman cult. It is a religion rather of gratitude and
tenderness; the dead being served by the household
as if they were actually present in the body. . . .
I fancy that if we were able to enter for a moment
into the vanished life of some old Greek city, we
should find the domestic religion there not less cheerful than the Japanese home-cult remains to-day. I
imagine that Greek children, three thousand years
ago, must have watched, like the Japanese children
of to-day, for a chance to steal some of the good
things offered to the ghosts of the ancestors; and I

fancy that Greek parents must have chidden quite as gently as Japanese parents chide in this era of Meiji—mingling reproof with instruction, and hinting of weird possibilities.

[1] Food presented to the dead may afterwards be eaten by the elders of the household, or given to pilgrims; but it is said that if children eat of it, they will grow up with feeble memories, and incapable of becoming scholars.

DEVELOPMENTS OF SHINTŌ

THE teaching of Herbert Spencer that the greater gods of a people — those figuring in popular imagination as creators, or as particularly directing certain elemental forces — represent a later development of ancestor-worship, is generally accepted to-day. Ancestral ghosts, considered as more or less alike in the time when primitive society had not yet developed class distinctions of any important character, subsequently become differentiated, as the society itself differentiates, into greater and lesser. Eventually the worship of some one ancestral spirit, or group of spirits, overshadows that of all the rest; and a supreme deity, or group of supreme deities, becomes evolved. But the differentiations of the ancestor cult must be understood to proceed in a great variety of directions. Particular ancestors of families engaged in hereditary occupations may develop into tutelar deities presiding over those occupations — patron gods of crafts and guilds. Out of other ancestral cults, through various processes of mental association, may be evolved the worship of deities of strength, of health, of long life, of particular products, of particular localities. When more light shall have been thrown upon the question of Japanese origins, it will probably be found that many of the lesser tutelar or patron gods now worshiped in the country were originally the gods of Chinese or Korean craftsmen; but I think that Japanese mythology, as a whole, will prove to offer few important exceptions to the evolutional law. Indeed, Shintō presents us with a mythological hierarchy of which the development can be satisfactorily explained by that law alone.

Besides the Ujigami, there are myriads of superior and of inferior deities. There are the primal deities, of whom only the names are mentioned — apparitions of the period of chaos; and there are the gods of creation, who gave shape to the land. There are the gods of earth and sky, and the gods of the sun and moon. Also there are gods, beyond counting, supposed to preside over all things good or evil in human life — birth and marriage and death, riches and poverty, strength and disease. . . . It can scarcely be supposed that all this mythology was developed out of the old ancestor-cult in Japan itself: more probably its evolution began on the Asiatic continent. But the evolution of the national cult — that form of Shintō which became the state religion — seems to have been Japanese, in the strict meaning of the word. This cult is the worship of the gods from whom the Emperors claim descent — the worship of the "Imperial ancestors." It appears that the early Emperors of Japan — the "heavenly sovereigns," as they are called in the old records — were not emperors at all in the true meaning of the term, and did not even exercise universal authority. They were only the chiefs of the most powerful clan, or Uji, and their special ancestor cult had probably in that time no dominant influence. But eventually, when the chiefs of this great clan really became supreme rulers of the land, their clan cult spread everywhere, and overshadowed, without abolishing, all the other cults. Then arose the national mythology.

We therefore see that the course of Japanese ancestor-worship, like that of Aryan ancestor-worship, exhibits those three successive stages of development before mentioned. It may be assumed that on coming from the continent to their present island-home, the race brought with them a rude form of ancestor-worship, consisting of little more than rites and sacrifices performed at the graves of the dead. When the land had been portioned out among the various clans, each of which had its own ancestor cult, all the people of the district belonging to any particular clan would eventually adopt the religion of the clan ancestor; and thus arose the thousand cults of the Ujigami. Still later, the special cult of the most powerful clan developed into a national religion — the worship of the Goddess of the Sun, from whom the supreme ruler claimed descent. Then, under Chinese influence, the domestic form of ancestor-worship was established in lieu of the primitive family cult: thereafter offerings and prayers were made regularly in the home, where the ancestral tablets represented the tombs of the family dead. But offerings were still made, on special occasions, at the graves; and the three Shintō forms of the cult, together with later forms of Buddhist introduction, continued to exist; and they rule the life of the nation to-day.

It was the cult of the supreme ruler that first gave to the people a written account of traditional beliefs. The mythology of the reigning house furnished the scriptures of Shintō, and established ideas linking together all the existing forms of ancestor-worship. All Shintō traditions were by these writings blended into one mythological history — explained upon the basis of one legend. The whole mythology is contained in two books, of which English translations have been made. The oldest is entitled "Ko-ji-ki," or "Records of Ancient Matters"; and it is supposed to have been compiled in the year 712 A.D. The other and much larger work is called "Nihongi," "Chronicles of Nihon [Japan]," and dates from about 720 A.D. Both works profess to be histories; but a large portion of them is mythological, and either begins with a story of creation. They were compiled, mostly, from oral traditions we are told, by Imperial order. It is said that a yet earlier work, dating from the seventh century, may have been drawn upon; but this has been lost. No great antiquity can, therefore, be claimed for the texts as they stand; but they contain traditions which must be very much older — possibly thousands of years older. The "Ko-ji-ki" is said to have been written from the dictation of an old man of marvelous memory; and the Shintō theologian Hirata would have us believe that traditions thus preserved are especially trustworthy. "It is probable," he wrote, "that those ancient traditions, preserved for us by exercise of memory, have for that very reason come down to us in greater detail than if they had been recorded in documents. Besides, men must have had much stronger memories in the days before they acquired the habit of trusting to written characters for facts which they wished to remember — as is shown at the present time in the case of the illiterate, who have to depend on memory alone." We must smile at Hirata's good faith in the changelessness of oral tradition; but I believe that folk-lorists would discover, in the character of the older myths, intrinsic evidence of immense antiquity. Chinese influence is discernible in both works; yet certain parts have a particular quality not to be found, I imagine, in anything Chinese — a primeval artlessness, a weirdness, and a strangeness having nothing in common with other mythical literature. For example, we have, in the story of Izanagi, the world-maker, visiting the shades to recall his dead spouse, a myth that seems to be purely Japanese. The archaic naïveté of the recital must impress anybody who studies the literal translation. I shall present only the substance of the legend, which has been recorded in a number of different versions:[1]

When the time came for the Fire-God, Kagu-Tsuchi, to be born, his mother, Izanami-no-Mikoto, was burnt, and suffered change, and departed. Then Izanagi-no-Mikoto was wroth and said, "Oh! that I should have given my loved younger sister in exchange for a single child!" He crawled at her head and he crawled at her feet, weeping and lamenting; and the tears which he shed fell down and became a deity. . . . Thereafter Izanagi-no-Mikoto went after Izanami-no-Mikoto into the Land of Yomi, the world of the dead. Then Izanami-no-Mikoto, appearing still as she was when alive, lifted the curtain of the palace (of the dead), and came forth to meet him; and they talked together. And Izanagi-no Mikoto said to her: "I have come because I sorrowed for thee, my lovely younger sister. O my lovely younger sister, the lands that I and thou were making together are not yet finished; therefore come back!" Then Izanami-no-Mikoto made answer, saying, "My august lord and husband, lamentable it is that thou didst not come sooner — for now I have eaten of the cooking-range of Yomi. Nevertheless, as I am thus delightfully honored by thine entry here, my lovely elder brother, I wish to return with thee to the living world. Now I go to discuss the matter with the gods of Yomi. Wait thou here, and look not upon me." So having spoken, she went back; and Izanagi waited for her. But she tarried so long within that he became impatient. Then, taking the wooden comb that he wore in the left bunch of his hair, he broke off a tooth from one end of the comb and lighted it, and went in to look for Izanami-no-Mikoto. But he saw her lying swollen and festering among worms; and eight

[1] See for these different versions Aston's translation of the *Nihongi*, vol. I.

kinds of Thunder-Gods sat upon her. . . . And Izanagi, being overawed by that sight, would have fled away; but Izanami rose up, crying: "Thou hast put me to shame! Why didst thou not observe that which I charged thee? . . . Thou hast seen my nakedness; now I will see thine!" And she bade the Ugly Females of Yomi to follow after him, and slay him; and the eight Thunders also pursued him, and Izanami herself pursued him. . . . Then Izanagi-no-Mikoto drew his sword, and flourished it behind him as he ran. But they followed close upon him. He took off his black headdress and flung it down; and it became changed into grapes; and while the Ugly Ones were eating the grapes, he gained upon them. But they followed quickly; and he then took his comb and cast it down, and it became changed into bamboo sprouts; and while the Ugly Ones were devouring the sprouts, he fled on until he reached the mouth of Yomi. Then taking a rock which it would have required the strength of a thousand men to lift, he blocked therewith the entrance as Izanami came up. And standing behind the rock, he began to pronounce the words of divorce. Then, from the other side of the rock, Izanami cried out to him, "My dear lord and master, if thou dost so, in one day will I strangle to death a thousand of thy people!" And Izanagi-no-Mikoto answered her, saying, "My beloved younger sister, if thou dost so, I will cause in one day to be born fifteen hundred. . . ." But the deity Kukuri-hime-no-Kami then came, and spake to Izanami some word which she seemed to approve, and thereafter she vanished away. . . .

The strange mingling of pathos with nightmare-terror in this myth, of which I have not ventured to present all the startling naïveté, sufficiently proves its primitive character. It is a dream that some one really dreamed — one of those bad dreams in which the figure of a person beloved becomes horribly transformed; and it has a particular interest as expressing that fear of death and of the dead informing all primitive ancestor-worship. The whole pathos and weirdness of the myth, the vague monstrosity of the fancies, the formal use of terms of endearment in the moment of uttermost loathing and fear — all impress one as unmistakably Japanese. Several other myths scarcely less remarkable are to be found in the "Ko-ji-ki" and "Nihongi"; but they are mingled with legends of so light and graceful a kind that it is scarcely possible to believe these latter to have been imagined by the same race. The story of the magical jewels and the visit to the sea-god's palace, for example, in the second book of the "Nihongi," sounds oddly like an Indian fairy-tale; and it is not unlikely that the "Ko-ji-ki" and "Nihongi" both contain myths derived from various alien sources. At all events their mythical chapters present us with some curious problems which yet remain unsolved. Otherwise the books are dull reading, in spite of the light which they shed upon ancient customs and beliefs; and, generally speaking, Japanese mythology is unattractive. But to dwell here upon the mythology, at any length, is unnecessary; for its relation to Shintō can be summed up in the space of a single brief paragraph:

In the beginning neither force nor form was manifest; and the world was a shapeless mass that floated like a jelly-fish upon water. Then, in some way — we are not told how — earth and heaven became separated; dim gods appeared and disappeared; and at last there came into existence a male and a female deity, who gave birth and shape to things. By this pair, Izanagi and Izanami, were produced the islands of Japan, and the generations of the gods, and the deities of the Sun and Moon. The descendants of these creating deities, and of the gods whom they brought into being, were the 8000 (or 80,000) myriads of gods worshiped by Shintō. Some went to dwell in the blue Plain of High Heaven; others remained on earth and became the ancestors of the Japanese race.

Such is the mythology of the "Ko-ji-ki" and the "Nihongi," stated in the briefest possible way. At first it appears that there were two classes of gods recognized: celestial and terrestrial; and the old Shintō rituals (norito) maintain this distinction. But it is a curious fact that the celestial gods of this mythology do not represent celestial forces; and that the gods who are really identified with celestial phenomena are classed as terrestrial gods — having been born or "produced" upon earth. The Sun and Moon, for example, are said to have been born in Japan — though afterwards placed in heaven; the Sun-Goddess, Ama-terasu-no-oho-Kami, having been produced from the left eye of Izanagi, and the Moon-God, Tsuki-yomi-no-Mikoto, having been produced from the right eye of Izanagi when, after his visit to the under-world, he washed himself at the mouth of a river in the island of Tsukushi. The Shintō scholars of the eighteenth and nineteenth centuries established some order in this chaos of fancies by denying all distinction between the celestial and terrestrial gods, except as regarded the accident of birth. They also denied the old distinction between the so-called Age of the Gods (Kami-yo), and the subsequent period of the Emperors. It was true, they said, that the early rulers of Japan were gods; but so were also the later rulers. The whole Imperial line, the "Sun's Succession," represented one unbroken descent from the Goddess of the Sun. Hirata wrote: "There exists no hard-and-fast line between the Age of the Gods and the present age; and there exists no justification whatever for drawing one, as the 'Nihongi' does." Of course this position involved the doctrine of a divine descent for the whole race — inasmuch as, according to the old mythology, the first Japanese were all descendants of gods — and that doctrine Hirata boldly accepted. All the Japanese, he averred, were of divine origin, and for that reason superior to the people of all other countries. He even held that their divine descent could be proved without difficulty. These are his words: "The descendants of the gods who accompanied Ninigi-no-Mikoto [grandson of the Sun-Goddess, and supposed founder of the Imperial House] — as well as the offspring of the successive Mikados, who entered

235

the ranks of the subjects of the Mikados, with the names of Taira, Minamoto, and so forth — have gradually increased and multiplied. Although numbers of Japanese cannot state with certainty from what gods they are descended, all of them have tribal names (kabané), which were originally bestowed on them by the Mikados; and those who make it their province to study genealogies can tell, from a man's ordinary surname, who his remotest ancestor must have been." All the Japanese were gods in this sense; and their country was properly called the "Land of the Gods" — Shinkoku or Kami-no-kuni. Are we to understand Hirata literally? I think so — but we must remember that there existed in feudal times large classes of people, outside of the classes officially recognized as forming the nation, who were not counted as Japanese, nor even as human beings: these were pariahs, and reckoned as little better than animals. Hirata probably referred to the four great classes only — samurai, farmers, artisans, and merchants. But even in that case what are we to think of his ascription of divinity to the race, in view of the moral and physical feebleness of human nature? The moral side of the question is answered by the Shintō theory of evil deities, "gods of crookedness," who were alleged to have "originated from the impurities contracted by Izanagi during his visit to the under-world." As for the physical weakness of men, that is explained by a legend of Ninigi-no-

Mikoto, divine founder of the Imperial House. The Goddess of Long Life, Iha-naga-himé (Rock-Long-Princess), was sent to him for wife; but he rejected her because of her ugliness; and that unwise proceeding brought about "the present shortness of the lives of men." Most mythologies ascribe vast duration to the lives of early patriarchs or rulers: the farther we go back into mythological history, the longer-lived are the sovereigns. To this general rule Japanese mythology presents no exception. The son of Ninigi-no-Mikoto is said to have lived five hundred and eighty years at his palace of Takachiho; but that, remarks Hirata, "was a short life compared with the lives of those who lived before him." Thereafter men's bodies declined in force; life gradually became shorter and shorter; yet in spite of all degeneration the Japanese still show traces of their divine origin. After death they enter into a higher divine condition, without, however, abandoning this world. . . . Such were Hirata's views. Accepting the Shintō theory of origins, this ascription of divinity to human nature proves less inconsistent than it appears at first sight; and the modern Shintōist may discover a germ of scientific truth in the doctrine which traces back the beginnings of life to the Sun.

More than any other Japanese writer, Hirata has enabled us to understand the hierarchy of Shintō mythology — corresponding closely, as we might have expected, to the ancient ordination of Japanese society. In the lowermost ranks are the spirits of common people, worshiped only at the household shrine or at graves. Above these are the gentile gods or Ujigami — ghosts of old rulers now worshiped as tutelar gods. All Ujigami, Hirata tells us, are under the control of the Great God of Izumo — Oho-kuni-nushi-no-Kami — and, "acting as his agents, they rule the fortunes of human beings before their birth, during their life, and after their death." This means that the ordinary ghosts obey, in the world invisible, the commands of the clangods or tutelar deities; that the conditions of communal worship during life continue after death. The following extract from Hirata will be found of interest — not only as showing the supposed relation of the individual to the Ujigami, but also as suggesting how the act of abandoning one's birthplace was formerly judged by common opinion:

When a person removes his residence, his original Ujigami has to make arrangements with the Ujigami of the place whither he transfers his abode. On such occasions it is proper to take leave of the old god, and to pay a visit to the temple of the new god as soon as possible after coming within his jurisdiction. The apparent reasons which a man imagines to have induced him to change his abode may be many; *but the real reasons cannot be otherwise than that either he has offended his Ujigami, and is therefore expelled, or that the Ujigami of another place has negotiated his transfer. . . .*[1]

It would thus appear that every person was sup-

[1] Translated by Satow. The italics are mine.

posed to be the subject, servant, or retainer of some Ujigami, both during life and after death.

There were, of course, various grades of these clan-gods, just as there were various grades of living rulers, lords of the soil. Above ordinary Ujigami ranked the deities worshiped in the chief Shintō temples of the various provinces, which temples were termed "Ichi-no-miya," or temples of the first grade. These deities appear to have been in many cases spirits of princes or greater daimyō, formerly ruling extensive districts; but all were not of this category. Among them were deities of elements or elemental forces — Wind, Fire, and Sea — deities also of longevity, of destiny, and of harvests — clan-gods, perhaps, originally, though their real history had been long forgotten. But above all other Shintō divinities ranked the gods of the Imperial Cult — the supposed ancestors of the Mikados.

Of the higher forms of Shintō worship, that of the Imperial Ancestors proper is the most important, being the State cult; but it is not the oldest. There are two supreme cults: that of the Sun-Goddess, represented by the famous shrines of Isé; and the Izumo cult, represented by the great temple of Kitzuki. This Izumo temple is the centre of the more ancient cult. It is dedicated to Oho-kuni-nushi-no-Kami, first ruler of the Province of the Gods, and offspring of the brother of the Sun-Goddess. Dispossessed of his realm in favor of the founder of the Imperial dynasty, Oho-kuni-nushi-

no-Kami became the ruler of the Unseen World —
that is to say the World of Ghosts. Unto his shadowy dominion the spirits of all men proceed after
death; and he rules over all of the Ujigami. We
may therefore term him the Emperor of the Dead.
"You cannot hope," Hirata says, "to live more
than a hundred years, under the most favorable
circumstances; but as you will go to the Unseen
Realm of Oho-kuni-nushi-no-Kami after death, and
be subject to him, learn betimes to bow down before
him." . . . That weird fancy expressed in the wonderful fragment by Coleridge, "The Wanderings of
Cain," would therefore seem to have actually
formed an article of ancient Shintō faith: "The
Lord is God of the living only: the dead have
another God." . .

The God of the Living in Old Japan was, of course,
the Mikado — the deity incarnate, Arahito-gami —
and his palace was the national sanctuary, the Holy
of Holies. Within the precincts of that palace was
the Kashiko-Dokoro (Place of Awe), the private
shrine of the Imperial Ancestors, where only the
court could worship — the public form of the same
cult being maintained at Isé. But the Imperial
House worshiped also by deputy (and still so worships) both at Kitzuki and Isé, and likewise at
various other great sanctuaries. Formerly a great
number of temples were maintained, or partly
maintained, from the Imperial revenues. All Shintō
temples of importance used to be classed as greater

and lesser shrines. There were 304 of the first rank, and 2828 of the second rank. But multitudes of temples were not included in this official classification, and depended upon local support. The recorded total of Shintō shrines to-day is upwards of 195,000.

We have thus — without counting the great Izumo cult of Oho-kuni-nushi-no-Kami — four classes of ancestor-worship: the domestic religion, the religion of the Ujigami, the worship at the chief shrines (Ichi-no-miya) of the several provinces, and the national cult at Isé. All these cults are now linked together by tradition; and the devout Shintōist worships the divinities of all, collectively, in his daily morning prayer. Occasionally he visits the chief shrine of his province; and he makes a pilgrimage to Isé if he can. Every Japanese is expected to visit the shrines of Isé once in his lifetime, or to send thither a deputy. Inhabitants of remote districts are not all able, of course, to make the pilgrimage; but there is no village which does not, at certain intervals, send pilgrims either to Kitzuki or to Isé on behalf of the community — the expense of such representation being defrayed by local subscription. And, furthermore, every Japanese can worship the supreme divinities of Shintō in his own house, where upon a "god-shelf" (Kami-dana) are tablets inscribed with the assurance of their divine protection — holy charms obtained from the priests of Isé or of Kitzuki. In the case of the Isé cult, such tablets are commonly made from the wood of the holy shrines themselves, which, according to primal custom, must be rebuilt every twenty years — the timber of the demolished structures being then cut into tablets for distribution throughout the country.

Another development of ancestor-worship — the cult of gods presiding over crafts and callings — deserves special study. Unfortunately we are as yet little informed upon the subject. Anciently this worship must have been more definitely ordered and maintained than it is now. Occupations were hereditary; artisans were grouped into guilds — perhaps we might even say castes; — and each guild or caste then probably had its patron deity. In some cases the craft-gods may have been ancestors of Japanese craftsmen; in other cases they were perhaps of Korean or Chinese origin — ancestral gods of immigrant artisans, who brought their cults with them to Japan. Not much is known about them. But it is tolerably safe to assume that most, if not all of the guilds, were at one time religiously organized, and that apprentices were adopted not only in a craft, but into a cult. There were corporations of weavers, potters, carpenters, arrow-makers, bow-makers, smiths, boat-builders, and other tradesmen; and the past religious organization of these is suggested by the fact that certain occupations assume a religious character even to-day. For example, the carpenter still builds according to Shintō tradition: he dons a priestly costume at a certain stage of the work, performs rites, and chants invocations, and places the new house under the protection of the gods. But the occupation of the swordsmith was in old days the most sacred of crafts: he worked in priestly garb, and practiced Shintō rites of purification while engaged in the making of a good blade. Before his smithy was then suspended the sacred rope of rice-straw (shimé-nawa), which is the oldest symbol of Shintō: none even of his family might enter there, or speak to him; and he ate only of food cooked with holy fire.

The 195,000 shrines of Shintō represent, however, more than clan cults or guild cults or national cults. . . . Many are dedicated to different spirits of the same god; for Shintō holds that the spirit of either a man or a god may divide itself into several spirits, each with a different character. Such separated spirits are called "waka-mi-tama" (august-divided-spirits). Thus the spirit of the Goddess of Food, Toyo-uké-bimé, separated itself into the God of Trees, Kukunochi-no-Kami, and into the Goddess of Grasses, Kayanu-himé-no-Kami. Gods and men were supposed to have also a Rough Spirit and a Gentle Spirit; and Hirata remarks that the Rough Spirit of Oho-kuni-nushi-no-Kami was worshiped at one temple, and his Gentle

243

Spirit at another.[1] . . . Also we have to remember
that great numbers of Ujigami temples are dedicated to the same divinity. These duplications or
multiplications are again offset by the fact that in
some of the principal temples a multitude of different deities are enshrined. Thus the number of
Shintō temples in actual existence affords no indi-
cation whatever of the actual number of gods worshiped, nor of the variety of their cults. Almost
every deity mentioned in the "Ko-ji-ki" or "Nihongi" has a shrine somewhere; and hundreds of
others — including many later apotheoses — have
their temples. Numbers of temples have been dedicated, for example, to historical personages — to
spirits of great ministers, captains, rulers, scholars,
heroes, and statesmen. The famous minister of
the Empress Jingō, Take-no-uji-no-Sukuné — who
served under six successive sovereigns, and lived to
the age of three hundred years — is now invoked in
many a temple as a giver of long life and great wisdom. The spirit of Sugiwara-no-Michizané, once
minister to the Emperor Daigō, is worshiped as the
god of calligraphy, under the name of Tenjin, or
Temmangu: children everywhere offer to him the
first examples of their handwriting, and deposit in
receptacles, placed before his shrine, their worn-out
writing-brushes. The Soga brothers, victims and

[1] Even men had the Rough and the Gentle Spirit; but a god had three
distinct spirits — the Rough, the Gentle, and the Bestowing — respectively termed "Arami-tama," "Nigi-mi-tama," and "Saki-mi-
tama." (See Satow's *Revival of Pure Shintau*.)

heroes of a famous twelfth-century tragedy, have become gods to whom people pray for the mainte- nance of fraternal harmony. Kato Kiyomasa, the determined enemy of Jesuit Christianity, and Hidé- yoshi's greatest captain, has been apotheosized both by Buddhism and by Shintō. Iyéyasu is worshiped under the appellation of Tōshōgu. In fact most of the great men of Japanese history have had temples erected to them; and the spirits of the daimyō were, in former years, regularly worshiped by the subjects of their descendants and successors.

Besides temples to deities presiding over indus- tries and agriculture — or deities especially invoked by the peasants, such as the Goddess of Silkworms, the Goddess of Rice, the Gods of Wind and Weather — there are to be found in almost every part of the country what I may call propitiatory temples. These latter Shintō shrines have been erected by way of compensation to spirits of persons who suf- fered great injustice or misfortune. In these cases the worship assumes a very curious character, the worshiper always appealing for protection against the same kind of calamity or trouble as that from which the apotheosized person suffered during life. In Izumo, for example, I found a temple dedicated to the spirit of a woman, once a prince's favorite. She had been driven to suicide by the intrigues of jealous rivals. The story is that she had very beau- tiful hair; but it was not quite black, and her enemies used to reproach her with its color. Now mothers having children with brownish hair pray to her that the brown may be changed to black; and offerings are made to her of tresses of hair and Tōkyō colored prints, for it is still remembered that she was fond of such prints. In the same province there is a shrine erected to the spirit of a young wife who pined away for grief at the absence of her lord. She used to climb a hill to watch for his return, and the shrine was built upon the place where she waited; and wives pray there to her for the safe return of absent husbands. . . . An almost similar kind of propitiatory worship is practiced in cemeteries. Public pity seeks to apotheosize those urged to suicide by cruelty, or those executed for offenses which, although legally criminal, were inspired by patriotic or other motives commanding sympathy. Before their graves offerings are laid and prayers are murmured. Spirits of unhappy lovers are commonly invoked by young people who suffer from the same cause. . . . And among other forms of propitiatory worship I must mention the old custom of erecting small shrines to spirits of animals — chiefly domestic animals — either in recognition of dumb service rendered and ill-rewarded, or as a compensation for pain unjustly inflicted.

Yet another class of tutelar divinities remains to be noticed — those who dwell within or about the houses of men. Some are mentioned in the old

mythology, and are probably developments of
Japanese ancestor-worship; some are of alien origin;
some do not appear to have any temples; and some
represent little more than what is called Animism.
This class of divinities corresponds rather to the
Roman "dii genitales" than to the Greek δαίμονες.
Suijin-Sama, the God of Wells; Kojin, the God of
the Cooking-Range (in almost every kitchen there
is either a tiny shrine for him, or a written charm
bearing his name); the Gods of the Cauldron and
Saucepan, Kudo-no-Kami and Kobé-no-Kami (anciently called Okitsuhiko and Okitsuhimé); the
Master of Ponds, Iké-no-Nushi, supposed to make
apparition in the form of a serpent; the Goddess
of the Rice-Pot, O-Kama-Sama; the Gods of the
Latrina, who first taught men how to fertilize their
fields (these are commonly represented by little
figures of paper, having the forms of a man and a
woman, but faceless); the Gods of Wood and Fire
and Metal; the Gods likewise of Gardens, Fields,
Scarecrows, Bridges, Hills, Woods, and Streams;
and also the Spirits of Trees (for Japanese mythology has its dryads): most of these are undoubtedly
of Shintō. On the other hand, we find the roads
under the protection of Buddhist deities chiefly.
I have not been able to learn anything regarding
gods of boundaries — "termes," as the Latins called
them; and one sees only images of the Buddhas at
the limits of village territories. But in almost every
garden, on the north side, there is a little Shintō

shrine, facing what is called the "Ki-Mon," or "Demon-Gate" — that is to say, the direction from which, according to Chinese teaching, all evils come; and these little shrines, dedicated to various Shintō deities, are supposed to protect the home from evil spirits. The belief in the Ki-Mon is obviously a Chinese importation.

One may doubt, however, if Chinese influence alone developed the belief that every part of a house — every beam of it — and every domestic utensil has its invisible guardian. Considering this belief, it is not surprising that the building of a house — unless the house be in foreign style — is still a religious act, and that the functions of a master-builder include those of a priest.

This brings us to the subject of Animism. (I doubt whether any evolutionist of the contemporary school holds to the old-fashioned notion that animism preceded ancestor-worship — a theory involving the assumption that belief in the spirits of inanimate objects was evolved before the idea of a human ghost had yet been developed.) In Japan it is now as difficult to draw the line between animistic beliefs and the lowest forms of Shintō as to establish a demarcation between the vegetable and the animal worlds; but the earliest Shintō literature gives no evidence of such a developed animism as that now existing. Probably the development was gradual, and largely influenced by Chinese beliefs. Still, we read in the "Ko-ji-ki" of "evil gods who glittered like fireflies or were disorderly as mayflies," and of "demons who made rocks, and stumps of trees, and the foam of the green waters to speak" — showing that animistic or fetichistic notions were prevalent to some extent before the period of Chinese influence. And it is significant that where animism is associated with persistent worship (as in the matter of the reverence paid to strangely shaped stones or trees), the form of the worship is, in most cases, Shintō. Before such objects there is usually to be seen the model of a Shintō gateway — torii. . . . With the development of animism, under Chinese and Korean influence, the man of Old Japan found himself truly in a world of spirits and demons. They spoke to him in the sound of tides and of cataracts, in the moaning of wind and the whispers of leafage, in the crying of birds, and the trilling of insects, in all the voices of nature. For him all visible motion — whether of waves or grasses or shifting mist or drifting cloud — was ghostly; and the never moving rocks — nay, the very stones by the wayside — were informed with viewless and awful being.

WORSHIP AND PURIFICATION

WE have seen that, in Old Japan, the world of the living was everywhere ruled by the world of the dead — that the individual, at every moment of his existence, was under ghostly supervision. In his home he was watched by the spirits of his fathers; without it, he was ruled by the god of his district. All about him, and above him, and beneath him were invisible powers of life and death. In his conception of nature all things were ordered by the dead — light and darkness, weather and season, winds and tides, mist and rain, growth and decay, sickness and health. The viewless atmosphere was a phantom-sea, an ocean of ghost; the soil that he tilled was pervaded by spirit-essence; the trees were haunted and holy; even the rocks and the stones were infused with conscious life. . . . How might he discharge his duty to the infinite concourse of the invisible?

Few scholars could remember the names of all the greater gods, not to speak of the lesser; and no mortal could have found time to address those greater gods by their respective names in his daily prayer. The later Shintō teachers proposed to simplify the duties of the faith by prescribing one brief daily prayer to the gods in general, and special prayers to a few gods in particular; and in thus doing they were most likely confirming a custom already established by necessity. Hirata wrote: "As the number of the gods who possess different functions is very great, it will be convenient to worship by name the most important only, and to include the rest in a general petition." He pre-scribed ten prayers for persons having time to re-peat them, but lightened the duty for busy folk — observing: "Persons whose daily affairs are so mul-titudinous that they have not time to go through all the prayers, may content themselves with adoring (1) the residence of the Emperor, (2) the domestic god-shelf — Kamidana, (3) the spirits of their ancestors, (4) their local patron god — Ujigami, (5) the deity of their particular calling." He advised that the following prayer should be daily repeated before the "god-shelf":

Reverently adoring the great god of the two palaces of Isé in the first place — the eight hundred myriads of celestial gods — the eight hundred myriads of terrestrial gods — the fifteen hundred myriads of gods to whom are consecrated the great and small temples in all provinces, all islands, and all places of the Great Land of Eight Islands — the fifteen hundred myriads of gods whom they cause to serve them, and the gods of branch palaces and branch temples — and Sohodo-no-Kami[1] whom I have invited to the shrine set up on this divine shelf, and to whom I offer praises day by day — I pray with awe that they will deign to correct the unwilling faults which,

[1] Sohodo-no-Kami is the God of Scarecrows — protector of the fields.

heard and seen by them, I have committed; and that, blessing and favoring me according to the powers which they severally wield, they will cause me to follow the divine example, and to perform good works in the Way.[1]

This text is interesting as an example of what Shintō's greatest expounder thought a Shintō prayer should be; and, excepting the reference to Sohodo-no-Kami, the substance of it is that of the morning prayer still repeated in Japanese households. But the modern prayer is very much shorter. . . . In Izumo, the oldest Shintō province, the customary morning worship offers perhaps the best example of the ancient rules of devotion. Immediately upon rising, the worshiper performs his ablutions; and after having washed his face and rinsed his mouth, he turns to the sun, claps his hands, and with bowed head reverently utters the simple greeting: "Hail to thee this day, August One!" In thus adoring the sun he is also fulfilling his duty as a subject — paying obeisance to the Imperial Ancestor. . . . The act is performed out of doors, not kneeling, but standing; and the spectacle of this simple worship is impressive. I can now see in memory — just as plainly as I saw with my eyes many years ago, off the wild Oki coast — the naked figure of a young fisherman erect at the prow of his boat, clapping his hands in salutation to the rising sun, whose ruddy glow transformed him into a statue of bronze. Also I retain a vivid memory of pilgrim figures

[1] Translated by Satow.

poised upon the topmost crags of the summit of Fuji, clapping their hands in prayer, with faces to the east. . . . Perhaps ten thousand — twenty thousand — years ago all humanity so worshiped the Lord of Day. . . .

After having saluted the sun, the worshiper returns to his house, to pray before the Kamidana and before the tables of the ancestors. Kneeling, he invokes the great gods of Isé or of Izumo, the gods of the chief temples of his province, the god of his parish-temple also (Ujigami), and finally all the myriads of the deities of Shintō. These prayers are not said aloud. The ancestors are thanked for the foundation of the home; the higher deities are invoked for aid and protection. . . . As for the custom of bowing in the direction of the Emperor's palace, I am not able to say to what extent it survives in the remoter districts; but I have often seen the reverence performed.

Once, too, I saw the reverence done immediately in front of the gates of the palace in Tōkyō by country-folk on a visit to the capital. They knew me, because I had often sojourned in their village; and on reaching Tōkyō they sought me out, and found me. I took them to the palace; and before the main entrance they removed their hats, and bowed, and clapped their hands — just as they would have done when saluting the gods or the rising sun — and this with a simple and dignified reverence that touched me not a little.

WORSHIP AND PURIFICATION

The duties of morning worship, which include the placing of offerings before the tablets, are not the only duties of the domestic cult. In a Shintō household, where the ancestors and the higher gods are separately worshiped, the ancestral shrine may be said to correspond with the Roman "lararium"; while the "god-shelf," with its taima or o-nusa (symbols of those higher gods especially revered by the family), may be compared with the place accorded by Latin custom to the worship of the Penates. Both Shintō cults have their particular feast-days; and, in the case of the ancestor-cult, the feast-days are occasions of religious assembly — when the relatives of the family should gather to celebrate the domestic rite. . . . The Shintōist must also take part in the celebration of the festivals of the Uji-gami, and must at least aid in the celebration of the nine great national holidays related to the national cult; these nine, out of a total eleven, being occasions of Imperial Ancestor-worship.

The nature of the public rites varied according to the rank of the gods. Offerings and prayers were made to all; but the greater deities were worshiped with exceeding ceremony. To-day the offerings usually consist of food and rice-wine, together with symbolic articles representing the costlier gifts of woven stuffs presented by ancient custom. The ceremonies include processions, music, singing, and dancing. At the very small shrines there are few ceremonies — only offerings of food are presented. But at the great temples there are hierarchies of priests and priestesses (miko) — usually daughters of priests; and the ceremonies are elaborate and solemn. It is particularly at the temples of Isé (where, down to the fourteenth century, the high priestess was a daughter of emperors), or at the great temple of Izumo, that the archaic character of the ceremonial can be studied to most advantage. There, in spite of the passage of that huge wave of Buddhism, which for a period almost submerged the more ancient faith, all things remain as they were a score of centuries ago; — Time, in those haunted precincts, would seem to have slept, as in the enchanted palaces of fairy-tale. The mere shapes of the buildings, weird and tall, startle by their unfamiliarity. Within, all is severely plain and pure: there are no images, no ornaments, no symbols visible — except those strange paper-cuttings (gohei), suspended to upright rods, which are symbols of offerings and also tokens of the viewless. By the number of them in the sanctuary, you know the number of the deities to whom the place is consecrate. There is nothing imposing but the space, the silence, and the suggestion of the past. The innermost shrine is veiled: it contains, perhaps, a mirror of bronze, an ancient sword, or other object enclosed in multiple wrappings: that is all. For this faith, older than icons, needs no images: its gods are ghosts; and the void stillness of its shrines compels more awe than tangible representation could inspire. Very strange, to Western eyes at least, are the rites, the forms of the worship, the shapes of sacred objects. Not by any modern method must the sacred fire be lighted — the fire that cooks the food of the gods: it can be kindled only in the most ancient of ways, with a wooden fire-drill. The chief priests are robed in the sacred color — white — and wear headdresses of a shape no longer seen elsewhere: high caps of the kind formerly worn by lords and princes. Their assistants wear various colors, according to grade; and the faces of none are completely shaven; — some wear full beards, others the mustache only. The actions and attitudes of these hierophants are dignified, yet archaic, in a degree difficult to describe. Each movement is regulated by tradition; and to perform well the functions of a Kannushi, a long disciplinary preparation is necessary. The office is hereditary; the training begins in boyhood; and the impassive deportment eventually acquired is really a wonderful thing. Officiating, the Kannushi seems rather a statue than a man — an image moved by invisible strings; — and, like the gods, he never winks. Not at least observably. . . . Once, during a great Shintō procession, several Japanese friends, and I myself, undertook to watch a young priest on horseback, in order to see how long he could keep from winking; and none of us were able to detect the slightest movement of eyes or eyelids, notwithstanding that the priest's horse became restive during the time that we were watching.

The principal incidents of the festival ceremonies within the great temples are the presentation of the offerings, the repetition of the ritual, and the dancing of the priestesses. Each of these performances retains a special character rigidly fixed by tradition. The food-offerings are served upon archaic vessels of unglazed pottery (red earthenware mostly): boiled rice pressed into cones of the form of a sugar-loaf, various preparations of fish and of edible seaweed, fruits and fowls, rice-wine presented in jars of immemorial shape. These offerings are carried into the temple upon white wooden trays of curious form, and laid upon white wooden tables of equally curious form; — the faces of the bearers being covered, below the eyes, with sheets of white paper, in order that their breath may not contaminate the food of the gods; and the trays, for like reason, must be borne at arms' length. . . . In ancient times the offerings would seem to have included things much more costly than food — if we may credit the testimony of what are probably the oldest documents extant in the Japanese tongue, the Shintō rituals, or norito.[1] The following excerpt from Satow's translation of the ritual prayer to the Wind-Gods of

[1] Several have been translated by Satow, whose opinion of their antiquity is here cited; and translations have also been made into German.

257

WORSHIP AND PURIFICATION

Tatsuta is interesting, not only as a fine example of the language of the norito, but also as indicating the character of the great ceremonies in early ages, and the nature of the offerings:

As the great offerings set up for the Youth-God, I set up various sorts of offerings: for clothes, bright cloth, glittering cloth, soft cloth, and coarse cloth — and the five kinds of things, a mantlet, a spear, a horse furnished with a saddle; — for the Maiden-God I set up various sorts of offerings — providing clothes, a golden thread-box, a golden tatari, a golden skein-holder, bright cloth, glittering cloth, soft cloth, and coarse cloth, and the five kinds of things, a horse furnished with a saddle; — as to Liquor, I raise high the beer-jars, fill and range-in-a-row the bellies of the beer-jars; soft grain and coarse grain; — as to things which dwell in the hills, things soft of hair and things coarse of hair; — as to things which grow in the great field-plain, sweet herbs and bitter herbs; — as to things which dwell in the blue sea-plain, things broad of fin and things narrow of fin — down to the weeds of the offing and weeds of the shore. And if the sovereign gods will take these great offerings which I set up — piling them up like a range of hills — peacefully in their hearts, as peaceful offerings and satisfactory offerings; and if the sovereign gods, deigning not to visit the things produced by the great People of the region under heaven with bad winds and rough waters, will ripen and bless them — I will at the autumn service set up the first fruits, raising high the beer-jars, filling and ranging-in-rows the bellies of the beer-jars — and drawing them hither in juice and in ear, in many hundred rice-plants and a thousand rice-plants. And for this purpose the princes and councillors and all the functionaries, the servants of the six farms of the country of Yamato — even to the males and females of them — have all come and assembled in the fourth month of this year, and, plunging down the root of the neck cormorant-wise in the presence of the sovereign gods, fulfill their praise as the Sun of to-day rises in glory. . . .

The offerings are no longer piled up "like a range of hills," nor do they include "all things dwelling in the mountains and in the sea"; but the imposing ritual remains, and the ceremony is always impressive. Not the least interesting part of it is the sacred dance. While the gods are supposed to be partaking of the food and wine set out before their shrines, the girl-priestesses, robed in crimson and white, move gracefully to the sound of drums and flutes — waving fans, or shaking bunches of tiny bells as they circle about the sanctuary. According to our Western notions, the performance of the miko could scarcely be called dancing; but it is a graceful spectacle, and very curious — for every step and attitude is regulated by traditions of unknown antiquity. As for the plaintive music, no Western ear can discern in it anything resembling a real melody; but the gods should find delight in it, because it is certainly performed for them to-day exactly as it used to be performed twenty centuries ago.

I speak of the ceremonies especially as I have witnessed them in Izumo: they vary somewhat according to cult and province. At the shrines of Isé, Kasuga, Kompira, and several others which I visited, the ordinary priestesses are children; and when they have reached the nubile age, they retire from the service. At Kitzuki the priestesses are grown-up women: their office is hereditary; and they are permitted to retain it even after marriage.

Formerly the miko was more than a mere officiant: the songs which she is still obliged to learn indicate that she was originally offered to the gods as a bride. Even yet her touch is holy; the grain sown by her hand is blessed. At some time in the past she seems to have been also a pythoness: the spirits of the gods possessed her and spoke through her lips. All the poetry of this most ancient of religions centres in the figure of its little Vestal — child-bride of ghosts — as she flutters, like some wonderful white-and-crimson butterfly, before the shrine of the Invisible. Even in these years of change, when she must go to the public school, she continues to represent all that is delightful in Japanese girlhood; for her special home-training keeps her reverent, innocent, dainty in all her little ways, and worthy to remain the pet of the gods.

The history of the higher forms of ancestor-worship in other countries would lead us to suppose that the public ceremonies of the Shintō-cult must include some rite of purification. As a matter of fact, the most important of all Shintō ceremonies is the ceremony of purification — "o-harai," as it is called, which term signifies the casting-out or expulsion of evils. . . . In ancient Athens a corresponding ceremony took place every year; in Rome, every four years. The o-harai is performed twice every year — in the sixth month and the twelfth month by the ancient calendar. It used to be not less obligatory than the Roman lustration; and the idea behind the obligation was the same as that which inspired the Roman laws on the subject. . . . So long as men believe that the welfare of the living depends upon the will of the dead — that all happenings in the world are ordered by spirits of different characters, evil as well as good — that every bad action lends additional power to the viewless forces of destruction, and therefore endangers the public prosperity — so long will the necessity of a public purification remain an article of common faith. The presence in any community of even one person who has offended the gods, consciously or unwillingly, is a public misfortune, a public peril. Yet it is not possible for all men to live so well as never to vex the gods by thought, word, or deed — through passion or ignorance or carelessness. "Every one," declares Hirata, "is certain to commit accidental offenses, however careful he may be. . . . Evil acts and words are of two kinds: those of which we are conscious, and those of which we are not conscious. . . . It is better to assume that we have committed such unconscious offenses." Now it should be remembered that for the man of Old Japan — as for the Greek or the Roman citizen of early times — religion consisted chiefly in the exact observance of multitudinous custom; and that it was therefore difficult to know whether, in performing the duties of the several cults, one had not inadvertently displeased the Unseen. As a means of maintaining and assuring the religious purity of the people, periodical lustration was consequently deemed indispensable.

From the earliest period Shintō exacted scrupulous cleanliness — indeed, we might say that it regarded physical impurity as identical with moral impurity, and intolerable to the gods. It has always been, and still remains, a religion of ablutions. The Japanese love of cleanliness — indicated by the universal practice of daily bathing, and by the irreproachable condition of their homes — has been maintained, and was probably initiated, by their religion. Spotless cleanliness being required by the rites of ancestor-worship — in the temple, in the person of the officiant, and in the home — this rule of purity was naturally extended by degrees to all the conditions of existence. And besides the great periodical ceremonies of purification, a multitude of minor lustrations were exacted by the cult. This was the case also, it will be remembered, in the early Greek and Roman civilizations: the citizen had to submit to purification upon almost every important occasion of existence. There were lustrations indispensable at birth, marriage, and death; lustrations on the eve of battle; lustrations, at regular periods, of the dwelling, estate, district, or city. And, as in Japan, no one could approach a temple without a preliminary washing of hands. But ancient Shintō exacted more than the Greek or the Roman cult: it required the erection of special houses for birth — "parturition houses"; special houses for the consummation of marriage — "nuptial huts"; and special buildings for the dead — "mourning houses." Formerly women were obliged during the period of menstruation, as well as during the time of confinement, to live apart. These harsher archaic customs have almost disappeared, except in one or two remote districts, and in the case of certain priestly families; but the general rules as to purification, and as to the times and circumstances forbidding approach to holy places, are still everywhere obeyed. Purity of heart is not less insisted upon than physical purity; and the great rite of lustration, performed every six months, is of course a moral purification. It is performed not only at the great temples, and at all the Ujigami, but likewise in every home.[1]

[1] On the Kamidana, or "god-shelf," there is usually placed a kind of oblong paper box containing fragments of the wands used by the priests of Isé at the great national purification ceremony, or o-harai. This box is commonly called by the name of the ceremony, o-harai, or "august purification," and is inscribed with the names of the great gods of Isé. The presence of this object is supposed to protect the home; but it should be replaced by a new o-harai at the expiration of six months; for the virtue of the charm is supposed to last only during the interval between two official purifications. This distribution to thousands of homes of fragments of the wands, used to "drive away evils" at the time of the Isé lustration, represents of course the supposed extension of the high-priest's protection to those homes until the time of the next o-harai.

WORSHIP AND PURIFICATION

The modern domestic form of the o-harai is very simple. Each Shintō parish-temple furnishes to all its Ujiko, or parishioners, small paper-cuttings called "hitogata" ("mankind-shapes"), representing figures of men, women, and children as in silhouette — only that the paper is white, and folded curiously. Each household receives a number of hitogata corresponding to the number of its members — "men-shapes" for the men and boys, "women-shapes" for the women and girls. Each person in the house touches his head, face, limbs, and body with one of these hitogata; repeating the while a Shintō invocation, and praying that any misfortune or sickness incurred by reason of offenses involuntarily committed against the gods (for in Shintō belief sickness and misfortune are divine punishments) may be mercifully taken away. Upon each hitogata is then written the age and sex (not the name) of the person for whom it was furnished; and when this has been done, all are returned to the parish-temple, and there burnt, with rites of purification. Thus the community is "lustrated" every six months.

In the old Greek and Latin cities lustration was accompanied with registration. The attendance of every citizen at the ceremony was held to be so necessary that one who willfully failed to attend might be whipped and sold as a slave. Non-attendance involved loss of civic rights. It would seem that in Old Japan also every member of a community was obliged to be present at the rite; but I have not been able to learn whether any registration was made upon such occasions. Probably it would have been superfluous: the Japanese individual was not officially recognized; the family-group alone was responsible, and the attendance of the several members would have been assured by the responsibility of the group. The use of the hitogata, on which the name is not written, but only the sex and age of the worshiper, is probably modern, and of Chinese origin. Official registration existed, even in early times; but it appears to have had no particular relation to the o-harai; and the registers were kept, it seems, not by the Shintō, but by the Buddhist parish-priests. . . . In concluding these remarks about the o-harai, I need scarcely add that special rites were performed in cases of accidental religious defilement, and that any person judged to have sinned against the rules of the public cult had to submit to ceremonial purification.

Closely related by origin to the rites of purification are sundry ascetic practices of Shintō. It is not an essentially ascetic religion: it offers flesh and wine to its gods; and it prescribes only such forms of self-denial as ancient custom and decency require. Nevertheless, some of its votaries perform extraordinary austerities on special occasions — austerities which always include much cold-water bathing. It is not uncommon for the very fervent worshiper to invoke the gods as he stands naked under the ice-cold rush of a cataract in midwinter. . . . But the most curious phase of this Shintō asceticism is represented by a custom still prevalent in remote districts. According to this custom a community yearly appoints one of its citizens to devote himself wholly to the gods on behalf of the rest. During the term of his consecration, this communal representative must separate from his family, must not approach women, must avoid all places of amusement, must eat only food cooked with sacred fire, must abstain from wine, must bathe in fresh cold water several times a day, must repeat particular prayers at certain hours, and must keep vigil upon certain nights. When he has performed these duties of abstinence and purification for the specified time, he becomes religiously free; and another man is then elected to take his place. The prosperity of the settlement is supposed to depend upon the exact observance by its representative of the duties prescribed: should any public misfortune occur, he would be suspected of having broken his vows. Anciently, in the case of a common misfortune, the representative was put to death. In the little town of Mionoséki, where I first learned of this custom, the communal representative is called "ichi-nen-gannushi" ("one-year god-master"); and his full term of vicarious atonement is twelve months. I was told that elders are usually appointed for this duty — young men very seldom. In ancient times such a communal representative was called by a name signifying "abstainer." References to the custom have been found in Chinese notices of Japan dating from a time before the beginning of Japanese authentic history.

Every persistent form of ancestor-worship has its system or systems of divination; and Shintō exemplifies the general law. Whether divination ever obtained in ancient Japan the official importance which it assumed among the Greeks and the Romans is at present doubtful. But long before the introduction of Chinese astrology, magic, and fortune-telling, the Japanese practiced various kinds of divination, as is proved by their ancient poetry, their records, and their rituals. We find mention also of official diviners, attached to the great cults. There was divination by bones, by birds, by rice, by barley-gruel, by footprints, by rods planted in the ground, and by listening in public ways to the speech of people passing by. Nearly all — probably all — of these old methods of divination are still in popular use. But the earliest form of official divination was performed by scorching the shoulder-blade of a deer, or other animal, and observing the cracks produced by the heat.[1] Tortoise-shells were after-

[1] Concerning this form of divination, Satow remarks that it was practiced by the Mongols in the time of Genghis Khan, and is still practiced by the Khirghiz Tartars — facts of strong interest in view of the probable origin of the early Japanese tribes.

For instances of ancient official divination see Aston's translation of the *Nihongi*, vol. 1, pp. 157, 189, 227, 229, 237.

wards used for the same purpose. Diviners were especially attached, it appears, to the Imperial Palace; and Motowori, writing in the latter half of the eighteenth century, speaks of divination as still being, in that epoch, a part of the Imperial function. "To the end of time," he said, "the Mikado is the child of the Sun-Goddess. His mind is in perfect harmony of thought and feeling with hers. He does not seek out new inventions; but he rules in accordance with precedents which date from the Age of the Gods; and if he is ever in doubt, he has recourse to divination, which reveals to him the mind of the great goddess."

Within historic times, at least, divination would not seem to have been much used in warfare — certainly not to the extent that it was used by the Greek and Roman armies. The greatest Japanese captains — such as Hidéyoshi and Nobunaga — were decidedly irreverent as to omens. Probably the Japanese, at an early period of their long military history, learned by experience that the general who conducts his campaign according to omens must always be at a hopeless disadvantage in dealing with a skillful enemy who cares nothing about omens.

Among the ancient popular forms of divination which still survive, the most commonly practiced in households is divination by dry rice. For the public, Chinese divination is still in great favor; but it is interesting to observe that the Japanese

fortune-teller invariably invokes the Shintō gods
before consulting his Chinese books, and maintains
a Shintō shrine in his reception-room.

We have seen that the developments of ancestor-
worship in Japan present remarkable analogies with
the developments of ancestor-worship in ancient
Europe — especially in regard to the public cult,
with its obligatory rites of purification.

But Shintō seems, nevertheless, to represent conditions of ancestor-worship less developed than
those which we are accustomed to associate with
early Greek and Roman life; and the coercion which
it exercised appears to have been proportionally
more rigid. The existence of the individual worshiper was ordered not merely in relation to the
family and the community, but even in relation to
inanimate things. Whatever his occupation might
be, some god presided over it; whatever tools he
might use, they had to be used in such manner as
tradition prescribed for all admitted to the craft-
cult. It was necessary that the carpenter should so
perform his work as to honor the deity of carpenters
— that the smith should fulfill his daily task so as to
honor the God of the Bellows — that the farmer
should never fail in respect to the Earth-God, and
the Food-God, and the Scarecrow God, and the
spirits of the trees about his habitation. Even the
domestic utensils were sacred: the servant could not
dare to forget the presence of the deities of the
cooking-range, the hearth, the cauldron, the brazier

— or the supreme necessity of keeping the fire pure. The professions, not less than the trades, were under divine patronage: the physician, the teacher, the artist — each had his religious duties to observe, his special traditions to obey. The scholar, for example, could not dare to treat his writing implements with disrespect, or put written paper to vulgar uses: such conduct would offend the God of Calligraphy. Nor were women ruled less religiously than men in their various occupations: the spinners and weaving-maidens were bound to revere the Weaving-Goddess and the Goddess of Silkworms; the sewing-girl was taught to respect her needles; and in all homes there was observed a certain holiday upon which offerings were made to the Spirits of Needles. In samurai families the warrior was commanded to consider his armor and his weapons as holy things: to keep them in beautiful order was an obligation of which the neglect might bring misfortune in the time of combat; and on certain days offerings were set before the bows and spears, arrows and swords, and other war-implements, in the alcove of the family guest-room. Gardens, too, were holy; and there were rules to be observed in their management, lest offense should be given to the Gods of Trees and Flowers. Carefulness, cleanliness, dustlessness, were everywhere enforced as religious obligations.

... It has often been remarked in these latter days that the Japanese do not keep their public offices, their railway stations, their new factory buildings, thus scrupulously clean. But edifices built in foreign style, with foreign material, under foreign supervision, and contrary to every local tradition, must seem to old-fashioned thinking God-forsaken places; and servants amid such unhallowed surroundings do not feel the invisible about them, the weight of pious custom, the silent claim of beautiful and simple things to human respect.

SOME THOUGHTS ABOUT ANCESTOR-WORSHIP

For twelve leagues, Ananda, around the Sala-Grove, there is no spot in size even as the pricking of the point of the tip of a hair, which is not pervaded by powerful spirits.　THE BOOK OF THE GREAT DECEASE

I

THE truth that ancestor-worship, in various unobtrusive forms, still survives in some of the most highly civilized countries of Europe, is not so widely known as to preclude the idea that any non-Aryan race actually practicing so primitive a cult must necessarily remain in the primitive stage of religious thought. Critics of Japan have pronounced this hasty judgment; and have professed themselves unable to reconcile the facts of her scientific progress, and the success of her advanced educational system, with the continuance of her ancestor-worship. How can the beliefs of Shintō coexist with the knowledge of modern science? How can the men who win distinction as scientific specialists still respect the household shrine or do reverence before the Shintō parish-temple? Can all this mean more than the ordered conservation of forms after the departure of faith? Is it not certain that with the further progress of education, Shintō, even as ceremonialism, must cease to exist?

Those who put such questions appear to forget

that similar questions might be asked about the continuance of any Western faith, and similar doubts expressed as to the possibility of its survival for another century. Really the doctrines of Shintō are not in the least degree more irreconcilable with modern science than are the doctrines of Orthodox Christianity. Examined with perfect impartiality, I would even venture to say that they are less irreconcilable in more respects than one. They conflict less with our human ideas of justice; and, like the Buddhist doctrine of karma, they offer some very striking analogies with the scientific facts of heredity — analogies which prove Shintō to contain an element of truth as profound as any single element of truth in any of the world's great religions. Stated in the simplest possible form, the peculiar element of truth in Shintō is the belief that the world of the living is directly governed by the world of the dead.

That every impulse or act of man is the work of a god, and that all the dead become gods, are the basic ideas of the cult. It must be remembered, however, that the term "Kami," although translated by the term "deity," "divinity," or "god," has really no such meaning as that which belongs to the English words: it has not even the meaning of those words as referring to the antique beliefs of Greece and Rome. It signifies that which is "above," "superior," "upper," "eminent," in the non-religious sense; in the religious sense it signifies a human spirit having obtained supernatural power after death. The dead are the "powers above," the "upper ones" — the Kami. We have here a conception resembling very strongly the modern Spiritualistic notion of ghosts — only that the Shintō idea is in no true sense democratic. The Kami are ghosts of greatly varying dignity and power — belonging to spiritual hierarchies like the hierarchies of ancient Japanese society. Although essentially superior to the living in certain respects, the living are, nevertheless, able to give them pleasure or displeasure, to gratify or to offend them — even sometimes to ameliorate their spiritual condition. Wherefore posthumous honors are never mockeries, but realities, to the Japanese mind. During the present year,[1] for example, several distinguished statesmen and soldiers were raised to higher rank immediately after their death; and I read only the other day, in the official gazette, that "His Majesty has been pleased to posthumously confer the Second Class of the Order of the Rising Sun upon Major-General Baron Yamane, who lately died in Formosa." Such imperial acts must not be regarded only as formalities intended to honor the memory of brave and patriotic men; neither should they be thought of as intended merely to confer distinction upon the family of the dead. They are essentially of Shintō, and exemplify that intimate sense of relation between the visible and invisible worlds which is the special religious characteristic of Japan among all civilized

[1] Written in September, 1895.

countries. To Japanese thought the dead are not less real than the living. They take part in the daily life of the people — sharing the humblest sorrows and the humblest joys. They attend the family repasts, watch over the well-being of the household, assist and rejoice in the prosperity of their descendants. They are present at the public pageants, at all the sacred festivals of Shintō, at the military games, and at all the entertainments especially provided for them. And they are universally thought of as finding pleasure in the offerings made to them or the honors conferred upon them.

For the purpose of this little essay, it will be sufficient to consider the Kami as the spirits of the dead — without making any attempt to distinguish such Kami from those primal deities believed to have created the land. With this general interpretation of the term Kami, we return, then, to the great Shintō idea that all the dead still dwell in the world and rule it; influencing not only the thoughts and the acts of men, but the conditions of nature. "They direct," wrote Motowori, "the changes of the seasons, the wind and the rain, the good and the bad fortunes of states and of individual men." They are, in short, the viewless forces behind all phenomena.

II

THE most interesting sub-theory of this ancient spiritualism is that which explains the impulses and acts of men as due to the influence of the dead. This hypothesis no modern thinker can declare irrational, since it can claim justification from the scientific doctrine of psychological evolution, according to which each living brain represents the structural work of innumerable dead lives — each character a more or less imperfectly balanced sum of countless dead experiences with good and evil. Unless we deny psychological heredity, we cannot honestly deny that our impulses and feelings, and the higher capacities evolved through the feelings, have literally been shaped by the dead, and bequeathed to us by the dead; and even that the general direction of our mental activities has been determined by the power of the special tendencies bequeathed to us. In such a sense the dead are indeed our Kami; and all our actions are truly influenced by them. Figuratively we may say that every mind is a world of ghosts — ghosts incomparably more numerous than the acknowledged millions of the higher Shintō Kami; and that the spectral population of one grain of brain-matter more than realizes the wildest fancies of the mediæval schoolmen about the number of angels able to stand on the point of a needle. Scientifically we know that within one tiny living cell may be stored up the whole life of a race — the sum of all the past sensation of millions of years; perhaps even (who knows?) of millions of dead planets.

But devils would not be inferior to angels in the mere power of congregating upon the point of a needle. What of bad men and of bad acts in this theory of Shintō? Motowori made answer: "Whenever anything goes wrong in the world, it is to be attributed to the action of the evil gods called the Gods of Crookedness, whose power is so great that the Sun-Goddess and the Creator-God are sometimes powerless to restrain them; much less are human beings always able to resist their influence. The prosperity of the wicked, and the misfortunes of the good, which seem opposed to ordinary justice, are thus explained." All bad acts are due to the influence of evil deities; and evil men may become evil Kami. There are no self-contradictions in this simplest of cults [1] — nothing complicated or hard to be understood. It is not certain that all men guilty of bad actions necessarily become "gods of crookedness," for reasons hereafter to be seen; but all men, good or bad, become Kami, or influences. And all evil acts are the results of evil influences.

Now this teaching is in accord with certain facts of heredity. Our best faculties are certainly bequests from the best of our ancestors; our evil qualities are inherited from natures in which evil, or that

[1] I am considering only the pure Shintō belief as expounded by Shintō scholars. But it may be necessary to remind the reader that both Buddhism and Shintōism are blended in Japan, not only with each other, but with Chinese ideas of various kinds. It is doubtful whether the pure Shintō ideas now exist in their original form in popular belief. We are not quite clear as to the doctrine of multiple souls in Shintō — whether the psychical combination was originally thought of as dissolved by death. My own opinion, the result of investigation in different parts of Japan, is that the multiple soul was formerly believed to remain multiple after death.

which we now call evil, once predominated. The ethical knowledge evolved within us by civilization demands that we strengthen the high powers bequeathed us by the best experience of our dead, and diminish the force of the baser tendencies we inherit. We are under obligation to reverence and to obey our good Kami, and to strive against our gods of crookedness. The knowledge of the existence of both is old as human reason. In some form or other, the doctrine of evil and of good spirits in personal attendance upon every soul is common to most of the great religions. Our own mediæval faith developed the idea to a degree which must leave an impress on our language for all time; yet the faith in guardian angels and tempting demons evolutionally represents only the development of a cult once simple as the religion of the Kami. And this theory of mediæval faith is likewise pregnant with truth. The white-winged form that whispered good into the right ear, the black shape that murmured evil into the left, do not indeed walk beside the man of the nineteenth century, but they dwell within his brain; and he knows their voices and feels their urging as well and as often as did his ancestors of the Middle Ages.

The modern ethical objection to Shintō is that both good and evil Kami are to be respected.

Just as the Mikado worshiped the gods of heaven and of earth, so his people prayed to the good gods in order to obtain blessings, and performed rites in honor of the bad gods to avert their displeasure. . . . As there are bad as well as good gods, it is necessary to propitiate them with offerings of agreeable food, with the playing of harps and the blowing of flutes, with singing and dancing, and with whatever else is likely to put them in good-humor.[1]

As a matter of fact, in modern Japan, the evil Kami appear to receive few offerings or honors, notwithstanding this express declaration that they are to be propitiated. But it will now be obvious why the early missionaries characterized such a cult as devil-worship — although, to Shintō imagination, the idea of a devil, in the Western meaning of the word, never took shape. The seeming weakness of the doctrine is in the teaching that evil spirits are not to be warred upon — a teaching essentially repellent to Roman Catholic feeling. But between the evil spirits of Christian and of Shintō belief there is a vast difference. The evil Kami is only the ghost of a dead man, and is not believed to be altogether evil — since propitiation is possible. The conception of absolute, unmixed evil is not of the Far East. Absolute evil is certainly foreign to human nature, and therefore impossible in human ghosts. The evil Kami are not devils. They are simply ghosts, who influence the passions of men; and only in this sense the deities of the passions. Now Shintō is of all religions the most natural, and therefore in certain respects the most rational. It does not consider the passions necessarily evil in themselves, but evil only

1 Motowori, translated by Satow.

according to cause, conditions, and degrees of their indulgence. Being ghosts, the gods are altogether human — having the various good and bad qualities of men in varying proportions. The majority are good, and the sum of the influence of all is toward good rather than evil. To appreciate the rationality of this view requires a tolerably high opinion of mankind — such an opinion as the conditions of the old society of Japan might have justified. No pessimist could profess pure Shintōism. The doctrine is optimistic; and whoever has a generous faith in humanity will have no fault to find with the absence of the idea of implacable evil from its teaching.

Now it is just in the recognition of the necessity for propitiating the evil ghosts that the ethically rational character of Shintō reveals itself. Ancient experience and modern knowledge unite in warning us against the deadly error of trying to extirpate or to paralyze certain tendencies in human nature — tendencies which, if morbidly cultivated or freed from all restraint, lead to folly, to crime, and to countless social evils. The animal passions, the ape-and-tiger impulses, antedate human society, and are the accessories to nearly all crimes committed against it. But they cannot be killed; and they cannot be safely starved. Any attempt to extirpate them would signify also an effort to destroy some of the very highest emotional faculties with which they remain inseparably blended. The primitive impulses cannot even be numbed save at the cost of intellectual and emotional powers which give to human life all its beauty and all its tenderness, but which are, nevertheless, deeply rooted in the archaic soil of passion. The highest in us had its beginnings in the lowest. Asceticism, by warring against the natural feelings, has created monsters. Theological legislation, irrationally directed against human weaknesses, has only aggravated social disorders; and laws against pleasure have only provoked debaucheries. The history of morals teaches very plainly indeed that our bad Kami require some propitiation. The passions still remain more powerful than the reason in man, because they are incomparably older — because they were once all-essential to self-preservation — because they made that primal stratum of consciousness out of which the nobler sentiments have slowly grown. Never can they be suffered to rule; but woe to whosoever would deny their immemorial rights!

III

OUT of these primitive, but — as may now be perceived — not irrational beliefs about the dead, there have been evolved moral sentiments unknown to Western civilization. These are well worth considering, as they will prove in harmony with the most advanced conception of ethics — and especially with that immense though yet indefinite expansion of the sense of duty which has followed upon the understanding of evolution. I do not know that we have any reason to congratulate ourselves upon the absence from our lives of the sentiments in question; I am even inclined to think that we may yet find it morally necessary to cultivate sentiments of the same kind. One of the surprises of our future will certainly be a return to beliefs and ideas long ago abandoned upon the mere assumption that they contained no truth — beliefs still called barbarous, pagan, mediæval, by those who condemn them out of traditional habit. Year after year the researches of science afford us new proof that the savage, the barbarian, the idolater, the monk, each and all have arrived, by different paths, as near to some one point of eternal truth as any thinker of the nineteenth century. We are now learning, also, that the theories of the astrologers and of the alchemists were but partially, not totally, wrong. We have reason even to suppose that no dream of the invisible world has ever been dreamed — that no hypothesis of the unseen has ever been imagined — which future science will not prove to have contained some germ of reality.

Foremost among the moral sentiments of Shintō is that of loving gratitude to the past — a sentiment having no real correspondence in our own emotional life. We know our past better than the Japanese know theirs; we have myriads of books recording or considering its every incident and condition: but we cannot in any sense be said to love it or to feel grateful to it. Critical recognitions of its merits and of its defects; some rare enthusiasms excited by its beauties; many strong denunciations of its mistakes: these represent the sum of our thoughts and feelings about it. The attitude of our scholarship in reviewing it is necessarily cold; that of our art, often more than generous; that of our religion, condemnatory for the most part. Whatever the point of view from which we study it, our attention is mainly directed to the work of the dead — either the visible work that makes our hearts beat a little faster than usual while looking at it, or the results of their thoughts and deeds in relation to the society of their time. Of past humanity as unity — of the millions long-buried as real kindred — we either think not at all, or think only with the same sort of curiosity that we give to the subject of extinct races. We do indeed find interest in the record of some individual lives that have left large marks in history; our emotions are stirred by the memories of great captains, statesmen, discoverers, reformers — but only because the magnitude of that which they accomplished appeals to our own ambitions, desires, egotisms, and not at all to our altruistic sentiments in ninety-nine cases out of a hundred. The nameless dead to whom we owe most we do not trouble ourselves about — we feel no gratitude, no love to them. We even find it difficult to persuade ourselves that the love of ancestors can possibly be a real, powerful, penetrating, life-moulding, religious emotion in any form of human society — which it certainly is in Japan. The mere idea is utterly foreign to our ways of thinking, feeling, acting. A partial reason for this, of course, is that we have no common faith in the existence of an active spiritual relation between our ancestors and ourselves. If we happen to be irreligious, we do not believe in ghosts. If we are profoundly religious, we think of the dead as removed from us by judgment — as absolutely separated from us during the period of our lives. It is true that among the peasantry of Roman Catholic countries there still exists a belief that the dead are permitted to return to earth once a year — on the night of All Souls. But even according to this belief they are not considered as related to the living by any stronger bond than memory; and they are thought of — as our collections of folk-lore bear witness — rather with fear than love.

In Japan the feeling toward the dead is utterly different. It is a feeling of grateful and reverential love. It is probably the most profound and powerful of the emotions of the race — that which especially directs national life and shapes national character. Patriotism belongs to it. Filial piety depends upon it. Family love is rooted in it. Loyalty is based upon it. The soldier who, to make a path for his comrades through the battle, deliberately flings away his life with a shout of "Teikoku manzai!" — the son or daughter who unmurmuring sacrifices all the happiness of existence for the sake, perhaps, of an undeserving or even cruel parent; the partisan who gives up friends, family, and fortune, rather than break the verbal promise made in other years to a now poverty-stricken master; the wife who ceremoniously robes herself in white, utters a prayer, and thrusts a sword into her throat to atone for a wrong done to strangers by her husband — all these obey the will and hear the approval of invisible witnesses. Even among the skeptical students of the new generation, this feeling survives many wrecks of faith, and the old sentiments are still uttered: "Never must we cause shame to our ancestors"; "it is our duty to give honor to our ancestors." During my former engagement as a teacher of English, it happened more than once that ignorance of the real meaning behind such phrases prompted me to change them in written composition. I would suggest, for example, that the expression, "to do honor *to the memory of* our ancestors," was more correct than the phrase given. I remember one day even attempting to explain why we ought not to speak of ancestors exactly as if they were living parents! Perhaps my pupils suspected me of trying to meddle with their beliefs; for the Japanese never think of an ancestor as having become "only a memory": their dead are alive.

Were there suddenly to arise within us the absolute certainty that our dead are still with us — seeing every act, knowing our every thought, hearing each word we utter, able to feel sympathy with us or anger against us, able to help us and delighted to receive our help, able to love us and greatly needing our love — it is quite certain that our conceptions of life and duty would be vastly changed. We should have to recognize our obligations to the past in a very solemn way. Now, with the man of the Far East, the constant presence of the dead has been a matter of conviction for thousands of years: he speaks to them daily; he tries to give them happiness; and, unless a professional criminal, he never quite forgets his duty towards them. No one, says Hirata, who constantly discharges that duty, will ever be disrespectful to the gods or to his living parents. "Such a man will also be loyal to his friends, and kind and gentle with his wife and children; for the essence of this devotion is in truth filial piety." And it is in this sentiment that the secret of much strange feeling in Japanese character must be sought. Far more foreign to our world of sentiment than the splendid courage with which death is faced, or the equanimity with which the most trying sacrifices are made, is the simple deep emotion of the boy who, in the presence of a Shintō shrine never seen before, suddenly feels the tears spring to his eyes. He is conscious in that moment of what we never emotionally recognize — the prodigious debt of the present to the past, and the duty of love to the dead.

KOKORO

IV

IF we think a little about our position as debtors, and our way of accepting that position, one striking difference between Western and Far-Eastern moral sentiment will become manifest.

There is nothing more awful than the mere fact of life as mystery when that fact first rushes fully into consciousness. Out of unknown darkness we rise a moment into sunlight, look about us, rejoice and suffer, pass on the vibration of our being to other beings, and fall back again into darkness. So a wave rises, catches the light, transmits its motion, and sinks back into sea. So a plant ascends from clay, unfolds its leaves to light and air, flowers, seeds, and becomes clay again. Only, the wave has no knowledge; the plant has no perceptions. Each human life seems no more than a parabolic curve of motion out of earth and back to earth; but in that brief interval of change it perceives the universe. The awfulness of the phenomenon is that nobody knows anything about it. No mortal can explain this most common, yet most incomprehensible of all facts — life in itself; yet every mortal who can think has been obliged betimes to think about it in relation to self.

I come out of mystery; I see the sky and the land, men and women and their works; and I know that I must return to mystery; and merely what this means not even the greatest of philosophers — not even Mr. Herbert Spencer — can tell me. We are all of us riddles to ourselves and riddles to each other; and space and motion and time are riddles; and matter is a riddle. About the before and the after neither the newly born nor the dead have any message for us. The child is dumb; the skull only grins. Nature has no consolation for us. Out of her formlessness issue forms which return to formlessness — that is all. The plant becomes clay; the clay becomes a plant. When the plant turns to clay, what becomes of the vibration which was its life? Does it go on existing viewlessly, like the forces that shape spectres of frondage in the frost upon a window-pane?

Within the horizon-circle of the infinite enigma, countless lesser enigmas, old as the world, awaited the coming of man. Œdipus had to face one Sphinx; humanity, thousands of thousands — all crouching among bones along the path of Time, and each with a deeper and a harder riddle. All the sphinxes have not been satisfied; myriads line the way of the future to devour lives yet unborn; but millions have been answered. We are now able to exist without perpetual horror because of the relative knowledge that guides us — the knowledge won out of the jaws of destruction.

All our knowledge is bequeathed knowledge. The dead have left us record of all they were able to learn about themselves and the world — about the laws of death and life — about things to be acquired and things to be avoided — about ways of making existence less painful than Nature willed it — about right and wrong and sorrow and happiness — about the error of selfishness, the wisdom of kindness, the obligation of sacrifice. They left us information of everything they could find out concerning climates and seasons and places — the sun and moon and stars — the motions and the composition of the universe. They bequeathed us also their delusions which long served the good purpose of saving us from falling into greater ones. They left us the story of their errors and efforts, their triumphs and failures, their pains and joys, their loves and hates — for warning or example. They expected our sympathy, because they toiled with the kindest wishes and hopes for us, and because they made our world. They cleared the land; they extirpated monsters; they tamed and taught the animals most useful to us.

The mother of Kullervo awoke within her tomb, and from the deeps of the dust she cried to him — "I have left thee the Dog, tied to a tree, that thou mayest go with him to the chase." [1]

They domesticated likewise the useful trees and plants; and they discovered the places and the powers of the metals. Later they created all that we call civilization — trusting us to correct such mistakes as they could not help making. The sum of

[1] Kalevala; thirty-sixth Rune.

their toil is incalculable; and all that they have given us ought surely to be very sacred, very precious, if only by reason of the infinite pain and thought which it cost. Yet what Occidental dreams of saying daily, like the Shintō believer?

Ye forefathers of the generations, and of our families, and of our kindred — unto you, the founders of our homes, we utter the gladness of our thanks.

None. It is not only because we think the dead cannot hear, but because we have not been trained for generations to exercise our powers of sympathetic mental representation except within a very narrow circle — the family circle. The Occidental family circle is a very small affair indeed compared with the Oriental family circle. In this nineteenth century the Occidental family is almost disintegrated; it practically means little more than husband, wife, and children well under age. The Oriental family means not only parents and their blood-kindred, but grandparents and their kindred, and great-grandparents, and all the dead behind them. This idea of the family cultivates sympathetic representation to such a degree that the range of the emotion belonging to such representation may extend, as in Japan, to many groups and sub-groups of living families, and even, in time of national peril, to the whole nation as one great family: a feeling much deeper than what we call patriotism. As a religious emotion the feeling is infinitely extended to all the past; the blended sense of love, of loyalty, and of gratitude is not less real, though necessarily more vague, than the feeling to living kindred.

In the West, after the destruction of antique society, no such feeling could remain. The beliefs that condemned the ancients to hell, and forbade the praise of their works — the doctrine that trained us to return thanks for everything to the God of the Hebrews — created habits of thought and habits of thoughtlessness, both inimical to every feeling of gratitude to the past. Then, with the decay of theology and the dawn of larger knowledge, came the teaching that the dead had no choice in their work — they had obeyed necessity, and we had only received from them of necessity the results of necessity. And to-day we still fail to recognize that the necessity itself ought to compel our sympathies with those who obeyed it, and that its bequeathed results are as pathetic as they are precious. Such thoughts rarely occur to us even in regard to the work of the living who serve us. We consider the cost of a thing purchased or obtained to ourselves; about its cost in effort to the producer we do not allow ourselves to think: indeed, we should be laughed at for any exhibition of conscience on the subject. And our equal insensibility to the pathetic meaning of the work of the past, and to that of the work of the present, largely explains the wastefulness of our civilization — the reckless consumption by luxury of the labor of years in the pleasure of an hour — the inhumanity of the thousands of unthinking rich, each of whom dissipates yearly in the gratification of totally unnecessary wants the price of a hundred human lives. The cannibals of civilization are unconsciously more cruel than those of savagery, and require much more flesh. The deeper humanity — the cosmic emotion of humanity — is essentially the enemy of useless luxury, and essentially opposed to any form of society which places no restraints upon the gratifications of sense or the pleasures of egotism.

In the Far East, on the other hand, the moral duty of simplicity of life has been taught from very ancient times, because ancestor-worship had developed and cultivated this cosmic emotion of humanity which we lack, but which we shall certainly be obliged to acquire at a later day, simply to save ourselves from extermination. Two sayings of Iyeyasu exemplify the Oriental sentiment. When virtually master of the empire, this greatest of Japanese soldiers and statesmen was seen one day cleaning and smoothing with his own hands an old dusty pair of silk hakama or trousers. "What you see me do," he said to a retainer, "I am not doing because I think of the worth of the garment in itself, but because I think of what it needed to produce it. It is the result of the toil of a poor woman; and that is why I value it. *If we do not think, while using things, of the time and effort required to make them — then our want of consideration puts us on a level with the beasts.*" Again, in the days of his greatest wealth, we hear of him rebuking his wife for wishing to furnish him too often with new clothing. "When I think," he protested, "of the multitudes around me, and of the generations to come after me, I feel it my duty to be very sparing, for their sake, of the goods in my possession." Nor has this spirit of simplicity yet departed from Japan. Even the Emperor and Empress, in the privacy of their own apartments, continue to live as simply as their subjects, and devote most of their revenue to the alleviation of public distress.

v

IT is through the teachings of evolution that there will ultimately be developed in the West a moral recognition of duty to the past like that which ancestor-worship created in the Far East. For even to-day whoever has mastered the first principles of the new philosophy cannot look at the commonest product of man's handiwork without perceiving something of its evolutional history. The most ordinary utensil will appear to him, not the mere product of individual capacity on the part of carpenter or potter, smith or cutler, but the product of experiment continued through thousands of years with methods, with materials, and with forms. Nor will it be possible for him to consider the vast time and toil necessitated in the evolution of any mechanical appliance, and yet experience no generous sentiment. Coming generations *must* think of the material bequests of the past in relation to dead humanity.

ABOUT ANCESTOR-WORSHIP

But in the development of this "cosmic emotion" of humanity, a much more powerful factor than recognition of our material indebtedness to the past will be the recognition of our psychical indebtedness. For we owe to the dead our immaterial world also — the world that lives within us — the world of all that is lovable in impulse, emotion, thought. Whosoever understands scientifically what human goodness is, and the terrible cost of making it, can find in the commonest phases of the humblest lives that beauty which is divine, and can feel that in one sense our dead are truly gods.

So long as we supposed the woman soul one in itself — a something specially created to fit one particular physical being — the beauty and the wonder of mother-love could never be fully revealed to us. But with deeper knowledge we must perceive that the inherited love of myriads of millions of dead mothers has been treasured up in one life; that only thus can be interpreted the infinite sweetness of the speech which the infant hears — the infinite tenderness of the look of caress which meets its gaze. Unhappy the mortal who has not known these; yet what mortal can adequately speak of them! Truly is mother-love divine; for everything by human recognition called divine is summed up in that love; and every woman uttering and transmitting its highest expression is more than the mother of man: she is the *Mater Dei*.

KOKORO

Needless to speak here about the ghostliness of first love, sexual love, which is illusion — because the passion and the beauty of the dead revive in it, to dazzle, to delude, and to bewitch. It is very, very wonderful; but it is not all good, because it is not all true. The real charm of woman in herself is that which comes later — when all the illusions fade away to reveal a reality, lovelier than any illusion, which has been evolving behind the phantom-curtain of them. What is the divine magic of the woman thus perceived? Only the affection, the sweetness, the faith, the unselfishness, the intuitions of millions of buried hearts. All live again; all throb anew, in every fresh warm beat of her own.

Certain amazing faculties exhibited in the highest social life tell in another way the story of soul structure built up by dead lives. Wonderful is the man who can really "be all things to all men," or the woman who can make herself twenty, fifty, a hundred different women — comprehending all, penetrating all, unerring to estimate all others; seeming to have no individual self, but only selves innumerable; able to meet each varying personality with a soul exactly toned to the tone of that to be encountered. Rare these characters are, but not so rare that the traveler is unlikely to meet one or two of them in any cultivated society which he has a chance of studying. They are essentially multiple beings — so visibly multiple that even those who think of the Ego as single have to describe them as "highly complex." Nevertheless this manifestation of forty or fifty different characters in the same person is a phenomenon so remarkable (especially remarkable because it is commonly manifested in youth long before relative experience could possibly account for it) that I cannot but wonder how few persons frankly realize its signification.

So likewise with what have been termed the "intuitions" of some forms of genius — particularly those which relate to the representation of the emotions. A Shakespeare would always remain incomprehensible on the ancient soul-theory. Taine attempted to explain him by the phrase, "a perfect imagination"; and the phrase reaches far into the truth. But what is the meaning of a perfect imagination? Enormous multiplicity of soul-life — countless past existences revived in one. Nothing else can explain it. . . . It is not, however, in the world of pure intellect that the story of psychical complexity is most admirable: it is in the world which speaks to our simplest emotions of love, honor, sympathy, heroism.

"But by such a theory," some critic may observe, "the source of impulses to heroism is also the source of the impulses that people jails. Both are of the dead." This is true. We inherited evil as well as good. Being composites only — still evolving, still becoming — we inherit imperfections. But the survival of the fittest in impulses is certainly proven by the average moral condition of humanity — using the word "fittest" in its ethical sense. In spite of all the misery and vice and crime, nowhere so terribly developed as under our own so-called Christian civilization, the fact must be patent to any one who has lived much, traveled much, and thought much, that the mass of humanity is good, and therefore that the vast majority of impulses bequeathed us by past humanity is good. Also it is certain that the more normal a social condition, the better its humanity. Through all the past the good Kami have always managed to keep the bad Kami from controlling the world. And with the acceptation of this truth, our future ideas of wrong and of right must take immense expansion. Just as a heroism, or any act of pure goodness for a noble end, must assume a preciousness heretofore unsuspected — so a real crime must come to be regarded as a crime less against the existing individual or society, than against the sum of human experience, and the whole past struggle of ethical aspiration. Real goodness will, therefore, be more prized, and real crime less leniently judged. And the early Shintō teaching, that no code of ethics is necessary — that the right rule of human conduct can always be known by consulting the heart — is a teaching which will doubtless be accepted by a more perfect humanity than that of the present.

VI

"EVOLUTION," the reader may say, "does indeed show through its doctrine of heredity that the living are in one sense really controlled by the dead. But it also shows that the dead are within us, not without us. They are part of us; there is no proof that they have any existence which is not our own. Gratitude to the past would, therefore, be gratitude to ourselves; love of the dead would be self-love. So that your attempt at analogy ends in the absurd."

No. Ancestor-worship in its primitive form may be a symbol only of truth. It may be an index or foreshadowing only of the new moral duty which larger knowledge must force upon us: the duty of reverence and obedience to the sacrificial past of human ethical experience. But it may also be much more. The facts of heredity can never afford but half an explanation of the facts of psychology. A plant produces ten, twenty, a hundred plants without yielding up its own life in the process. An animal gives birth to many young, yet lives on with all its physical capacities and its small powers of thought undiminished. Children are born; and the parents survive them. Inherited the mental life certainly is, not less than the physical; yet the reproductive cells, the least specialized of all cells, whether in plant or in animal, never take away, but only repeat the parental being. Continually multiplying, each conveys and transmits the whole experience of a race;

yet leaves the whole experience of the race behind it. Here is the marvel inexplicable: the self-multiplication of physical and psychical being — life after life thrown off from the parent life, each to become complete and reproductive. Were all the parental life given to the offspring, heredity might be said to favor the doctrine of materialism. But like the deities of Hindoo legend, the Self multiplies and still remains the same, with full capacities for continued multiplication. Shintō has its doctrine of souls multiplying by fission; but the facts of psychological emanation are infinitely more wonderful than any theory.

The great religions have recognized that heredity could not explain the whole question of self — could not account for the fate of the original residual self. So they have generally united in holding the inner independent of the outer being. Science can no more fully decide the issues they have raised than it can decide the nature of Reality-in-itself. Again we may vainly ask, What becomes of the forces which constituted the vitality of a dead plant? Much more difficult the question, What becomes of the sensations which formed the psychical life of a dead man? — since nobody can explain the simplest sensation. We know only that during life certain active forces within the body of the plant or the body of the man adjusted themselves continually to outer forces; and that after the interior forces could no longer respond to the pressure of the exterior forces

— then the body in which the former were stored was dissolved into the elements out of which it had been built up. We know nothing more of the ultimate nature of those elements than we know of the ultimate nature of the tendencies which united them. But we have more right to believe the ultimates of life persist after the dissolution of the forms they created, than to believe they cease. The theory of spontaneous generation (misnamed, for only in a qualified sense can the term "spontaneous" be applied to the theory of the beginnings of mundane life) is a theory which the evolutionist must accept, and which can frighten none aware of the evidence of chemistry that matter itself is in evolution. The real theory (not the theory of organized life beginning in bottled infusions, but of the life primordial arising upon a planetary surface) has enormous — nay, infinite — spiritual significance. It requires the belief that all potentialities of life and thought and emotion pass from nebula to universe, from system to system, from star to planet or moon, and again back to cyclonic storms of atomicity; it means that tendencies survive sunburnings — survive all cosmic evolutions and disintegrations. The elements are evolutionary products only; and the difference of universe from universe must be the creation of tendencies — of a form of heredity too vast and complex for imagination. There is no chance. There is only law. Each fresh evolution must be influenced by previous evolutions — just as each individual human life is influenced by the experience of all the lives in its ancestral chain. Must not the tendencies even of the ancestral forms of matter be inherited by the forms of matter to come; and may not the acts and thoughts of men even now be helping to shape the character of future worlds? No longer is it possible to say that the dreams of the Alchemists were absurdities. And no longer can we even assert that all material phenomena are not determined, as in the thought of the ancient East, by soul-polarities.

Whether our dead do or do not continue to dwell without us as well as within us — a question not to be decided in our present undeveloped state of comparative blindness — certain it is that the testimony of cosmic facts accords with one weird belief of Shintō: the belief that all things are determined by the dead — whether by ghosts of men or ghosts of worlds. Even as our personal lives are ruled by the now viewless lives of the past, so doubtless the life of our Earth, and of the system to which it belongs, is ruled by ghosts of spheres innumerable: dead universes — dead suns and planets and moons — as forms long since dissolved into the night, but as forces immortal and eternally working.

Back to the Sun, indeed, like the Shintōist, we can trace our descent; yet we know that even there the beginning of us was not. Infinitely more remote in time than a million sun-lives was that beginning — if it can truly be said there was a beginning.

The teaching of Evolution is that we are one with that unknown Ultimate, of which matter and human mind are but ever-changing manifestations. The teaching of Evolution is also that each of us is many, yet that all of us are still one with each other and with the cosmos; that we must know all past humanity not only in ourselves, but likewise in the preciousness and beauty of every fellow-life; that we can best love ourselves in others; that we shall best serve ourselves in others; that forms are but veils and phantoms; and that to the formless Infinite alone really belong all human emotions, whether of the living or the dead.

KITZUKI: THE MOST ANCIENT SHRINE OF JAPAN

SHINKOKU is the sacred name of Japan — Shinkoku, "The Country of the Gods"; and of all Shinkoku the most holy ground is the land of Izumo. Hither from the blue Plain of High Heaven first came to dwell awhile the Earth-Makers, Izanagi and Izanami, the parents of gods and of men; somewhere upon the border of this land was Izanami buried; and out of this land into the black realm of the dead did Izanagi follow after her, and seek in vain to bring her back again. And the tale of his descent into that strange nether world, and of what there befell him, is it not written in the Kojiki?[1] And of all legends primeval concerning the Underworld this story is one of the weirdest — more weird than even the Assyrian legend of the Descent of Ishtar.

Even as Izumo is especially the province of the gods, and the place of the childhood of the race by whom Izanagi and Izanami are yet worshiped, so is Kitzuki of Izumo especially the city of the gods, and its immemorial temple the earliest home of the ancient faith, the great religion of Shintō.

[1] The most ancient book extant in the archaic tongue of Japan. It is the most sacred scripture of Shintō. It has been admirably translated, with copious notes and commentaries, by Professor Basil Hall Chamberlain, of Tōkyō.

KITZUKI

Now to visit Kitzuki has been my most earnest ambition since I learned the legends of the Kojiki concerning it; and this ambition has been stimulated by the discovery that very few Europeans have visited Kitzuki, and that none have been admitted into the great temple itself. Some, indeed, were not allowed even to approach the temple court. But I trust that I shall be somewhat more fortunate; for I have a letter of introduction from my dear friend Nishida Sentarō, who is also a personal friend of the high pontiff of Kitzuki. I am thus assured that even should I not be permitted to enter the temple — a privilege accorded to but few among the Japanese themselves — I shall at least have the honor of an interview with the Guji, or Spiritual Governor of Kitzuki, Senke Takanori, whose princely family trace back their descent to the Goddess of the Sun.[1]

I

I LEAVE Matsue for Kitzuki early in the afternoon of a beautiful September day; taking passage upon a tiny steamer in which everything, from engines to awnings, is lilliputian. In the cabin one must kneel. Under the awnings one cannot possibly

[1] The genealogy of the family is published in a curious little book with which I was presented at Kitzuki. Senke Takanori is the eighty-first Pontiff Governor (formerly called Kokuzō) of Kitzuki. His lineage is traced back through sixty-five generations of Kokuzō and sixteen generations of earthly deities to Ama-terasu and her brother Susanoō-no-mikoto.

stand upright. But the miniature craft is neat and pretty as a toy model, and moves with surprising swiftness and steadiness. A handsome naked boy is busy serving the passengers with cups of tea and with cakes, and setting little charcoal furnaces before those who desire to smoke: for all of which a payment of about three quarters of a cent is expected.

I escape from the awnings to climb upon the cabin roof for a view; and the view is indescribably lovely. Over the lucent level of the lake we are steaming toward a far-away heaping of beautiful shapes, colored with that strangely delicate blue which tints all distances in the Japanese atmosphere — shapes of peaks and headlands looming up from the lake verge against a porcelain-white horizon. They show no details whatever. Silhouettes only they are — masses of absolutely pure color. To left and right, framing in the Shinjiko, are superb green surgings of wooded hills. Great Yakuno-San is the loftiest mountain before us, northwest. Southeast, behind us, the city has vanished; but proudly towering beyond looms Daisen — enormous, ghostly blue and ghostly white, lifting the cusps of its dead crater into the region of eternal snow. Over all arches a sky of color faint as a dream.

There seems to be a sense of divine magic in the very atmosphere, through all the luminous day, brooding over the vapory land, over the ghostly blue of the flood — a sense of Shintō. With my

fancy full of the legends of the Kojiki, the rhythmic
chant of the engines comes to my ears as the rhythm
of a Shintō ritual mingled with the names of gods:

Koto-shiro-nushi-no-Kami,
Oho-kuni-nushi-no-Kami.

II

THE great range on the right grows loftier as we
steam on; and its hills, always slowly advancing
toward us, begin to reveal all the rich details of
their foliage. And lo! on the tip of one grand wood-
clad peak is visible against the pure sky the many-
angled roof of a great Buddhist temple. That is
the temple of Ichibata, upon the mountain Ichibata-
yama, the temple of Yakushi-Nyorai, the Physician
of Souls. But at Ichibata he reveals himself more
specially as the healer of bodies, the Buddha who
giveth sight unto the blind. It is believed that
whosoever has an affection of the eyes will be made
well by praying earnestly at that great shrine; and
thither from many distant provinces do afflicted
thousands make pilgrimage, ascending the long
weary mountain path and the six hundred and
forty steps of stone leading to the windy temple
court upon the summit, whence may be seen one
of the loveliest landscapes in Japan. There the
pilgrims wash their eyes with the water of the sacred
spring, and kneel before the shrine and murmur
the holy formula of Ichibata: "On-koro-koro-sen-
dai-matōki-sowaka"—words of which the meaning

has long been forgotten, like that of many a Buddhist invocation; Sanscrit words transliterated into Chinese, and thence into Japanese, which are understood by learned priests alone, yet are known by heart throughout the land, and uttered with the utmost fervor of devotion.

I descend from the cabin roof, and squat upon the deck, under the awnings, to have a smoke with Akira. And I ask:

"How many Buddhas are there, O Akira? Is the number of the Enlightened known?"

"Countless the Buddhas are," makes answer Akira; "yet there is truly but one Buddha; the many are forms only. Each of us contains a future Buddha. Alike we all are except in that we are more or less unconscious of the truth. But the vulgar may not understand these things, and so seek refuge in symbols and in forms."

"And the Kami — the deities of Shintō?"

"Of Shintō I know little. But there are eight hundred myriads of Kami in the Plain of High Heaven — so says the Ancient Book. Of these, three thousand one hundred and thirty and two dwell in the various provinces of the land; being enshrined in two thousand eight hundred and sixty-one temples. And the tenth month of our year is called the 'No-God-Month,' because in that month all the deities leave their temples to assemble in the province of Izumo, at the great temple of Ki-tzuki; and for the same reason that month is called

in Izumo, and only in Izumo, the 'God-is-Month.'
But educated persons sometimes call it the 'God-
Present-Festival,' using Chinese words. Then it is believed the serpents come from the sea to the land,
and coil upon the sambo, which is the table of the
gods, for the serpents announce the coming; and the
Dragon-King sends messengers to the temples of Izanagi and Izanami, the parents of gods and men."

"O Akira, many millions of Kami there must be
of whom I shall always remain ignorant, for there
is a limit to the power of memory; but tell me something of the gods whose names are most seldom uttered, the deities of strange places and of strange
things, the most extraordinary gods."

"You cannot learn much about them from me,"
replies Akira. "You will have to ask others more
learned than I. But there are gods with whom it is
not desirable to become acquainted. Such are the
God of Poverty, and the God of Hunger, and the
God of Penuriousness, and the God of Hindrances
and Obstacles. These are of dark color, like the
clouds of gloomy days, and their faces are like the
faces of gaki." [1]

"With the God of Hindrances and Obstacles, O
Akira, I have had more than a passing acquaintance.
Tell me of the others."

"I know little about any of them," answers
Akira, "excepting Bimbogami. It is said there are

[1] In Sanscrit "pretas." The gaki are the famished ghosts of that
Circle of Torment in hell whereof the penance is hunger; and the mouths
of some are "smaller than the points of needles."

two gods who always go together — Fuku-no-Kami, who is the God of Luck, and Bimbogami, who is the God of Poverty. The first is white, and the second is black."

"Because the last," I venture to interrupt, "is only the shadow of the first. Fuku-no-Kami is the Shadow-Caster, and Bimbogami the Shadow; and I have observed, in wandering about this world, that wherever the one goeth, eternally followeth after him the other."

Akira refuses his assent to this interpretation, and resumes:

"When Bimbogami once begins to follow any one it is extremely difficult to be free from him again. In the village of Umitsu, which is in the province of Omi, and not far from Kyōto, there once lived a Buddhist priest who during many years was grievously tormented by Bimbogami. He tried oftentimes without avail to drive him away; then he strove to deceive him by proclaiming aloud to all the people that he was going to Kyōto. But instead of going to Kyōto he went to Tsuruga, in the province of Echizen; and when he reached the inn at Tsuruga there came forth to meet him a boy lean and wan like a gaki. The boy said to him, 'I have been waiting for you'; — and the boy was Bimbogami.

"There was another priest who for sixty years had tried in vain to get rid of Bimbogami, and who resolved at last to go to a distant province.

On the night after he had formed this resolve he had a strange dream, in which he saw a very much emaciated boy, naked and dirty, weaving sandals of straw (waraji), such as pilgrims and runners wear; and he made so many that the priest wondered, and asked him, 'For what purpose are you making so many sandals?' And the boy answered, 'I am going to travel with you. I am Bimbogami.'"

"Then is there no way, Akira, by which Bimbogami may be driven away?"

"It is written," replies Akira, "in the book called Jizō-Kyō-Kosui that the aged Enjobo, a priest dwelling in the province of Owari, was able to get rid of Bimbogami by means of a charm. On the last day of the last month of the year he and his disciples and other priests of the Shingon sect took branches of peach-trees and recited a formula, and then, with the branches, imitated the action of driving a person out of the temple, after which they shut all the gates and recited other formulas. The same night Enjobo dreamed of a skeleton priest in a broken temple weeping alone, and the skeleton priest said to him, 'After I had been with you for so many years, how could you drive me away?' But always thereafter until the day of his death, Enjobo lived in prosperity."

III

For an hour and a half the ranges to left and right alternately recede and approach. Beautiful blue shapes glide toward us, change to green, and then, slowly drifting behind us, are all blue again. But the far mountains immediately before us — immovable, unchanging — always remain ghosts. Suddenly the little steamer turns straight into the land — a land so low that it came into sight quite unexpectedly — and we puff up a narrow stream between rice-fields to a queer, quaint, pretty village on the canal bank — Shōbara. Here I must hire jinrikisha to take us to Kitzuki.

There is not time to see much of Shōbara if I hope to reach Kitzuki before bedtime, and I have only a flying vision of one long wide street (so picturesque that I wish I could pass a day in it), as our kuruma rush through the little town into the open country, into a vast plain covered with rice-fields. The road itself is only a broad dike, barely wide enough for two jinrikisha to pass each other upon it. On each side the superb plain is bounded by a mountain range shutting off the white horizon. There is a vast silence, an immense sense of dreamy peace, and a glorious soft vapory light over everything, as we roll into the country of Hyasugi to Kaminawoë. The jagged range on the left is Shusai-yama, all sharply green, with the giant Daikoku-yama overtopping all; and its peaks bear the names of gods. Much more remote, upon our right, enormous, pansy-purple, tower the shapes of the Kita-yama, or northern range; filing away in tremendous procession toward the sunset, fading more and more as they stretch west, to vanish suddenly at last, after the ghostliest conceivable manner, into the uttermost day.

All this is beautiful; yet there is no change while hours pass. Always the way winds on through miles of rice-fields, white-speckled with paper-winged shafts which are arrows of prayer. Always the voice of frogs — a sound as of infinite bubbling. Always the green range on the left, the purple on the right, fading westward into a tall file of tinted spectres which always melt into nothing at last, as if they were made of air. The monotony of the scene is broken only by our occasional passing through some pretty Japanese village, or by the appearance of a curious statue or monument at an angle of the path, a roadside Jizō, or the grave of a wrestler, such as may be seen on the bank of the Hiagawa, a huge slab of granite sculptured with the words, "Ikumo Matsu kikusuki."

But after reaching Kandogori, and passing over a broad but shallow river, a fresh detail appears in the landscape. Above the mountain chain on our left looms a colossal blue silhouette, almost saddle-shaped, recognizable by its outline as a once mighty volcano. It is now known by various names, but it was called in ancient times Sa-hime-yama; and it has its Shintō legend.

It is said that in the beginning the God of Izumo, gazing over the land, said, "This new land of Izumo is a land of but small extent, so I will make it a larger land by adding unto it." Having so said, he looked about him over to Korea, and there he saw land which was good for the purpose. With a great rope he dragged therefrom four islands, and added the land of them to Izumo. The first island was called Ya-o-yo-ne, and it formed the land where Kitzuki now is. The second island was called Sada-no-kuni, and is at this day the site of the holy temple where all the gods do yearly hold their second assembly, after having first gathered together at Kitzuki. The third island was called in its new place Kura-mi-no-kuni, which now forms Shimane-gori. The fourth island became that place where stands the temple of the great god at whose shrine are delivered unto the faithful the charms which protect the rice-fields.[1]

Now in drawing these islands across the sea into their several places the god looped his rope over the mighty mountain of Daisen and over the mountain Sa-hime-yama; and they both bear the marks of that wondrous rope even unto this day. As for the rope itself, part of it was changed into the long island of ancient times [2] called Yomi-ga-hama, and a part into the Long Beach of Sono.

After we pass the Hori-kawa the road narrows

[1] Mionoseki.
[2] Now solidly united with the mainland. Many extraordinary changes, of rare interest to the physiographer and geologist, have actually taken place along the coast of Izumo and in the neighborhood of the great lake. Even now, each year some change occurs. I have seen several very strange ones.

and becomes rougher and rougher, but always draws nearer to the Kita-yama range. Toward sundown we have come close enough to the great hills to discern the details of their foliage. The path begins to rise; we ascend slowly through the gathering dusk. At last there appears before us a great multitude of twinkling lights. We have reached Kitzuki. the holy city.

IV

OVER a long bridge and under a tall torii we roll into upward-sloping streets. Like Enoshima, Kitzuki has a torii for its city gate; but the torii is not of bronze. Then a flying vision of open lamp-lighted shop-fronts, and lines of luminous shōji under high-tilted eaves, and Buddhist gateways guarded by lions of stone, and long, low, tile-coped walls of temple courts overtopped by garden shrubbery, and Shintō shrines prefaced by other tall torii; but no sign of the great temple itself. It lies toward the rear of the city proper, at the foot of the wooded mountains; and we are too tired and hungry to visit it now. So we halt before a spacious and comfortable-seeming inn — the best, indeed, in Kitzuki — and rest ourselves and eat, and drink saké out of exquisite little porcelain cups, the gift of some pretty singing-girl to the hotel. Thereafter, as it has become much too late to visit the Guji, I send to his residence by a messenger my letter of introduction, with an humble request in Akira's handwriting, that I may be allowed to present myself at the house before noon the next day.

Then the landlord of the hotel, who seems to be a very kindly person, comes to us with lighted paper lanterns, and invites us to accompany him to the Oho-yashiro.

Most of the houses have already closed their wooden sliding doors for the night, so that the streets are dark, and the lanterns of our landlord indispensable; for there is no moon, and the night is starless. We walk along the main street for a distance of about six squares, and then, making a turn, find ourselves before a superb bronze torii, the gateway to the great temple avenue.

V

EFFACING colors and obliterating distances, night always magnifies by suggestion the aspect of large spaces and the effect of large objects. Viewed by the vague light of paper lanterns, the approach to the great shrine is an imposing surprise — such a surprise that I feel regret at the mere thought of having to see it to-morrow by disenchanting day: a superb avenue lined with colossal trees, and ranging away out of sight under a succession of giant torii, from which are suspended enormous shime-nawa, well worthy the grasp of that Heavenly-Hand-Strength Deity whose symbols they are. But, more than by the torii and their festooned symbols,

315

the dim majesty of the huge avenue is enhanced by the prodigious trees — many perhaps thousands of years old — gnarled pines whose shaggy summits are lost in darkness. Some of the mighty trunks are surrounded with a rope of straw: these trees are sacred. The vast roots, far-reaching in every direction, look in the lantern-light like a writhing and crawling of dragons.

The avenue is certainly not less than a quarter of a mile in length; it crosses two bridges and passes between two sacred groves. All the broad lands on either side of it belong to the temple. Formerly no foreigner was permitted to pass beyond the middle torii. The avenue terminates at a lofty wall pierced by a gateway resembling the gateways of Buddhist temple courts, but very massive. This is the entrance to the outer court; the ponderous doors are still open, and many shadowy figures are passing in or out.

Within the court all is darkness, against which pale yellow lights are gliding to and fro like a multitude of enormous fireflies — the lanterns of pilgrims. I can distinguish only the looming of immense buildings to left and right, constructed with colossal timbers. Our guide traverses a very large court, passes into a second, and halts before an imposing structure whose doors are still open. Above them, by the lantern glow, I can see a marvelous frieze of dragons and water, carved in some rich wood by the hand of a master. Within I can see the symbols of Shintō, in a side shrine on the left; and directly before us the lanterns reveal a surface of matted floor vaster than anything I had expected to find. Therefrom I can divine the scale of the edifice which I suppose to be the temple. But the landlord tells us this is not the temple, but only the Haiden or Hall of Prayer, before which the people make their orisons. By day, through the open doors, the temple can be seen. But we cannot see it to-night, and but few visitors are permitted to go in. "The people do not enter even the courts of the great shrine, for the most part," interpret Akira; "they pray before it at a distance. Listen!"

All about me in the shadow I hear a sound like the plashing and dashing of water — the clapping of many hands in Shintō prayer.

"But this is nothing," says the landlord; "there are but few here now. Wait until to-morrow, which is a festival day."

As we wend our way back along the great avenue, under the torii and the giant trees, Akira interprets for me what our landlord tells him about the sacred serpent.

"The little serpent," he says, "is called by the people the august Dragon-Serpent; for it is sent by the Dragon-King to announce the coming of the gods. The sea darkens and rises and roars before the coming of Ryū-ja-Sama. Ryū-ja-Sama we call it because it is the messenger of Ryūgū-jō, the palace of the dragons; but it is also called Hakuja, or the White Serpent." [1]

"Does the little serpent come to the temple of its own accord?"

"Oh, no. It is caught by the fishermen. And only one can be caught in a year, because only one is sent; and whoever catches it and brings it either to the Kitzuki-no-oho-yashiro, or to the temple Sada-jinja, where the gods hold their second assembly during the Kami-ari-zuki, receives one hyō [2] of rice in recompense. It costs much labor and time to catch a serpent; but whoever captures one is sure to become rich in after time." [3]

[1] The Hakuja, or White Serpent, is also the servant of Benten, or Ben-zai-ten, Goddess of Love, of Beauty, of Eloquence, and of the Sea. "The Hakuja has the face of an ancient man, with white eyebrows, and wears upon its head a crown." Both goddess and serpent can be identified with ancient Indian mythological beings, and Buddhism first introduced both into Japan. Among the people, especially perhaps in Izumo, certain divinities of Buddhism are often identified, or rather confused, with certain Kami, in popular worship and parlance.

Since this sketch was written, I have had opportunity of seeing a Ryū-ja within a few hours after its capture. It was between two and three feet long, and about one inch in diameter at its thickest girth. The upper part of the body was a very dark brown, and the belly yellowish white; toward the tail there were some beautiful yellowish mottlings. The body was not cylindrical, but curiously four-sided, — like those elaborately woven whip-lashes which have four edges. The tail was flat and triangular, like that of certain fish. A Japanese teacher, Mr. Watanabe, of the Normal School of Matsue, identified the little creature as a hydrophid of the species called *Pelamis bicolor*. It is so seldom seen, however, that I think the foregoing superficial description of it may not be without interest to some readers.

[2] Ippyo, one hyō; 2½ hyō make one koku = 5.13 bushels. The word hyō means also the bag made to contain one hyō.

[3] Either at Kitzuki or at Sada it is possible sometimes to buy a serpent. On many a "household-god-shelf" in Matsue the little serpent

"There are many deities enshrined at Kitzuki, are there not?" I ask.

"Yes; but the great deity of Kitzuki is Oho-kuni-nushi-no-Kami,[1] whom the people more commonly call Daikoku. Here also is worshiped his son, whom many call Ebisu. These deities are usually pictured together: Daikoku seated upon bales of rice, holding the Red Sun against his breast with one hand, and in the other grasping the magical mallet of which a single stroke gives wealth; and Ebisu bearing a fishing-rod, and holding under his arm a great tai-fish. These gods are always represented with smiling faces; and both have great ears, which are the sign of wealth and fortune."

VI

A LITTLE wearied by the day's journeying, I get to bed early, and sleep as dreamlessly as a plant

may be seen. I saw one that had become brittle and black with age, but was excellently preserved by some process of which I did not learn the nature. It had been admirably posed in a tiny wire cage, made to fit exactly into a small shrine of white wood, and must have been, when alive, about two feet four inches in length. A little lamp was lighted daily before it, and some Shintō formula recited by the poor family to whom it belonged.

[1] Translated by Professor Chamberlain the "Deity Master-of-the-Great-Land" — one of the most ancient divinities of Japan, but in popular worship confounded with Daikoku, God of Wealth. His son, Koto-shiro-nushi-no-Kami, is similarly confounded with Ebisu, or Yebisu, the patron of honest labor. The origin of the Shintō custom of clapping the hands in prayer is said by some Japanese writers to have been a sign given by Koto-shiro-nushi-no-Kami.

Both deities are represented by Japanese art in a variety of ways. Some of the twin images of them sold at Kitzuki are extremely pretty as well as curious.

until I am awakened about daylight by a heavy, regular, bumping sound, shaking the wooden pillow on which my ear rests — the sound of the katsu of the kometsuki beginning his eternal labor of rice-cleaning. Then the pretty musume of the inn opens the chamber to the fresh mountain air and the early sun, rolls back all the wooden shutters into their casings behind the gallery, takes down the brown mosquito net, brings a hibachi with freshly kindled charcoal for my morning smoke, and trips away to get our breakfast.

Early as it is when she returns, she brings word that a messenger has already arrived from the Guji, Senke Takanori, high descendant of the Goddess of the Sun. The messenger is a dignified young Shintō priest, clad in the ordinary Japanese full costume, but wearing also a superb pair of blue silken hakama, or Japanese ceremonial trousers, widening picturesquely towards the feet. He accepts my invitation to a cup of tea, and informs me that his august master is waiting for us at the temple.

This is delightful news, but we cannot go at once. Akira's attire is pronounced by the messenger to be defective. Akira must don fresh white tabi and put on hakama before going into the august presence: no one may enter thereinto without hakama. Happily Akira is able to borrow a pair of hakama from the landlord; and, after having arranged ourselves as neatly as we can, we take our way to the temple, guided by the messenger.

VII

I AM agreeably surprised to find, as we pass again under a magnificent bronze torii which I admired the night before, that the approaches to the temple lose very little of their imposing character when seen for the first time by sunlight. The majesty of the trees remains astonishing; the vista of the avenue is grand; and the vast spaces of groves and grounds to right and left are even more impressive than I had imagined. Multitudes of pilgrims are going and coming; but the whole population of a province might move along such an avenue without jostling. Before the gate of the first court a Shintō priest in full sacerdotal costume waits to receive us: an elderly man, with a pleasant kindly face. The messenger commits us to his charge, and vanishes through the gateway, while the elderly priest, whose name is Sasa, leads the way.

Already I can hear a heavy sound, as of surf, within the temple court; and as we advance the sound becomes sharper and recognizable — a volleying of handclaps. And passing the great gate, I see thousands of pilgrims before the Haiden, the same huge structure which I visited last night. None enter there: all stand before the dragon-swarming doorway, and cast their offerings into the money-chest placed before the threshold; many making contribution of small coin, the very poorest throwing only a handful of rice into the box.[1] Then they clap their hands and bow their heads before the threshold, and reverently gaze through the Hall of Prayer at the loftier edifice, the Holy of Holies, beyond it. Each pilgrim remains but a little while, and claps his hands but four times; yet so many are coming and going that the sound of the clapping is like the sound of a cataract.

Passing by the multitude of worshipers to the other side of the Haiden, we find ourselves at the foot of a broad flight of iron-bound steps leading to the great sanctuary — steps which I am told no European before me was ever permitted to approach. On the lower steps the priests of the temple, in full ceremonial costume, are waiting to receive us. Tall men they are, robed in violet and purple silks shot through with dragon-patterns in gold. Their lofty fantastic headdresses, their voluminous and beautiful costume, and the solemn immobility of their hierophantic attitudes make them at first sight seem marvelous statues only. Somehow or other there comes suddenly back to me the memory of a strange French print I used to wonder at when a child, representing a group of Assyrian astrologers. Only their eyes move as we approach. But as I reach the steps all simultaneously salute me with a

[1] Very large donations are made to this temple by wealthy men. The wooden tablets without the Haiden, on which are recorded the number of gifts and the names of the donors, mention several recent presents of one thousand yen, or dollars; and donations of five hundred yen are not uncommon. The gift of a high civil official is rarely less than fifty yen.

most gracious bow, for I am the first foreign pilgrim to be honored by the privilege of an interview in the holy shrine itself with the princely hierophant, their master, descendant of the Goddess of the Sun — he who is still called by myriads of humble worshipers in the remoter districts of this ancient province Ikigami, "the living deity." Then all become absolutely statuesque again.

I remove my shoes, and am about to ascend the steps, when the tall priest who first received us before the outer gate indicates, by a single significant gesture, that religion and ancient custom require me, before ascending to the shrine of the god, to perform the ceremonial ablution. I hold out my hands; the priest pours the pure water over them thrice from a ladle-shaped vessel of bamboo with a long handle, and then gives me a little blue towel to wipe them upon, a votive towel with mysterious white characters upon it. Then we all ascend; I feeling very much like a clumsy barbarian in my ungraceful foreign garb.

Pausing at the head of the steps, the priest inquires my rank in society. For at Kitzuki hierarchy and hierarchical forms are maintained with a rigidity as precise as in the period of the gods; and there are special forms and regulations for the reception of visitors of every social grade. I do not know what flattering statements Akira may have made about me to the good priest; but the result is that I can rank only as a common person — which veracious fact doubtless saves me from some formalities which would have proved embarrassing, all ignorant as I still am of that finer and more complex etiquette in which the Japanese are the world's masters.

VIII

THE priest leads the way into a vast and lofty apartment opening for its entire length upon the broad gallery to which the stairway ascends. I have barely time to notice, while following him, that the chamber contains three immense shrines, forming alcoves on two sides of it. Of these, two are veiled by white curtains reaching from ceiling to matting — curtains decorated with perpendicular rows of black disks about four inches in diameter, each disk having in its centre a golden blossom. But from before the third shrine, in the farther angle of the chamber, the curtains have been withdrawn; and these are of gold brocade, and the shrine before which they hang is the chief shrine, that of Oho-kuni-nushi-no-Kami. Within are visible only some of the ordinary emblems of Shintō, and the exterior of that Holy of Holies into which none may look. Before it a long low bench, covered with strange objects, has been placed, with one end toward the gallery and one toward the alcove. At the end of this bench, near the gallery, I see a majestic bearded figure, strangely coifed and robed all in white, seated upon the matted floor in hierophantic attitude. Our priestly guide motions us to take our places in front of him and to bow down before him. For this is Senke Takanori, the Guji of Kitzuki, to whom even in his own dwelling none may speak save on bended knee, descendant of the Goddess of the Sun, and still by multitudes revered in thought as a being superhuman. Prostrating myself before him, according to the customary code of Japanese politeness, I am saluted in return with that exquisite courtesy which puts a stranger immediately at ease. The priest who acted as our guide now sits down on the floor at the Guji's left hand; while the other priests, who followed us to the entrance of the sanctuary only, take their places upon the gallery without.

IX

SENKE TAKANORI is a youthful and powerful man. As he sits there before me in his immobile hieratic pose, with his strange lofty headdress, his heavy curling beard, and his ample snowy sacerdotal robe broadly spreading about him in statuesque undulations, he realizes for me all that I had imagined, from the suggestion of old Japanese pictures, about the personal majesty of the ancient princes and heroes. The dignity alone of the man would irresistibly compel respect; but with that feeling of respect there also flashes through me at once the thought of the profound reverence paid him by the population of the most ancient province of Japan, the idea of the immense spiritual power in his

325

hands, the tradition of his divine descent, the sense of the immemorial nobility of his race; — and my respect deepens into a feeling closely akin to awe. So motionless he is that he seems a sacred statue only — the temple image of one of his own deified ancestors. But the solemnity of the first few moments is agreeably broken by his first words, uttered in a low rich basso, while his dark, kindly eyes remain motionlessly fixed upon my face. Then my interpreter translates his greeting — large fine phrases of courtesy — to which I reply as I best know how, expressing my gratitude for the exceptional favor accorded me.

"You are, indeed," he responds through Akira, "the first European ever permitted to enter into the Oho-yashiro. Other Europeans have visited Kitzuki and a few have been allowed to enter the temple court; but you only have been admitted into the dwelling of the god. In past years, some strangers who desired to visit the temple out of common curiosity only were not allowed to approach even the court; but the letter of Mr. Nishida, explaining the object of your visit, has made it a pleasure for us to receive you thus."

Again I express my thanks; and after a second exchange of courtesies the conversation continues through the medium of Akira.

"Is not this great temple of Kitzuki," I inquire, "older than the temples of Ise?"

"Older by far," replies the Guji; "so old, indeed,

that we do not well know the age of it. For it was first built by order of the Goddess of the Sun, in the time when deities alone existed. Then it was exceedingly magnificent; it was three hundred and twenty feet high. The beams and the pillars were larger than any existing timber could furnish; and the framework was bound together firmly with a rope made of taku [1] fibre, one thousand fathoms long.

"It was first rebuilt in the time of the Emperor Sui-nin.[2] The temple so rebuilt by order of the Emperor Sui-nin was called the Structure of the Iron Rings, because the pieces of the pillars, which were composed of the wood of many great trees, had been bound fast together with huge rings of iron. This temple was also splendid, but far less splendid than the first, which had been built by the gods, for its height was only one hundred and sixty feet.

"A third time the temple was rebuilt, in the reign of the Empress Sai-mei; but this third edifice was only eighty feet high. Since then the structure of the temple has never varied; and the plan then followed has been strictly preserved to the least detail in the construction of the present temple.

"The Oho-yashiro has been rebuilt twenty-eight times; and it has been the custom to rebuild it every sixty-one years. But in the long period of

[1] Taku is the Japanese name for the paper mulberry.
[2] See the curious legend in Professor Chamberlain's translation of the Kojiki.

civil war it was not even repaired for more than a hundred years. In the fourth year of Tai-ei, one Amako Tsune Hisa, becoming Lord of Izumo, committed the great temple to the charge of a Buddhist priest, and even built pagodas about it, to the outrage of the holy traditions. But when the Amako family were succeeded by Moro Mototsugo, this latter purified the temple, and restored the ancient festivals and ceremonies which before had been neglected."

"In the period when the temple was built upon a larger scale," I ask, "were the timbers for its construction obtained from the forests of Izumo?"

The priest Sasa, who guided us into the shrine, makes answer:

"It is recorded that on the fourth day of the seventh month of the third year of Ten-in one hundred large trees came floating to the seacoast of Kitzuki, and were stranded there by the tide. With these timbers the temple was rebuilt in the third year of Ei-kyu; and that structure was called the Building-of-the-Trees-which-came-floating. Also in the same third year of Ten-in, a great tree-trunk, one hundred and fifty feet long, was stranded on the seashore near a shrine called Ube-no-yashiro at Miyanoshita-mura, which is in Inaba. Some people wanted to cut the tree; but they found a great serpent coiled around it, which looked so terrible that they became frightened, and prayed to the deity of Ube-no-yashiro to protect them; and the deity revealed himself, and said: 'Whensoever the great temple in Izumo is to be rebuilt, one of the gods of each province sends timber for the building of it, and this time it is my turn. Build quickly, therefore, with that great tree which is mine.' And therewith the god disappeared. From these and from other records we learn that the deities have always superintended or aided the building of the great temple of Kitzuki."

"In what part of the Oho-yashiro," I ask, "do the august deities assemble during the Kami-ari-zuki?"

"On the east and west sides of the inner court," replies the priest Sasa, "there are two long buildings called the Jiu-ku-sha. These contain nineteen shrines, no one of which is dedicated to any particular god; and we believe it is in the Jiu-ku-sha that the gods assemble."

"And how many pilgrims from other provinces visit the great shrine yearly?" I inquire.

"About two hundred and fifty thousand," the Guji answers. "But the number increases or diminishes according to the condition of the agricultural classes; the more prosperous the season, the larger the number of pilgrims. It rarely falls below two hundred thousand."

x

MANY other curious things the Guji and his chief priest then related to me; telling me the sacred name of each of the courts, and of the fences and holy groves and the multitudinous shrines and their divinities; even the names of the great pillars of the temple, which are nine in number, the central pillar being called the august Heart-Pillar of the Middle. All things within the temple grounds have sacred names, even the torii and the bridges.

The priest Sasa called my attention to the fact that the great shrine of Oho-kuni-nushi-no-Kami faces west, though the great temple faces east, like all Shintō temples. In the other two shrines of the same apartment, both facing east, are the first divine Kokuzō of Izumo, his seventeenth descendant, and the father of Nominosukune, wise prince and famous wrestler. For in the reign of the Emperor Sui-nin one Kehaya of Taima had boasted that no man alive was equal to himself in strength. Nominosukune, by the emperor's command, wrestled with Kehaya, and threw him down so mightily that Kehaya's ghost departed from him. This was the beginning of wrestling in Japan; and wrestlers still pray unto Nominosukune for power and skill.

There are so many other shrines that I could not enumerate the names of all their deities without wearying those readers unfamiliar with the traditions and legends of Shintō. But nearly all those divinities who appear in the legend of the Master of the Great Land are still believed to dwell here with him, and here their shrines are: the beautiful one, magically born from the jewel worn in the

tresses of the Goddess of the Sun, and called by
men the Torrent-Mist Princess; and the daughter
of the Lord of the World of Shadows, she who loved
the Master of the Great Land, and followed him out
of the place of ghosts to become his wife; and the
deity called "Wondrous-Eight-Spirits," grandson
of the "Deity of Water-Gates," who first made a
fire-drill and platters of red clay for the august ban-
quet of the god at Kitzuki; and many of the heavenly kindred of these.

XI

THE priest Sasa also tells me this:

When Naomasu, grandson of the great Iyeyasu,
and first daimyō of that mighty Matsudaira family
who ruled Izumo for two hundred and fifty years,
came to this province, he paid a visit to the Temple
of Kitzuki, and demanded that the miya of the
shrine within the shrine should be opened that he
might look upon the sacred objects — upon the
shintai, or body of the deity. And this being an
impious desire, both of the Kokuzō [1] unitedly pro-

[1] From a remote period there have been two Kokuzō in theory, although but one incumbent. Two branches of the same family claim
ancestral right to the office — the rival houses of Senke and Kitajima.
The government has decided always in favor of the former; but the
head of the Kitajima family has usually been appointed Vice-Kokuzō.
A Kitajima to-day holds the lesser office.

The term Kokuzō is not, correctly speaking, a spiritual, but rather
a temporal title. The Kokuzō has always been the emperor's deputy
to Kitzuki — the person appointed to worship the deity in the emperor's stead; but the real spiritual title of such a deputy is that still
borne by the present Guji — "Mitsuye-Shiro."

tested against it. But despite their remonstrances and their pleadings, he persisted angrily in his demand, so that the priests found themselves compelled to open the shrine. And the miya being opened, Naomasu saw within it a great awabi [1] of nine holes — so large that it concealed everything behind it. And when he drew still nearer to look, suddenly the awabi changed itself into a huge serpent more than fifty feet in length; [2] and it massed its black coils before the opening of the shrine, and hissed like the sound of raging fire, and looked so terrible, that Naomasu and those with him fled away — having been able to see naught else. And ever thereafter Naomasu feared and reverenced the god.

XII

THE Guji then calls my attention to the quaint relics lying upon the long low bench between us, which is covered with white silk: a metal mirror, found in preparing the foundation of the temple when rebuilt many hundred years ago; magatama jewels of onyx and jasper; a Chinese flute made of jade; a few superb swords, the gifts of shōguns and emperors; helmets of splendid antique workmanship; and a bundle of enormous arrows with double-pointed heads of brass, fork-shaped and keenly edged.

[1] *Haliotis tuberculata,* or "sea-ear." The curious shell is pierced with a row of holes, which vary in number with the age and size of the animal it shields.

[2] Literally, "ten hirō," or Japanese fathoms.

After I have looked at these relics and learned something of their history, the Guji rises and says to me, "Now we will show you the ancient fire-drill of Kitzuki, with which the sacred fire is kindled."

Descending the steps, we pass again before the Haiden, and enter a spacious edifice on one side of the court, of nearly equal size with the Hall of Prayer. Here I am agreeably surprised to find a long handsome mahogany table at one end of the main apartment into which we are ushered, and mahogany chairs placed all about it for the reception of guests. I am motioned to one chair, my interpreter to another; and the Guji and his priests take their seats also at the table. Then an attendant sets before me a handsome bronze stand about three feet long, on which rests an oblong something carefully wrapped in snow-white cloths. The Guji removes the wrappings; and I behold the most primitive form of fire-drill known to exist in the Orient.[1] It is simply a very thick piece of solid white plank, about two and a half feet long, with a line of holes drilled along its upper edge, so that the upper part of each hole breaks through the sides of the plank. The sticks which produce the fire, when fixed in the holes and rapidly rubbed between the palms of the hands, are made of a lighter kind of white wood; they are about two feet long, and as thick as a common lead pencil.

[1] The fire-drill used at the Shintō temples of Ise is far more complicated in construction, and certainly represents a much more advanced stage of mechanical knowledge than the Kitzuki fire-drill indicates.

KITZUKI

While I am yet examining this curious simple utensil, the invention of which tradition ascribes to the gods, and modern science to the earliest childhood of the human race, a priest places upon the table a light, large wooden box, about three feet long, eighteen inches wide, and four inches high at the sides, but higher in the middle, as the top is arched like the shell of a tortoise. This object is made of the same hinoki wood as the drill; and two long slender sticks are laid beside it. I at first suppose it to be another fire-drill. But no human being could guess what it really is. It is called the koto-ita, and is one of the most primitive of musical instruments; the little sticks are used to strike it. At a sign from the Guji two priests place the box upon the floor, seat themselves on either side of it, and taking up the little sticks begin to strike the lid with them, alternately and slowly, at the same time uttering a most singular and monotonous chant. One intones only the sounds, "Ang! ang!" and the other responds, "Ong! ong!" The koto-ita gives out a sharp, dead, hollow sound as the sticks fall upon it in time to each utterance of "Ang! ang!" "Ong! ong!" [1]

[1] During a subsequent visit to Kitzuki I learned that the koto-ita is used only as a sort of primitive "tuning" instrument: it gives the right tone for the true chant which I did not hear during my first visit. The true chant, an ancient Shintō hymn, is always preceded by the performance above described.

XIII

THESE things I learn:

Each year the temple receives a new fire-drill; but the fire-drill is never made in Kitzuki, but in Kumano, where the traditional regulations as to the manner of making it have been preserved from the time of the gods. For the first Kokuzō of Izumo, on becoming pontiff, received the fire-drill for the great temple from the hands of the deity who was the younger brother of the Sun-Goddess, and is now enshrined at Kumano. And from his time the fire-drills for the Oho-yashiro of Kitzuki have been made only at Kumano.

Until very recent times the ceremony of delivering the new fire-drill to the Guji of Kitzuki always took place at the great temple of Oba, on the occasion of the festival called Unohi-matsuri. This ancient festival, which used to be held in the eleventh month, became obsolete after the Revolution everywhere except at Oba in Izumo, where Izanami-no-Kami, the mother of gods and men, is enshrined.

Once a year, on this festival, the Kokuzō always went to Oba, taking with him a gift of double rice-cakes. At Oba he was met by a personage called the Kame-da-yu, who brought the fire-drill from Kumano and delivered it to the priests at Oba. According to tradition, the Kame-da-yu had to act a somewhat ludicrous rôle, so that no Shintō priest ever cared to perform the part, and a man was hired for it. The duty of the Kame-da-yu was to find fault with the gift presented to the temple by the Kokuzō; and in this district of Japan there is still a proverbial saying about one who is prone to find fault without reason, "He is like the Kame-da-yu."

The Kame-da-yu would inspect the rice-cakes and begin to criticise them. "They are much smaller this year," he would observe, "than they were last year." The priests would reply: "Oh, you are honorably mistaken; they are in truth very much larger." "The color is not so white this year as it was last year; and the rice-flour is not finely ground." For all these imaginary faults of the mochi the priests would offer elaborate explanations or apologies.

At the conclusion of the ceremony the sakaki branches used in it were eagerly bid for, and sold at high prices, being believed to possess talismanic virtues.

XIV

IT nearly always happened that there was a great storm either on the day the Kokuzō went to Oba, or upon the day he returned therefrom. The journey had to be made during what is in Izumo the most stormy season (December by the new calendar). But in popular belief these storms were in some tremendous way connected with the divine personality of the Kokuzō, whose attributes would thus appear to present some curious analogy with those of the Dragon-God. Be that as it may, the great periodical storms of the season are still in this province called Kokuzō-aré;[1] and it is still the custom in Izumo to say merrily to the guest who arrives or departs in a time of tempest, "Why, you are like the Kokuzō!"

XV

THE Guji waves his hand, and from the farther end of the huge apartment there comes a sudden burst of strange music — a sound of drums and bamboo flutes; and turning to look, I see the musicians, three men, seated upon the matting, and a young girl with them. At another sign from the Guji the girl rises. She is barefooted and robed in snowy white, a virgin priestess. But below the hem of the white robe I see the gleam of hakama of crimson silk. She advances to a little table in the middle of the apartment, upon which a queer instrument is lying, shaped somewhat like a branch with twigs bent downward, from each of which hangs a little bell. Taking this curious object in both hands, she begins a sacred dance, unlike anything I ever saw before. Her every movement is a poem, because she is very graceful; and yet her performance could scarcely be called a dance, as we understand the word; it is rather a light swift walk within a circle, during which she shakes the instrument at regular

[1] The tempest of the Kokuzō.

337

intervals, making all the little bells ring. Her face remains impassive as a beautiful mask, placid and sweet as the face of a dreaming Kwannon; and her white feet are pure of line as the feet of a marble nymph. Altogether, with her snowy raiment and white flesh and passionless face, she seems rather a beautiful living statue than a Japanese maiden. And all the while the weird flutes sob and shrill, and the muttering of the drums is like an incantation.

What I have seen is called the Dance of the Miko, the Divineress.

XVI

THEN we visit the other edifices belonging to the temple: the storehouse; the library; the hall of assembly, a massive structure two stories high, where may be seen the portraits of the Thirty-Six Great Poets, painted by Tosano Mitsu Oki more than a thousand years ago, and still in an excellent state of preservation. Here we are also shown a curious magazine, published monthly by the temple — a record of Shintō news, and a medium for the discussion of questions relating to the archaic texts.

After we have seen all the curiosities of the temple, the Guji invites us to his private residence near the temple to show us other treasures — letters of Yoritomo, of Hideyoshi, of Iyeyasu; documents in the handwriting of the ancient emperors and the great shōguns, hundreds of which precious manuscripts he keeps in a cedar chest. In case of fire the immediate removal of this chest to a place of safety would be the first duty of the servants of the household.

Within his own house, the Guji, attired in ordinary Japanese full dress only, appears no less dignified as a private gentleman than he first seemed as pontiff in his voluminous snowy robe. But no host could be more kindly or more courteous or more generous. I am also much impressed by the fine appearance of his suite of young priests, now dressed, like himself, in the national costume; by the handsome, aquiline, aristocratic faces, totally different from those of ordinary Japanese — faces suggesting the soldier rather than the priest. One young man has a superb pair of thick black moustaches, which is something rarely to be seen in Japan.

At parting our kind host presents me with the ofuda, or sacred charms given to pilgrims — two pretty images of the chief deities of Kitzuki — and a number of documents relating to the history of the temple and of its treasures.

XVII

HAVING taken our leave of the kind Guji and his suite, we are guided to Inasa-no-hama, a little sea-bay at the rear of the town, by the priest Sasa, and another kannushi. This priest Sasa is a skilled poet and a man of deep learning in Shintō history

and the archaic texts of the sacred books. He re-
lates to us many curious legends as we stroll along
the shore.

This shore, now a popular bathing resort — bor-
dered with airy little inns and pretty tea-houses —
is called Inasa because of a Shintō tradition that
here the god Oho-kuni-nushi-no-Kami, the Master-
of-the-Great-Land, was first asked to resign his
dominion over the land of Izumo in favor of Masa-
ka-a-katsu-kachi-hayabi-ame-no-oshi-ho-mimi-no-
mikoto; the word Inasa signifying "Will you consent or not?" [1] In the thirty-second section of the
first volume of the Kojiki the legend is written:
I cite a part thereof:

The two deities (Tori-bune-no-Kami and Take-mika-
dzu-chi-no-wo-no-Kami), descending to the little shore
of Inasa in the land of Izumo, drew their swords ten
handbreadths long, and stuck them upside down on
the crest of a wave, and seated themselves cross-legged
upon the points of the swords, and asked the Deity Master-of-the-Great-Land, saying: "The Heaven-Shining-
Great-August-Deity and the High-Integrating-Deity
have charged us and sent us to ask, saying: 'We have
deigned to charge our august child with thy dominion, as
the land which he should govern. So how is thy heart!'"
He replied, saying: "I am unable to say. My son Ya-
he-koto-shiro-nushi-no-Kami will be the one to tell you."
. . . So they asked the Deity again, saying: "Thy son
Koto-shiro-nushi-no-Kami has now spoken thus. Hast

[1] That is, according to Motoöri, the commentator. Or more briefly
"No or yes?" This is, according to Professor Chamberlain, a mere
fanciful etymology; but it is accepted by Shintō faith, and for that
reason only is here given.

thou other sons who should speak?" He spoke again, saying: "There is my other son, Take-mi-na-gata-no-Kami." . . . While he was thus speaking the Deity Take-mi-na-gata-no-Kami came up [from the sea], bearing on the tips of his fingers a rock which it would take a thousand men to lift, and said, "I should like to have a trial of strength."

Here, close to the beach, stands a little miya called Inasa-no-kami-no-yashiro, or, the Temple of the God of Inasa; and therein Take-mika-dzu-chi-no-Kami, who conquered in the trial of strength, is enshrined. And near the shore the great rock which Take-mi-na-gata-no-Kami lifted upon the tips of his fingers, may be seen rising from the water. And it is called Chihikinoiha.

We invite the priests to dine with us at one of the little inns facing the breezy sea; and there we talk about many things, but particularly about Kitzuki and the Kokuzō.

XVIII

ONLY a generation ago the religious power of the Kokuzō extended over the whole of the province of the gods; he was in fact as well as in name the Spiritual Governor of Izumo. His jurisdiction does not now extend beyond the limits of Kitzuki, and his correct title is no longer Kokuzō, but Guji.[1]

[1] The title of Kokuzō, indeed, still exists, but it is now merely honorary, having no official duties connected with it. It is actually borne by Baron Senke, the father of Senke Takanori, residing in the capital. The active religious duties of the Mitsuye-shiro now devolve upon the Guji.

KITZUKI

Yet to the simple-hearted people of remoter districts he is still a divine or semi-divine being, and is mentioned by his ancient title, the inheritance of his race from the epoch of the gods. How profound a reverence was paid to him in former ages can scarcely be imagined by any who have not long lived among the country folk of Izumo. Outside of Japan perhaps no human being, except the Dalai Lama of Thibet, was so humbly venerated and so religiously beloved. Within Japan itself only the Son of Heaven, the "Tenshi-Sama," standing as mediator "between his people and the Sun," received like homage; but the worshipful reverence paid to the Mikado was paid to a dream rather than to a person, to a name rather than to a reality, for the Tenshi-Sama was ever invisible as a deity "divinely retired," and in popular belief no man could look upon his face and live.[1] Invisibility and mystery vastly enhanced the divine legend of the Mikado. But the Kokuzō, within his own province, though visible to the multitude and often journeying among the people, received almost equal devotion; so that his material power, though rarely, if ever, exercised, was scarcely less than that of the Daimyō of Izumo himself. It was indeed large enough to render him a person with whom the shōgunate would have deemed it wise policy to

[1] As late as 1890 I was told by a foreign resident, who had traveled much in the interior of the country, that in certain districts many old people may be met with who still believe that to see the face of the emperor is "to become a Buddha"; that is, to die.

342

remain upon good terms. An ancestor of the present Guji even defied the great Taikō Hideyoshi, refusing to obey his command to furnish troops with the haughty answer that he would receive no order from a man of common birth.[1] This defiance cost the family the loss of a large part of its estates by confiscation, but the real power of the Kokuzō remained unchanged until the period of the new civilization.

Out of many hundreds of stories of a similar nature, two little traditions may be cited as illustrations of the reverence in which the Kokuzō was formerly held.

It is related that there was a man who, believing himself to have become rich by favor of the Daikoku of Kitzuki, desired to express his gratitude by a gift of robes to the Kokuzō. The Kokuzō courteously declined the proffer; but the pious worshiper persisted in his purpose, and ordered a tailor to make the robes. The tailor, having made them, demanded a price that almost took his patron's breath away. Being asked to give his reason for demanding such a price, he made answer: "Having made robes for the Kokuzō, I cannot hereafter make garments for any other person. Therefore I must have money enough to support me for the rest of my life."

The second story dates back to about one hundred and seventy years ago.

[1] Hideyoshi, as is well known, was not of princely extraction.

KITZUKI

Among the samurai of the Matsue clan in the time of Nobukori, fifth daimyō of the Matsudaira family, there was one Sughihara Kitoji, who was stationed in some military capacity at Kitzuki. He was a great favorite with the Kokuzō, and used often to play at chess with him. During a game, one evening, this officer suddenly became as one paralyzed, unable to move or speak. For a moment all was anxiety and confusion; but the Kokuzō said: "I know the cause. My friend was smoking, and although smoking disagrees with me, I did not wish to spoil his pleasure by telling him so. But the Kami, seeing that I felt ill, became angry with him. Now I shall make him well." Whereupon the Kokuzō uttered some magical word, and the officer was immediately as well as before.

XIX

ONCE more we are journeying through the silence of this holy land of mists and of legends; wending our way between green leagues of ripening rice white-sprinkled with arrows of prayer, between the far processions of blue and verdant peaks whose names are the names of gods. We have left Kitzuki far behind. But as in a dream I still see the mighty avenue, the long succession of torii with their colossal shimenawa, the majestic face of the Guji, the kindly smile of the priest Sasa, and the girl priestess in her snowy robes dancing her beautiful ghostly dance. It seems to me that I can still hear the sound of the clapping of hands, like the crashing of a torrent. I cannot suppress some slight exultation at the thought that I have been allowed to see what no other foreigner has been privileged to see — the interior of Japan's most ancient shrine, and those sacred utensils and quaint rites of primitive worship so well worthy the study of the anthropologist and the evolutionist.

But to have seen Kitzuki as I saw it is also to have seen something much more than a single wonderful temple. To see Kitzuki is to see the living centre of Shintō, and to feel the life-pulse of the ancient faith, throbbing as mightily in this nineteenth century as ever in that unknown past whereof the Kojiki itself, though written in a tongue no longer spoken, is but a modern record.[1] Buddhism, changing form or slowly decaying through the centuries, might seem doomed to pass away at last from this Japan to which it came only as an alien faith; but Shintō, unchanging and vitally unchanged, still remains all dominant in the land of its birth, and only seems to gain in power and dignity with time.[2] Buddhism has a voluminous theology, a profound philosophy, a literature vast as the sea. Shintō has no philosophy, no code of

[1] The Kojiki dates back, as a written work, only to A.D. 712. But its legends and records are known to have existed in the form of oral literature from a much more ancient time.

[2] In certain provinces of Japan Buddhism practically absorbed Shintō in other centuries, but in Izumo Shintō absorbed Buddhism; and now that Shintō is supported by the state there is a visible tendency to eliminate from its cult certain elements of Buddhist origin.

ethics, no metaphysics; and yet, by its very immateriality, it can resist the invasion of Occidental religious thought as no other Orient faith can. Shintō extends a welcome to Western science, but remains the irresistible opponent of Western religion; and the foreign zealots who would strive against it are astounded to find the power that foils their uttermost efforts indefinable as magnetism and invulnerable as air. Indeed the best of our scholars have never been able to tell us what Shintō is. To some it appears to be merely ancestor-worship, to others ancestor-worship combined with nature-worship; to others, again, it seems to be no religion at all; to the missionary of the more ignorant class it is the worst form of heathenism. Doubtless the difficulty of explaining Shintō has been due simply to the fact that the sinologists have sought for the source of it in books: in the Kojiki and the Nihongi, which are its histories; in the Norito, which are its prayers; in the commentaries of Motowori and Hirata, who were its greatest scholars. But the reality of Shintō lives not in books, nor in rites, nor in commandments, but in the national heart, of which it is the highest emotional religious expression, immortal and ever young. Far underlying all the surface crop of quaint superstitions and artless myths and fantastic magic there thrills a mighty spiritual force, the whole soul of a race with all its impulses and powers and intuitions. He who would know what Shintō is must learn to know that mysterious soul in which the sense of beauty and the power of art and the fire of heroism and magnetism of loyalty and the emotion of faith have become inherent, immanent, unconscious, instinctive.

Trusting to know something of that Oriental soul in whose joyous love of nature and of life even the unlearned may discern a strange likeness to the soul of the old Greek race, I trust also that I may presume some day to speak of the great living power of that faith now called Shintō, but more anciently Kami-no-michi, or "The Way of the Gods."

INDEX

INDEX

sects, 12; old rites, 15; rites of ancestor-worship, 214, 215, 219, 220; temples, 23

Buddhist, doctrine, 71, 132, 133; explained and commented, 30; graveyard, 181; idealism, 142 n.; identity, 93; impermanency, 89; lion (guardian), 175, 177, 184; metaphysics, 125; ontology, 71, 72; philosophy, 55, 62, 126; philosophical, popular misconception of, 29; point of view, 6; a religion of metaphysicians, 49; Sutras, 30; teaching of, 33; texts, 125, 140; words of, 119

Buddhists, 141 n., 142 n.

Buddhist priests, civil functions of, 27, 114, 115, 116, 117

Butsudan, 214, 215

Chamberlain, Basil Hall, 303, 319, 327, 340

China, 7; arts, brought to Japan by Buddhism, 12; characters, 99, 174, 176, 186; civilization, 27; effect of religion of filial piety, 222; influence and establishment of domestic cult, 228, 229, 230, 248, 249, 277

Christian doctrine, 128, 135; orthodox, 273; civilization, 297

Cho (Leapers), 78

Chu-U (disembodied state), 16 n., 95

Cleanliness, love of, 262

Cloudiness, the, 76

Coleridge, Samuel T., *The Wanderings of Cain*, 240

Concept of life, 120

Confucianism, in Japan, 8, 11

Conscience and Buddhism, 19

Consciousness, 51, 53

Contemporary Buddhism in Japan, the general thought of, 73

Cosmos, the, 97, 136, 139; apparition, 96; attribute of, 90; emotion of, 294, 300

Coulanges, N. D. Fustel de, *La Cite Antique*, 200, 207, 224

Creator, 90; God of, 277

Dai-Butsu, the great Buddha Statue, 163

Daikoku, 181; -yama, Mt., 311

Daisen, Mt., 305, 313

Dances of the Festival of the Dead, 25 n.

Dead, all supposed to become gods, 199, 200, 218; Buddhist belief of, 16 n., 92, 219, 220; control of human life, 204, 219, 250; the early Japanese idea of, 198; feelings of, 283, 284; offerings of food to, 202, 203; in Shinto concept, 32, 203, 217, 218, 290

Death, 131; according to Shinto belief, 201, 202; custom of leaving house, 207, 208, 209

Delusion, 62

Desire, the world of, 73; of life, 131

Destruction of the twelve Nidanas, the doctrine of, 54

Dhyana, 1; sect of, 1; texts of, 1 (see Zen, 1-6)

Diamond-Cutter, the, 50, 55, 62

Divination, System of, 268-270

Domestic cult, 195-225; Buddhism and, 9, 10; existing forms of, 214 ff.; importance of rites, 216; relation to conduct, 217 n.

Dragons, sculptured, 148; -Goddess, 172; of Benten, 180

Dust, 95, 96

350

INDEX

INDEX

INDEX

INDEX

INDEX